THE JOHN PHILLIPS COMMENTARY SERIES

# *Exploring* GALATIANS

*An Expository Commentary*

JOHN PHILLIPS

kregel
PUBLICATIONS

Grand Rapids, MI 49501

*Exploring Galatians: An Expository Commentary*



Published in 2004 by Kregel Publications, a division of Kregel, Inc., 2450 Oak Industrial Dr. NE, Grand Rapids, MI 49505.



Scripture quotations are from the King James Version of the Holy Bible.

**Library of Congress Cataloging-in-Publication Data**
Phillips, John.
Exploring Galatians: an expository commentary /by John Phillips.
p. cm.
1. Bible N.T. Galatians—Commentaries. I. Title.
BS2685.53 .P49 2004
227'.4077—dc22 2004016158

ISBN 978-0-8254-3397-9

Printed in the United States of America

8 9 10 11 / 26 25 24 23

# Contents

# Preface

Long before they became the nation known to Paul, the Galatians (identified at times with the Celts) left their mark on a number of nations, including Switzerland, Italy, Germany, and the British Isles.

Still restless, they moved on again. They burned Rome, invaded Asia Minor, and spread out all over the peninsula.

In 190 B.C., some Galatian mercenaries joined Antiochus III in his campaign against Rome. They were defeated at the Battle of Magnesia. Having punished them, the Romans then granted them a measure of autonomy, which, eventually, expanded into a single kingdom.

At the Battle of Actium in 31 B.C., they sided with Augustus, betraying Anthony and leaving him to his fate. Consequently, the Romans expanded their territory into the Galatia with which we are familiar from our New Testament.

In Paul's day, the term *Galatia* applied to both the original Galatian territory and the larger Roman province. Scholars disagree as to the sense in which the word is used in Acts 16:6 and 18:23 and Paul's epistle to the Galatians. If "Galatia" meant the Roman province, then Paul evangelized it on his first missionary journey. If it meant the old territory of Galatia, then Paul evangelized it on his second missionary journey. The view taken in this commentary is that the churches that Paul addresses in this epistle were the churches that he planted in southern Galatia on his first missionary journey.[1]

The Galatians had welcomed Paul with open arms and had received him, indeed, "as an angel of God" (Gal. 4:14). Had it been possible, they would have

1. Readers who are interested in a discussion of the two views are referred to F. F. Bruce, *The Epistle to the Galatians* (Grand Rapids: Eerdmans, 1982), 1–32.

"plucked out [their] own eyes, and have given them to [him]" (4:15). But that hospitable attitude did not last. They became prejudiced against Paul by false teachers who persuaded them to embrace "another gospel" (1:6). They had been "bewitched," Paul said (3:1), and had become as ready to "bite and devour one another" (5:15) as they were to change teachers and gospels. The Galatians were brave and enthusiastic, but they were susceptible to quick impressions and sudden changes.

Yet Paul loved them. He was not the kind of man to write them off just because false teachers had hypnotized them. No, indeed! Paul's response was to seize his pen and dash off this letter, perhaps the first of all his letters. In so doing, he has done us a service, too, because we still have those among us who would like to make us bow to legalism, Judaism, or some other kindred error.

# Complete Outline

Part 1: Introduction (1:1–2)

- A. Paul's personal signature (1:1a)
- B. Paul's privileged status (1:1b–c)
  - 1. His denial (1:1b)
  - 2. His delight (1:1c)
- C. Paul's present supporters (1:2a)
- D. Paul's peremptory start (1:2b)

Part 2: An Explanation (1:3–2:21)

- A. The declaration of the gospel (1:3–5)
  - 1. Simple grace (1:3)
    - a. The sincerity of the greeting (1:3a)
    - b. The significance of the greeting (1:3b)
  - 2. Saving grace (1:4a–b)
    - a. A fresh view of our Savior (1:4a)
    - b. A fresh view of our salvation (1:4b)
  - 3. Sovereign grace (1:4c–5)
    - a. The government of God (1:4c)
    - b. The glory of God (1:5)
- B. The distortion of the gospel (1:6–10)
  - 1. Paul's astonishment (1:6)
  - 2. Paul's assessment (1:7)
  - 3. Paul's assertion (1:8–10)
    - a. The branded heretic (1:8–9)
      - (1) Whether apostle (1:8a)

- (2) Whether angel (1:8b)
- (3) Whether anyone (1:9)

b. The beloved herald (1:10)

- (1) Who he sought to persuade (1:10a)
- (2) Who he sought to please (1:10b)

C. The distinctives of the gospel (1:11–24)

1. Paul's distinctive reception of the gospel (1:11–17)

a. His claim (1:11–12)

- (1) What Paul denied (1:11–12a)
  - (a) It was not conceived for him by man (1:11)
  - (b) It was not received by him from man (1:12a)
- (2) What Paul declared (1:12b)

b. His conversion (1:13–16b)

- (1) Paul as a religious man (1:13–14)
  - (a) How zealously he persecuted the Christian faith (1:13)
  - (b) How zealously he practiced the Jewish faith (1:14)
    - i. Paul and his contemporaries (1:14a)
    - ii. Paul and his convictions (1:14b)
- (2) Paul as a regenerated man (1:15–16b)
  - (a) How he was separated (1:15a)
  - (b) How he was saved (1:15b)
  - (c) How he was sanctified (1:16a)
  - (d) How he was sent (1:16b)

c. His concealment (1:16c–17)

- (1) His resolve (1:16c–17a)
  - (a) Not to confer with the laity of the church (1:16c)
  - (b) Not to contact the leaders of the church (1:17a)
- (2) His retirement (1:17b)
- (3) His return (1:17c)

2. Paul's distinctive reputation in the gospel (1:18–24)

a. His acceptance in Jerusalem (1:18–19)

- (1) When he went (1:18a)
- (2) Why he went (1:18b–19)
  - (a) The intentional meeting with Peter (1:18b)
  - (b) The incidental meeting with James (1:19)

b. His activities among Gentiles (1:20–21)

- (1) What he swore (1:20)
- (2) Where he served (1:21)

- c. His acknowledgment in Judea (1:22–24)
  - (1) The Jewish believers and their dreaded persecutor (1:22–23)
    - (a) His face was unknown to them (1:22)
    - (b) His fame was unquestioned by them (1:23)
  - (2) The Jewish believers and their delighted praise (1:24)

D. The defense of the gospel (2:1–21)

1. Paul's unwavering challenge to the church at Jerusalem: the center of Jewish Christianity (2:1–10)
   - a. The crucial test (2:1–3)
     - (1) The time (2:1)
       - (a) Paul's calendar (2:1a)
       - (b) Paul's companions (2:1b–c)
         - i. The gentle Barnabas (2:1b)
         - ii. The Gentile Titus (2:1c)
     - (2) The truth (2:2–3)
       - (a) Paul's guidance (2:2a)
       - (b) Paul's gospel (2:2b–3)
         - i. His presentation (2:2b)
         - ii. His precaution (2:2c–3)
           - *a.* His private audience (2:2c)
           - *b.* His personal acceptance (2:2d–3)
             - *1.* The acceptance of his message (2:2d)
             - *2.* The acceptance of his method (2:3)
   - b. The contested truth (2:4–5)
     - (1) How Paul faced his foes (2:4)
       - (a) Their mask removed (2:4a)
       - (b) Their method rebuked (2:4b)
       - (c) Their motive revealed (2:4c–d)
         - i. They were spies (2:4c)
         - ii. They wanted slaves (2:4d)
     - (2) How Paul fought his foes (2:5)
       - (a) His refusal (2:5a)
       - (b) His reason (2:5b)
   - c. The crowning triumph (2:6–10)
     - (1) Paul's message accepted (2:6–8)
       - (a) The big names (2:6)
         - i. Their reputation (2:6a–b)

*a.* Paul was unimpressed (2:6a)
*b.* Paul was unruffled (2:6b)
ii. Their repudiation (2:6c)
(b) The big news (2:7–8)
i. They acknowledged two respective arenas (2:7)
*a.* Paul's acknowledged sphere (2:7a)
*b.* Peter's acknowledged sphere (2:7b)
ii. They acknowledged two respected apostles (2:8)
*a.* Peter's successes acknowledged (2:8a)
*b.* Paul's successes acknowledged (2:8b)
(2) Paul's mission accepted (2:9–10)
(a) The pillars of the church (2:9)
i. Who they were (2:9a)
ii. What they welcomed (2:9b–c)
*a.* Their enlightenment (2:9b)
*b.* Their endorsement (2:9c)
(b) The poor of the church (2:10)
2. Paul's unwavering challenge to the church at Antioch: the center of Gentile Christianity (2:11–21)
a. Peter's conduct (2:11–13)
(1) Its critic (2:11)
(a) Paul's boldness (2:11a)
(b) Peter's blameworthiness (2:11b)
(2) Its character (2:12)
(a) Peter's fellowship with the Gentiles (2:12a)
(b) Peter's fear of the Judaizers (2:12b)
(3) Its consequences (2:13)
(a) How believers were affected (2:13a)
(b) How Barnabas was affected (2:13b)
b. Paul's convictions (2:14–21)
(1) Paul's discernment of the problem (2:14)
(a) How he accosted Peter (2:14a)
(b) How he accused Peter (2:14b–c)
i. What he permitted in personal conduct (2:14b)
ii. What he proposed for Paul's converts (2:14c)
(2) Paul's discussion of the problem (2:15–21)
(a) The Law cannot bring us to redemption ground (2:15–18)

- i. The Jewish Christian position (2:15–16)
  - *a.* The Law cannot justify (2:15–16a)
  - *b.* The Lord can justify (2:16b)
- ii. The Jewish Christian problem (2:17–18)
  - *a.* What Jews believed about Gentile Christians (2:17a)
  - *b.* What Jesus brought to Gentile Christians (2:17b–18)

(b) The Law cannot bring us to resurrection ground (2:19–21)

- i. A principle (2:19)
- ii. A position (2:20)
  - *a.* Identified with Christ (2:20a)
  - *b.* Indwelt by Christ (2:20b–c)
    - *1.* A matchless life (2:20b)
    - *2.* A matchless love (2:20c)
- iii. A perspective (2:21)

PART 3: AN EXPOSITION (3:1–4:31)

A. How Paul interrogated the Galatians (3:1–5)

1. Regarding their seducers (3:1)
2. Regarding their salvation (3:2)
3. Regarding their sanctification (3:3)
4. Regarding their sufferings (3:4)
5. Regarding their signs (3:5)

B. How Paul instructed the Galatians (3:6–4:31)

1. Believers are the seed of Abraham (3:6–29)

a. The priority of grace (3:6–18)

(1) The conversion of Abraham (3:6–14)

(a) Abraham and the Seed (3:6–9)

- i. What Abraham did to be saved (3:6)
- ii. What all do to be saved (3:7–9)
  - *a.* The same faith (3:7)
  - *b.* The sure foundation (3:8)
  - *c.* The simple fact (3:9)

(b) Abraham and the Scripture (3:10–12)

- i. The curse (3:10)
- ii. The contrast (3:11)

- iii. The conclusion (3:12)
- (c) Abraham and the Savior (3:13–14)
    - i. The burden removed by Christ (3:13)
        - *a.* How the Law revealed the curse (3:13a)
        - *b.* How the Lord repealed the curse (3:13b)
    - ii. The blessing received by Christ (3:14)
- (2) The covenant with Abraham (3:15–18)
    - (a) The contract principle (3:15)
    - (b) The covenant promise (3:16–18)
        - i. The supreme goal of the Abrahamic covenant (3:16)
        - ii. The sublime guarantee of the Abrahamic covenant (3:17)
        - iii. The sole ground of the Abrahamic covenant (3:18)

b. The purpose of law (3:19–29)

- (1) To probe the soul for sin (3:19–22)
    - (a) The Law and its lesson (3:19a–b)
        - i. The transgression factor (3:19a)
        - ii. The time factor (3:19b)
    - (b) The Law and its limitations (3:20–22)
        - i. The Law as a contract (3:20)
            - *a.* The operation of a contract (3:20a)
            - *b.* The opposite to a contract (3:20b)
        - ii. The Law as a contrast (3:21–22)
            - *a.* It magnifies God's promise by its very failure (3:21)
            - *b.* It magnifies God's promise by its very function (3:22)
- (2) To prepare the soul for salvation (3:23–29)
    - (a) The Law (3:23–25)
        - i. The Law as a taskmaster (3:23)
        - ii. The Law as a schoolmaster (3:24–25)
            - *a.* The tutor's duty (3:24)
            - *b.* The tutor's dismissal (3:25)
    - (b) The Lord (3:26–29)
        - i. A new freedom (3:26)
        - ii. A new factor (3:27)
        - iii. A new fellowship (3:28)

iv. A new future (3:29)
2. Believers are the sons of God (4:1–31)
 a. Their birthright is declared (4:1–7)
  (1) The past: acceptance of spiritual minority (4:1–3)
   (a) The analogy (4:1–2)
    i. The minor and his status (4:1)
     *a.* Presently, under law (4:1a)
     *b.* Potentially, undisputed Lord (4:1b)
    ii. The minor and his servitude (4:2)
     *a.* The training element in it (4:2a)
     *b.* The time element in it (4:2b)
   (b) The application (4:3)
  (2) The present: access to spiritual maturity (4:4–7)
   (a) The advent of the Son of God (4:4–5a)
    i. The time: When He came (4:4)
    ii. The task: Why He came (4:5a)
   (b) The adoption of the sons of God (4:5b–7)
   We have received:
    i. Instant endorsement (4:5b)
    ii. Instant enablement (4:6)
    iii. Instant entitlement (4:7)
 b. Their betrayal is described (4:8–20)
  (1) Liberty surrendered (4:8–11)
   (a) Their past bondage (4:8)
    i. Their ignorance (4:8a)
    ii. Their idolatry (4:8b)
   (b) Their present bondage (4:9–11)
    i. Their enlightenment (4:9a)
    ii. Their enslavement (4:9b–11)
     *a.* Their decision (4:9b)
     *b.* Their desire (4:9c)
     *c.* Their deeds (4:10)
     *d.* Their danger (4:11)
  (2) Love suppressed (4:12–16)
   (a) Paul's plea (4:12)
   (b) Paul's preaching (4:13)
   (c) Paul's person (4:14–15)
    i. Their willingness to overlook his infirmity (4:14)

ii. Their wish to overcome his infirmity (4:15)
(d) Paul's perception (4:16)
(3) Loyalty subverted (4:17–20)
(a) The deceivers and their goal (4:17)
(b) The deceived and their good (4:18–20)
i. Paul's teaching (4:18)
ii. Paul's travail (4:19)
iii. Paul's trouble (4:20)
c. Their bondage is depicted (4:21–31)
(1) The approach (4:21)
(2) The appeal (4:22–27)
a. The text (4:22–23)
i. Two sons (4:22)
ii. Two situations (4:23)
b. The type (4:24–27)
i. The first covenant: enslavement (4:24–25) (Mount Sinai and the earthly Jerusalem)
ii. The final covenant: emancipation (4:26–27) (Mount Zion and the heavenly Jerusalem)
(3) The application (4:28–31)
a. The outlook (4:28)
b. The outrage (4:29)
c. The outlaw (4:30)
d. The outcome (4:31)

PART 4: AN EXHORTATION (5:1–6:10)
A. The law of liberty in Christ (5:1–15)
1. The foundation of our liberty (5:1–6)
a. That liberty attested (5:1)
(1) The demand (5:1a)
(2) The danger (5:1b)
b. That liberty attacked (5:2–6)
(1) The seriousness of the attack exposed (5:2)
(2) The seriousness of the attack explained (5:3–6)
(a) Terrible warnings (5:3–4)
i. Falling into debt (5:3)
*a.* The signature of circumcision (5:3a)
*b.* The significance of circumcision (5:3b)

- ii. Falling from grace (5:4)
  - *a.* The consequence (5:4a)
  - *b.* The cause (5:4b)
- (b) Triumphant waiting (5:5)
- (c) True working (5:6)

2. The foes of our liberty (5:7–12)
   - a. Their doctrine revealed (5:7–9)
     - (1) How it spoils (5:7–8)
     - (2) How it spreads (5:9)
   - b. Their doom revealed (5:10–12)
     - (1) Paul's confidence (5:10a)
     - (2) Paul's conviction (5:10b)
     - (3) Paul's condition (5:11–12)
       - (a) His persecution (5:11)
       - (b) His passion (5:12)
3. The frontiers of our liberty (5:13–15)
   - a. We are not free to indulge in carnality (5:13)
   - b. We are not free to indulge in conflict (5:14–15)
     - (1) The single word (5:14)
     - (2) The sarcastic warning (5:15)

B. The law of likeness to Christ (5:16–26)

1. The provision for Christlikeness (5:16–18)
   - a. A command (5:16)
   - b. A contrast (5:17)
   - c. A commitment (5:18)
2. The proofs of Christlikeness (5:19–23)
   - a. The sinful man revealed (5:19–21)
     - (1) Sexual sins (5:19)
     - (2) Spiritual sins (5:20a)
     - (3) Social sins (5:20b–21)
   - b. The spiritual man revealed (5:22–23)
     - (1) Emotional fruits of the Spirit (5:22a)
     - (2) Evidential fruits of the Spirit (5:22b)
     - (3) Elemental fruits of the Spirit (5:22c–23)
3. The practice of Christlikeness (5:24–26)
   - a. Death to the flesh (5:24)
   - b. Life in the Spirit (5:25–26)

C. The law of love for Christ (6:1–6)

1. The love that woos sympathetically (6:1–2)
    a. The backslider (6:1)
    b. The burden bearer (6:2)
2. The love that walks softly (6:3–5)
    a. Mark your own boundaries (6:3)
    b. Mind your own business (6:4)
    c. Move your own burden (6:5)
3. The love that works sincerely (6:6)

D. The law of life in Christ (6:7–10)
1. The law logically explained (6:7–8)
    a. The law of the soil (6:7)
    b. The law of the soul (6:8)
2. The law logically exploited (6:9–10)
    a. Patience required (6:9)
    b. Persistence required (6:10)
        (1) Doing good equally to the human family (6:10a)
        (2) Doing good especially to the heavenly family (6:10b)

PART 5: CONCLUSION (6:11–18)

A. Paul emphasizes the truth of Galatians positively (6:11)

B. Paul emphasizes the truth of Galatians persuasively (6:12–15)
1. The treacherous motives of the adversaries (6:12–13)
    a. Their insincerity (6:12a)
    b. Their insecurity (6:12b)
    c. Their inconsistency (6:13a)
    d. Their inferiority (6:13b)
2. The transparent motives of the apostle (6:14–15)
    a. He lived with his eye on Calvary (6:14)
    b. He lived with his eye on Christ (6:15)

C. Paul emphasizes the truth of Galatians practically (6:16)
1. The rule (6:16a)
2. The result (6:16b)
3. The realm (6:16c)

D. Paul emphasizes the truth of Galatians personally (6:17)

E. Paul emphasizes the truth of Galatians pastorally (6:18)

PART 1

# Introduction

## Galatians 1:1–2

Paul's epistle to the Galatians, in the Greek text, runs to approximately twenty-four hundred words—the length, indeed, of a small pamphlet. It shows us Paul's soul on fire. We catch glimpses of Paul's wide vision, keen logic, biting sarcasm, vehement indignation, warm love, and spiritual power.

The letter has been called a rough draft for his formal and far-reaching epistle to the Romans. The letter not only was aimed at silencing the Judaizers but also was designed to define, once and for all, just exactly what Christianity really is. Now and then, Paul calls on his readers to make a clear difference between the Law and the gospel and between works and faith. The Law had a curse for everyone who was under it; the gospel has a curse for everyone who would adulterate it. "The Gospel," says Govett, "is God's *one* remedy for the lost. How fearful a crime, therefore, to try to poison the well of salvation."[1]

Martin Luther loved this epistle. It is "my epistle," he said. "I have betrothed myself to it. It is my wife." The epistle to the Galatians became Luther's dagger to plunge into the heart of the papacy. It was his battle-ax in his ceaseless war with Rome.

"Liberty!" The thought occurs eleven times in this little letter. The name "Christ" occurs forty-three times. "Law" is referred to thirty-one times, "the flesh" crops up eighteen times, "the Spirit" is mentioned fifteen times, "faith" occurs twenty-two times, it appeals to "the Promise" ten times, the word *bondage* and its kindred words occur eleven times, and the cross is mentioned six times. Eight of fifteen instances of "works of the flesh," so deplored and rebuked by Paul in this epistle (5:20–21), are sins of strife.

A. Paul's personal signature (1:1a)

As he did with all of his epistles (except Hebrews), Paul begins Galatians with his signature—Paul! While he was on his way to Galatia, Paul dropped his Hebrew name, Saul, and picked up his Roman name, Paul. Mr. Little! That is what the name means. But there was nothing little about Paul. Shakespeare tells us that the conspirators against Caesar deplored the giant moral and political stature of their great adversary. His victories, genius, popularity with the people, and

1. R. Govett, *Govett on Galatians* (London: Thynne and Co., 1930), 6.

his grasp of power were formidable to them. "Why man, he doth bestride the world like a Colossus," Shakespeare has one of them say. And so he did. And so did Paul.

Paul's signature on a letter was worth millions, not in the coin of the realm but in spiritual terms. The name Paul on an epistle is like the name Mozart on a musical score, the name Rembrandt on a painting, the name Rockefeller on a check, or the word *sterling* on silver. It indicates its worth. Paul! He was the church's greatest thinker, the church's greatest missionary, the church's greatest apologist, the church's greatest theologian, the church's greatest enthusiast, and the church's greatest apostle. Paul!

Paul! As soon as they saw the name on the letter, the Galatians would see him in their mind's eye. They would recall at once the extraordinary Jew who spoke like a Roman and reasoned like a Greek. Paul! He was the man who could preach like an archangel, who was as bold as a lion, as tender as a nurse, as honest as the sunshine, wiser than Solomon, more patient than Job, and armed with spiritual authority and power. No foe could daunt him; no fear could haunt him. He had taken their little corner of the Roman world by storm! And how they had loved him! Paul!

The very name conjured the vision of a bold-eyed, eager-spirited, soft-spoken, openhanded, warmhearted, keen-witted, fearless Jew who had come into Pisidian Antioch, Iconium, Lystra, and Derbe—into city after city—to preach with passion, persuasion, and power a message for which their hearts had been hungry and their empty souls were longing for centuries. Paul! He was the man who turned the world upside down for God! His very signature seemed to summarize the man.

B. Paul's privileged status (1:1b–c)
   1. His denial (1:1b)

"An apostle, not of men, neither by man, but by Jesus Christ, and God the Father." Here we have none of those tender touches, common courtesies, and social flourishes that Paul used so often in his opening greetings. His very first words are an indignant denial of the lies that his enemies were telling about him, lies that the Galatians had been all too ready to entertain.

We can easily read between the lines of this letter. Jews from Jerusalem had been troubling the infant Galatian churches, just as they had been upsetting the older and more firmly established church in Syrian Antioch. We can almost hear them.

"Of course, you Gentiles must understand that this Paul is an upstart. He has no real authority, you know. He's a latecomer to the cause. Indeed, for some years he was its bitterest foe—we have widows in Jerusalem who can bear witness to that! Paul's not really an apostle at all, you know. We know that he talks about some vision he had on the Damascus road, but anyone can have visions.

"The Jerusalem church, of course, is the mother church. It was at Jerusalem that the church was born. Think of it—three thousand people, saved in a single day. Peter was the man God used for that. Peter, James, and John—they are the chief men among the brethren—at least James the Apostle is dead now, martyred by Herod; but James, the Lord's brother, has taken his place. There are only twelve apostles, you know. They are all men who spent time with Jesus in the days of His flesh. They heard His teaching firsthand. They saw all of His miracles. They observed Him; studied His character; witnessed His death, burial, and resurrection; and were appointed and commissioned to be His special messengers. They founded the Jerusalem church. They are the only ones who have the authority to define the gospel, say what it is and what its precepts and parameters are, accredit its agents, and define its mission. This man Paul is certainly not one of the Twelve; he never was. The true apostles received their authority from Christ. We'd hate to speculate where Paul got his."

It was a devastating attack. But that was no means all. Craftily, they would have to concede something to Paul. "Mind you," we can hear them say, "this Paul is very clever. He was trained to be a rabbi. Indeed, he even sat at the feet of Gamaliel, one of our greatest rabbis. He had a promising career in the Jew's religion. He is a man of uncommon talent. The Jerusalem apostles recognized that fact, so, after his conversion, they decided to let bygones be bygones. In spite of his leading role in the martyrdom of Stephen—Ah! There was a man for you, more than a match for this clever Saul of Tarsus when it came to debate—and in the persecution of the church, they forgave him in a true Christlike spirit, gave him the right hand of fellowship, and even decided to use his talents and zeal in the cause of Christ. They instructed him in the gospel and gave him their blessing."

They were lies, of course, all lies, cleverly mixed with truth—the way of error in all times and places from the very beginning. We can hear these enemies of Paul as they complete their attack.

"Well, when Paul launched out on his own, determined in his headstrong way to make a name for himself among the Gentiles, he made changes to the gospel. He could see that such old-fashioned (to his mind) biblical truths as circumcision, keeping the Sabbath, minding the traditions of the elders, abiding by the ritual requirements of the Mosaic Law would be unpalatable to the Gentiles. They always have been, of course. That is why so few Gentiles have ever become real proselytes of the Jewish religion. Well, Paul decided to jettison half of the Bible. He betrayed his own birth, background, and beliefs. He cast off his ancestral heritage and invented a lawless 'gospel' of his own. His 'gospel' is only half a gospel. It certainly does not have the endorsement of the true apostles and the mother church in Jerusalem. Why, not very long ago, Peter had a first-class row at Antioch with this Paul of yours over the whole question of the need for Gentiles to keep the Mosaic dietary laws."

No wonder Paul opened his epistle with a pen dipped in flame and fire.

"It wasn't like that at all!" he says. "What they say is not true. I *am* an apostle, every bit as much an apostle as Peter, John, or any of the others. But I did not receive my appointment and commission from either them or their accredited agents. I received it directly from 'Jesus Christ, and God the Father'—just as they received theirs. There is no particle of difference between my apostleship and theirs. Mine has been the mighty ordination of the nail-pierced hands."

2. His delight (1:1c)

But Paul delighted not in a position but in a Person. He was "an apostle . . . by Jesus Christ, and God the Father, who raised him from the dead." His delight was in a *risen* Christ. No less than nineteen times, Paul claims to be an apostle. He argues his claim in 1 Corinthians 9 and 2 Corinthians 12. One of the necessary marks of a genuine apostle was that he had to have been a witness of the resurrection of Christ (Acts 1:22). Paul's whole conversion experience was based on the fact that he personally saw the resurrected Christ. The raised and living Christ appeared to Paul (Acts 9:1–6), just as He had appeared to Peter (Luke 24:34). Paul's view of Christ was, thereafter, highly exalted. He ever after viewed Him as "the Lord from heaven" (1 Cor. 15:47). Paul's delight was not so much in the Lord, the One who trod these scenes of time, as a Man among men; his delight was in a *risen* Christ. Nobody ever appreciated this truth about Christ more or preached the Resurrection with greater conviction than Paul.

The death and resurrection of Christ had changed everything and rendered Judaism obsolete. When Christ died on the cross, God reached down from heaven and rent the temple veil (Matt. 27:51). Nothing could have been more conclusive than that—although not until Hebrews 10:19–20 was written would its theological implications be fully revealed. A risen Christ! A rent veil! Yes, indeed, Judaism as a religious system was obsolete.

This opening verse is the only direct reference in this epistle to the resurrection of Christ, but Paul's inclusion of it in his explosive opening remarks is a sure indication of his appreciation of its revolutionary significance and its bearing on the Galatian error. The whole issue of the letter is this: Moses or Christ? A dead and obsolete religious system or a living Man in the glory?

### C. Paul's present supporters (1:2a)

Paul did not stand alone in taking a stand against the Judaizers. He mentions "all the brethren which are with me" (1:2). He does not mention who was with him. Perhaps he was too indignant at the soon defection of his Galatian converts to want to include in this letter any of the warmer elements that are so common in the opening greetings in his other letters (1 Cor. 1:1; 2 Cor. 1:1; Phil. 1:1; Col. 1:1; 1 Thess. 1:1; 2 Thess. 1:1; Philem. 1). Almost every commentator has noted the curtness and abruptness of the way Paul begins this epistle. If this letter was written from Antioch, not long after the conclusion of Paul's first missionary journey, we might have expected, at least, the inclusion of the name of Barnabas. It might well be, however, that Paul's classical row with Barnabas over John Mark had already taken place (Acts 15:36–39), or at least was brewing. In that case, Paul might have been reluctant to ask Barnabas to endorse this letter. Indeed, the fact that Barnabas defected, however briefly, to Peter's side in the regrettable incident over table fellowship with Gentiles at Antioch (2:13), might have been another reason for leaving his name off the epistle. In any case, Paul wanted to avoid any hint that he might be sheltering behind someone else's authority.

### D. Paul's peremptory start (1:2b)

"Unto the churches of Galatia." This, then, was a circular letter addressed, as suggested, to the young churches in southern Galatia that he had planted a short while before on his first missionary journey.

At this point, it will be helpful to consider a possible sequence of events.

1. Paul, converted on the road to Damascus, remained in the Syrian capital long enough to regain his eyesight and to testify boldly for Christ in the synagogue (Acts 9:10–22).

2. He left Damascus for Arabia, where he stayed for some three years, thinking through the implications of the gospel (1:15–17).
3. He returned from Arabia to Damascus and witnessed for Christ in the city with such power that his enemies tried to kill him. He escaped by being let down over the city wall in a basket (1:17; Acts 9:23; 2 Cor. 11:32–33).
4. Three years after his conversion, with his theology fully developed, he visited Jerusalem, where Barnabus introduced him to the apostles. He spent two weeks with Peter and received a vision from the Lord warning him to leave Jerusalem and commissioning him to be the Apostle to the Gentiles. He escaped assassination by a precipitate flight to Caesarea (1:18–20; Acts 9:26–30; 22:17–21).
5. He left for Tarsus, where he labored for the Lord and was, seemingly, disinherited by his family (Acts 11:25; Phil. 3:7–8).
6. Needing a gifted leader for the revival in Antioch, Barnabas sought out Saul at Tarsus and brought him to Antioch to help in the evangelization of the city (Acts 11:26).
7. Paul, with Barnabas, paid a second visit to Jerusalem to bring famine relief to the believers. At that time, Herod Agrippa I was on the rampage. It is possible that on this occasion Paul met with the apostles to ensure that they understood his own apostleship and the content of his preaching. It is likely, too, that on this visit he took Titus to Jerusalem as a test case. Upon their return to Antioch, Paul and Barnabas took John Mark with them (Acts 11:27–30; Gal. 2:1–3).
8. Paul undertook his first evangelistic missionary journey, traveling through Cyprus and on to southern Galatia. He returned in triumph to Antioch (Acts 13:1–14:28) but not before Mark's defection.
9. Peter visited Antioch, where he had open fellowship with the Gentiles until some men from Judea ("from James") arrived in town. Peter then retreated into strict Judaism, causing consternation and confusion in the church. Paul rebuked Peter to his face. A hot dispute over the Law followed (2:11–14).
10. The Judaizers seem to have carried their legalism into Galatia at this time, infecting the infant Gentile churches that Paul planted.
11. Paul probably wrote his epistle to the Galatians at this time.
12. The church at Antioch decided to carry the whole vexing question of Judaizers to Jerusalem to be settled in conference.

13. The law-keeping issue was settled on a sound scriptural basis, and the decision of the Jerusalem council was confirmed by letter. Paul and Barnabas returned to Antioch and took Silas with them (Acts 15:23–34).
14. Paul and Barnabas decided on a second missionary journey but fell out over Barnabus's determination to take Mark with them.
15. Paul took Silas with him. He went first to Syria and Cilicia, where he, as Saul of Tarsus, had labored in seclusion after his first visit to Jerusalem. Then he went with Silas on to Galatia, penetrating into Old Galatia, this time in the north, before setting out for Europe and the West.

Paul's itinerary on his first missionary journey into southern Galatia can be visualized thus, as set forth in Acts 13:4–14:28:

- A. Departure from Antioch (13:4a)
  - B. Cyprus (13:4b–12)
    - C. Perga (13:13)
      - D. Antioch Pisidia (13:14–50)
        - E. Iconium (13:51–14:6a)
          - F. Lystra (14:6b–20a)
            - G. Derbe (14:20b)
          - F. Lystra (14:21a)
        - E. Iconium (14:21b)
      - D. Antioch Pisidia (14:21c–24)
    - C. Perga (14:25a)
  - B. Attalia (14:25b)
- A. Return to Antioch (14:25–28)

Paul, Barnabas, and young John Mark sailed from Cyprus and disembarked on the mainland of Asia Minor at Perga in Pamphylia. Ominous obstacles loomed ahead. Pamphylia was a low-lying country between the sea and the Taurus Mountains. It was sheltered by hills and watered by an abundance of rivers and streams. The climate was oppressive and enervating. Although Perga was one of the province's largest cities, it was hindered from fulfilling its destiny of becoming the chief port of Asia Minor by the ramparts of the mountains to the north. A temple of Diana corrupted the morals of the city.

In the distance loomed the snow-capped peaks of the Taurus Mountains, which had to be penetrated by means of narrow passes. Rickety bridges, robbers' castles, and rushing torrents were immediate dangers for the traveler. Not even the Roman army had succeeded wholly in overcoming them.

The intrepid traveler who braved these obstacles, however, had only just begun. The country to the north of the Taurus Mountains was a vast tableland of lofty peaks; scattered, lonely lakes; irregular mountain passes; and expanses of desert. The population was rough and rude and spoke an endless variety of dialects. No wonder John Mark decided to go home.

But Paul and Barnabas didn't turn back. They were made of sterner stuff. The lawless, marauding ways of the mountain folk were notorious. Some robber chiefs defied Rome and dared violent death in the mountain passes. There were perils of rivers and perils of robbers of which Paul would later write. Now they must be braved. He must force his own path through the Cilician Gates, armed with only his faith in Christ. There was a great fissure in the mountain chain ahead, a rent that ran from north to south for some eighty miles, and there stood the Cilician Gates. To secure them, Cyrus, Alexander, and other conquerors shed blood, but that was the way they must go, and go they did.

Like the conqueror he was, Paul, with his friend Barnabas, stormed the gates and arrived at Pisidian Antioch, the chief civil and military center of that part of Galatia. That city stood astride an important line of communication between Smyrna and Ephesus on the one hand and the Cilician Gates and Tarsus on the other hand. It lay three thousand six hundred feet above sea level. Augustus had made it a Roman colony, and, like all such transplants, it was typically Roman.

Paul always attached great importance to the evangelization of Roman colonies. They were always planted at strategic spots along the imperial highways. (Lystra, Troas, Philippi, Corinth, and Ptolemais are other Roman colony cities that we encounter in Acts.) Along with Greeks, Romans, and native Pisidians, Galatian Antioch contained its quota of Jews and a local synagogue. The local Jewish congregation was vigorous because they had made many proselytes and exerted considerable influence over the minds of the Gentile women of the city.

Following his customary practice, Paul headed straight for the synagogue at Antioch on his first Sabbath in town. As a distinguished rabbi from Jerusalem, he was invited to speak, and Luke records the sermon for us, Paul's first full-length sermon before a mission-field congregation. In it, he proclaimed Christ's death and the glad tidings of His resurrection. He pressed upon his audience the offer of God's free forgiveness of sins: "Be it known unto you therefore, men and brethren, that through this man is preached unto you the forgiveness of sins: And by him all that believe are justified from all things, from which ye could not be justified by the law of Moses" (Acts 13:38–39). Paul sensed a stiffening among the Jews at these words, and he concluded, "Beware therefore, lest that come upon you, which is spoken of in the prophets; Behold, ye despisers, and wonder, and perish: for I work a work in your days, a work which ye shall in no wise believe, though a man declare it unto you" (Acts 13:40–41).

The service broke up, and the Gentiles besieged Paul and Barnabus, pleading that he would preach the message to them. Many Jews and Jewish proselytes also flocked after the missionaries, who "persuaded them to continue in the grace of God" (Acts 13:43).

The following week was electric. The whole city talked of nothing else but the missionaries and their message. The next Sabbath saw the synagogue packed as practically the whole city thronged to hear the apostle. The success of Paul's preaching filled the Jews with envious rage, and they began to speak "against those things which were spoken by Paul, contradicting and blaspheming" (Acts 13:45).

Paul's reaction was typical. He shook off the dust of the synagogue against his Jewish enemies and turned his whole attention to the Gentiles, who received him with open arms. A revival broke out among the Gentiles, and the tidings of the gospel spread throughout the whole region. That only enraged the Jews still more. They "stirred up the devout and honourable women, and the chief men of the city, and raised persecution against Paul and Barnabas, and expelled them out of their coasts" (Acts 13:50).

Undaunted, the apostles headed for Iconium on the southeastern border of Phrygia. A crescent of snow-clad mountains enclosed the town to the west; well watered by abundant streams, it was a veritable garden city. To the north and east stretched the great Central Asia Minor plain. The city itself had been ruled successively by Seleucid, Galatian, and Pontic kings. It had been formally incorporated into the Roman Empire in A.D. 25, when Galatia became a Roman province.

The population was made up of pleasure-seeking Greeks, mostly attracted to the theatre and the marketplace, along with remnants of the older population, and by farmers who either came in occasionally from the country or resided in their own quarter of town. Some Roman officials were there, and they held themselves proud and aloof from the inhabitants of the conquered province. An old, established colony of Jews was there, and they were devoted to business during the week and the Law of Moses and the synagogue on the Sabbath.

Paul and Barnabas went straight to the synagogue "and so spake, that a great multitude both of the Jews and also of the Greeks believed" (14:1). Again, the envy of the unbelieving Jews was stirred; they, in turn, tried to turn the bulk of the Gentile population against the missionaries. Paul and Barnabas, however, simply dug in their heels: "Long time therefore abode they speaking boldly in the Lord, which gave testimony unto the word of his grace, and granted signs and wonders to be done by their hands" (Acts 14:3). The city took sides. In the end, the Jews stirred up violent persecution: "And when there was an assault made both of the Gentiles, and also of the Jews with their rulers, to use them despitefully, and to stone them, they were ware of it, and fled unto Lystra and Derbe, cities of Lycaonia . . ." (Acts 14:5–6).

Lycaonia was a bare, mountainous tract of country suitable only for raising sheep and goats. Lystra itself was off the main highway, on the banks of a stream that flowed through a valley on the southern border of the Lycaonian Plain. No mention is made of Jews in this town. Instead, at Lystra, Paul was confronted with raw paganism, superstition, and myth. The mythology of the region, however, was not refined and cultured, such as would appeal, for instance, to the Athenians. At Lystra, the missionaries faced the mythology and superstition of an uneducated and unsophisticated people. They met people who believed that Jupiter, father of the gods, occasionally visited earth.

Lystra was under the protection and patronage of Jupiter, who was supposed to haunt the city. The conspicuous temple of Jupiter stood by the city gates. In his travels, Jupiter was supposed to be accompanied by Mercury, the messenger of the gods. (The Greek names of Zeus and Hermes were the equivalent of the Latin names Jupiter and Mercurius.)

Undaunted by their persecution at Antioch and Iconium, Paul and Barnabus did not hesitate to preach the gospel at Lystra. Paul's keen eye soon spotted a lame man who had been handicapped from birth. With a word of command, Paul healed him. The reaction was unexpected. "The gods are come down to us!" the people had exclaimed, identifying Barnabas as Jupiter and Paul as Mercury (14:11–12). The news spread like wildfire through the town, and the priest of Jupiter hastily arranged for sacrifice to be offered to the startled missionaries. A horrified Paul and Barnabas were hard put to stop the sacrilege and to direct the attention of the excited mob to the true and living God. All of his efforts notwithstanding, Paul barely restrained the excited crowd from accomplishing its purpose.

Then the pendulum swung the other way. The Jews from Antioch and Iconium joined forces and descended on Lystra. They whipped up the mob, seized Paul, hustled him out of the city, stoned him, and left him for dead (Acts 14:19). The disciples that the evangelists had made stood around wringing their hands and lamenting Paul's untimely death when he "rose up" (the implication is that it was by divine power) and went back with them into the city.

The next day, Paul considered it expedient to go on to Derbe! This town was not far from the Black Mountain, which towers like an island from the surrounding Lycaonian plain. It took Paul and Barnabas only a few hours to walk the distance from Lystra. From the fact that Derbe is not mentioned in the list of places of which Paul reminds Timothy as being scenes of past sufferings (2 Tim. 3:11), some people have inferred that Paul's visit to Derbe was peaceful and free from persecution. Although that visit was a time of quiet and rest, Paul gave himself no rest from his master passion of soul winning. The fruit of the ministry of Paul and Barnabas at Derbe was the conversion of many disciples (Acts 14:21).

Then the missionaries retraced their steps, boldly revisiting Lystra, Iconium, and Antioch, places where they had experienced so many victories and such bitter persecution. Paul's first concern was never for his own safety but for the spiritual well-being of his converts. So he and Barnabas paid a visit to these towns on their way home, "confirming the souls of the disciples, and exhorting them to continue in the faith, and that we must through much tribulation enter into the kingdom of God. And when they had ordained them elders in every church, and had prayed with fasting, they commended them to the Lord, on whom they believed" (Acts 14:22–23).

Then they descended through the Pisidian Mountains to the Pamphylian Plain. They likely then headed north in the early spring and returned south from the highlands to the lowlands in the fall. They would thus arrive back to the plain about the time the people with cool mountain homes were returning from their summer retreat. Perga would be full of inhabitants. Paul had simply passed through this city on his outward journey; now he remained for a while. His preaching, however, seems to have had no conspicuous success.

So Paul and Barnabas turned homeward, not sailing this time but traveling instead across the plain of Attaleia back to Syrian Antioch. Thus, they had planted the first string of Galatian churches, the churches that Paul seems to address in this letter.

"Unto the churches of Galatia," Paul says abruptly and with none of his usual warmth and feeling. The situation was too critical and the news of the defection of his converts was too fresh in his mind for niceties. Paul could not wait to come to grips with the issues. He dipped his pen in the ink and plunged at once into the battle for their souls.

PART 2

# An Explanation

## Galatians 1:3–2:21

A. The declaration of the gospel (1:3–5)

1. Simple grace (1:3)

The epistle is in three parts. First, there is *an explanation,* in which Paul deals largely with matters of a historical nature. Then comes *an exposition,* in which Paul lays again the foundation of sound doctrine. Finally, there is *an exhortation,* in which Paul appeals for practical Christian living.

Paul's explanation begins with *a declaration,* in which he defines the significance of God's grace. Then he takes up *the distortion* of the gospel preached by the emissaries of Satan. Then he sets forth some of *the distinctions* of the gospel, how it came to him, and how it came to them. Finally, he underlines *his defense* of the gospel.

Simple grace! That is the essence of the New Testament gospel—simple grace: "Grace be to you and peace from God the Father, and from our Lord Jesus Christ."

*Grace! Peace!* These are the two great words of the gospel. Grace! That is God's wholly unconditional good will toward us. It is the basis upon which He saves us. Grace is God's unmerited favor that reaches out to us in all of our sin and need and gives us what we do not deserve—His unconditional, unearned salvation. Grace is God's love in action. Grace planned our salvation from before the foundation of the world. It was grace that the Judaizers so mercilessly attacked in Paul's Galatian churches. "Grace!" writes Paul. We can almost imagine his writing it in capital letters and underlining it. "Grace!" And peace! Peace means that the war is over. Grace means that we are reconciled with God. Peace means that all is well with our soul.

This grace and peace come from God the Father and from the Lord Jesus Christ. Thus, God the Father and God the Son are seen working together to make our salvation sure.

God the Father! What a wonderful name for God! Judaizers knew Him as Jehovah, *the God of covenant;* as Elohim, *the God of creation;* and as Adonai, the Sovereign Lord, *the God of command.* They knew Him as "the Lord God of your fathers, the God of Abraham, Isaac and Jacob." But the Galatians had been taught a higher truth than that. He was "God the Father."

Coeternal and coequal with God the Father is "our Lord Jesus Christ." He joins with the Father in bestowing the twin blessings of grace and peace upon His own.

Something was significant, too, about the words *our Lord Jesus Christ.* Later, when writing to the Romans, Paul warned, "Mark them which cause divisions and offences contrary to the doctrine which ye have learned; and avoid them. For they that are such serve not *our Lord Jesus Christ* . . ." (Rom. 16:17–18). They have a Christ in the cults, but He is not "our Lord Jesus Christ." *Our* Lord Jesus Christ is the eternal, uncreated, self-existing Son of the living God. *Our* Lord Jesus Christ created heaven and earth. *Our* Lord Jesus Christ was virgin born when He stepped out of eternity into time to become a Man among men. *Our* Lord Jesus Christ lived a sinless life. He raised the dead, cleansed the leper, and healed the sick. He fed the hungry multitudes. He changed water into wine, walked upon the waves, and stilled the storm. *Our* Lord Jesus Christ died an atoning death as a sacrifice for sin—the Just for us, the unjust—that He might bring us to God. *Our* Lord Jesus Christ was buried and remained in the tomb for three days and three nights. *Our* Lord Jesus was raised bodily from the dead and proved Himself alive after His passion by many infallible proofs. *Our* Lord Jesus Christ ascended bodily into heaven and now sits enthroned at God's right hand, exercising His ministry as our Great High Priest and as our Advocate with the Father. *Our* Lord Jesus Christ has sent His Holy Spirit into the world to call out a people for His name, a blood-bought bride, a church mystically one with Himself. *Our* Lord Jesus Christ is coming again, to receive His bride, to rule the world and, at last, to establish the kingdom to God. That is *our* Lord Jesus Christ.

They have a Christ in the cults, but he is not our Lord Jesus Christ. The Jehovah's Witnesses have a Christ, but he is not God the Son, nor did he rise from the dead because, according to them, his body was dissolved into gas in the tomb. Their Christ came back in 1914. He is not our Lord Jesus Christ.

The Mormons have a Christ. Their Christ was a polygamist, secretly married to Martha and Mary at the wedding of Cana of Galilee. He is not our Lord Jesus Christ.

The Seventh-day Adventists have a Christ, but he did not bear our sins in his own body on the tree. According to them, Satan was the scapegoat, and our sins were put on him. Their Christ is not our Lord Jesus Christ.

The Catholics have a Christ. The priest makes him by pronouncing five Latin words over a wafer of bread in the mass. That is not our Lord Jesus Christ.

The liberals have a Christ, but he was not virgin born, his miracles were sleights of hand, his life was only a good example, his death was an unfortunate martyrdom, and his resurrection was only a myth. Their Christ is not our Lord Jesus Christ.

The Judaizers who invaded the churches of Galatia had a Christ too. But he was a Christ who was unable to "save to the uttermost" all of those who come unto God through him; his grace and power was not sufficient for that! He required that, in addition to his own work, the Law of Moses be hung like a dead weight around the necks of all of those who would aspire to any hope of heaven.

"Our Lord Jesus Christ," wrote Paul in large letters (6:11). "Grace be to you and peace from God the Father, and from our Lord Jesus Christ."

2. Saving grace (1:4a–b)

Paul hurries on. He wants to get before his Galatian friends *a fresh view of our Savior:* "Who gave himself for our sins . . ." What are we to do about our sins?

In the Old Testament, Balak, king of Moab, had his own idea. He made his bids like a man in the market: "What will the Most High God take," he demanded, "to overlook my sins? I will offer Him burnt offerings, thousands of rams, rivers of oil, a Tigris, a Nile, a Euphrates of oil, ten thousand such rivers of oil. I will give my firstborn, all of my children, the fruit of my body for the sin of my soul" (Mic. 6:6–7).

F. W. Boreham, in one of his books, paints a vivid picture of Balak. He says that Balaam, carnal and pagan prophet that he was, knew enough of God to know that such offerings would be of no avail. He wrote,

> God's salvation, my Lord King, is not for sale, and even if it were, it could not be purchased in the kinds of things you offer in exchange. If salvation must be earned, if it can be purchased for a price, if human merits can be used as a barter price, try something else, something God can accept. Offer to God a life in which you have always done to others what you would have them do to you. Offer to Him a life in which you have loved mercy, a life that has always reached out with love and tenderness and compassion to those who have wronged you. And walk humbly with thy God. Offer to Him a life in which, like Enoch of old, you have always walked in step with God. There, my Lord King, if you think salvation can be earned, *that* is the price. That is heaven's irreducible minimum.

What are we to do about our sins? The Judaizers' ideas were like those of pagan King Balak and his hireling prophet Balaam. "Keep the Law of Moses," they said. "Be circumcised, sanctify the Sabbath, and observe the traditions of the elders and the rabbis."

"What are we to do about our sins?" Nothing! All of the doing was done at Calvary. God's grace is the answer to man's guilt. "Grace be to you . . . from our Lord Jesus Christ, who gave himself for our sins." Paul hastens to direct their gaze to the Savior.

He wants also to get before his Galatian friends *a fresh view of our salvation.* The Lord Jesus "gave himself for our sins, that he might deliver us from this present evil world. . . ." The word for "deliver" means "to rescue from danger." The word for "evil" is *ponēros,* which carries the idea of labor and pain, sorrow, malignant evil. The word for "world" is *aiōn,* literally "age." In other words, the Lord Jesus gave Himself for us to rescue us from this present age of malignant evil, an age controlled by its god, Satan (2 Cor. 4:4). The present age began with man's creation (Luke 1:70; John 9:32). Since man's fall this present evil age is one of spiritual darkness (Col. 1:13). Satan blinds its children to the light of the glorious gospel of Christ (2 Cor. 4:4). Christ-rejecting Judaism, with its bitter hostility to the gospel—a hostility that Paul had faced at Pisidian Antioch, Iconium, and Lystra—was part of Satan's world system, part of "this present evil world" from which Christ had delivered the Galatians.

3. Sovereign grace (1:4c–5)

Paul continues. Simple grace! Saving grace! And now sovereign grace! Paul's Galatian friends should realize that wrapped up in the counsels of God's grace is *God's government.* The grace that reaches out to deliver us is "according to the will of God and our Father." All of the initiative is with God the Father. Because God has a father heart, He reaches out to lost sinners of Adam's ruined race. That truth will be an everlasting wonder. In this age and this dark world of sin, we only dimly understand the wonders of God's grace. But when we arrive on heaven's shore and "know, even as we are known," our wonder and our awe will be complete. We shall express it in songs of loudest praise.

Ruth the Moabitess is an example. When she found herself at the feet of Boaz, she was overwhelmed by the loving-kindness and unmerited favor of that great prince of the house of Judah. She exclaimed, "Why have I found grace in thine eyes, that thou shouldest take knowledge of me, seeing I am a stranger?" (Ruth 2:10).

It was the same with Mephibosheth. He dwelt afar off in distant Lo-debar, the place of no pasture, a barren, inhospitable land. He was lame on both of his feet, the victim of a fall. He had no standing before God or man. He had been born into the family of Saul, David's most bitter foe, and he feared David for his very life. But what did David do? He said, "Is there not yet any of the house of Saul, that I may show the kindness of God unto him?" (2 Sam. 9:3). Then, sovereignly, and in grace surpassed only by the grace of God, David sent his messengers to find poor, lost Mephibosheth. It was all David's idea. It was David's love that flowed out to Mephibosheth. It was David who took the initiative. It was David's evangelists who found Mephibosheth and confronted him with the royal command of the king—"Come! Come, just as you are." So Mephibosheth responded. That was his part, all that he could do and all that the king expected him to do. He came to the king. He heard the gracious words of the king. He exclaimed, "What is thy servant, that thou shouldest look upon such a dead dog as I am?" (2 Sam. 9:8). Then he learned how far grace would go. He was adopted into the royal family. All of his lost estates were restored to him. He was given a place at the king's table "as one of the king's sons" (2 Sam. 9:11). No wonder, in later years, looking back on it all, he could say, "My lord the king is as an angel of God!" What sovereign grace did for Mephibosheth, sovereign grace has done for us. It is "according to the will of God and our Father." In the language of Samuel Medley's hymn "His Lovingkindness,"

> He saw me ruined by the fall
> Yet loved me notwithstanding all,
> He saved me from my lost estate
> His lovingkindness, O how great!

Paul, moreover, wanted his Galatian friends to know that wrapped up in God's grace is *God's glory.* "To whom be glory for ever and ever. Amen" (1:5).

Everything that God does ministers to His glory. God's grace is one of the factors in that vast equation of His glory. In creation, God displays His wisdom and power; in redemption, He displays His love and grace. The more we learn of God's grace, the more we glorify God. In the Apocalypse, the angelic hosts worship God with wonder and awe and exclaim, "Thou art worthy . . . for thou hast created all things . . ." (Rev. 4:11). That is as high as their worship can rise. They proclaim Him as the Lord of creation and raise their anthems to His wisdom and power. Then Jesus is introduced, and the whole song is lifted an octave higher. The blood-washed saints exclaim, "Thou art worthy . . . for thou wast slain, and hast redeemed us to God by thy blood" (Rev. 5:9). Their worship soars far above that of the angelic hosts and far above the "thrones and dominions" in the heavenly hierarchy. The ransomed children of Adam's ruined race proclaim Him as the Lamb of Calvary. They raise their anthems to His love and grace. The angelic hosts sing the song of *creation;* God's blood-washed throng sings the song of *redemption.* Thus, God's grace ministers eternally to God's glory. The redeemed will be exhibited to the angelic hosts eternally as trophies of God's grace. We, ourselves, will be the awesome proof to all of the orders and ranks of creation of the immeasurable vastness of God's grace. We shall sing:

God is love, I surely know,
By my Savior's depths of woe.
O how vile my low estate
Since my ransom was so great.[1]

The Judaizers wanted to spoil all of that by adding to God's grace the trumpery of their own beggarly ideas of how salvation ought to work. Like so many others in all ages, they thought that God's grace was not enough. They must add to it some effort of their own. No wonder Paul was indignant at what had happened to his beloved Galatians!

B. The distortion of the gospel (1:6–10)
   1. Paul's astonishment (1:6)

"I marvel that ye are so soon removed from him that called you into the grace of Christ unto another gospel." The word for "marvel" is *thaumazō.* It carries with it the idea of surprise at the unexpected. The news of the defection of the Galatians seems to have taken Paul off guard. He had not expected it. He had not long before left them. He had left them in good order, rejoicing in their "so great salvation" and triumphing over their foes. Their assemblies were in the care of handpicked elders. Their thanks and appreciation to God for him and Barnabas were full of the warmest regard and solicitude (4:15). What astonished Paul was not the fact that one or two of his converts had been led astray but the Galatians' wholesale abandonment of the truth. Perhaps, too, Paul had underestimated the courage of his Jewish enemies in Jerusalem. He might well have been surprised that they would dare the journey through the Taurus Mountains just to spread a

1. Robert C. Chapman, "Oh, My Savior Crucified," *Hymns of Worship and Remembrance* (Belle Chasse, LA: Truth and Praise, Inc., 1950), no. 171.

false gospel. If so, he had also underestimated the passion with which the Jerusalem Jews hated him, fired, as it was, by the fanaticism of error. He should have been aware of that, however, given his own former zeal in attacking the church.

"So soon!" he says. The word is *tacheōs,* which suggests that the defection had been hasty, a step taken without proper thought. The Galatians had been swept off their feet. After all, the Judaizers specialized in quoting Scripture. But they took texts out of context and ignored the dispensational dimension of the Scriptures. Error, especially when it is wrapped in Scripture and presented under cover of a false hermeneutic, can sound very much like the truth. People who are not instructed in the whole counsel of God can become an easy prey to false teachers. The whole so-called "charismatic" movement today thrives on such errors.

On the other hand, *tacheōs* can mean that only a little time had elapsed between the Galatians' acceptance of the gospel of grace and their abandonment of that truth for error. In the context, both meanings of the word seem to apply. The Galatians had only recently been evangelized. The good seed had barely taken root, had hardly come to fruit, and now this.

The word for "removed" is *metatithēmi,* which means "to desert," or to be moved from one position to another. The use of the present tense suggests that the abandonment of the truth by the Galatians was still in process and that it was not yet complete. Time still existed for the departure to be arrested. Hence, Paul's haste to get this letter on its way. Moreover, the use of the middle voice shows that Paul is putting the blame on his converts rather than on the false teachers. They should know better. We can be sure that Paul had well instructed them in the truth of God's grace.

2. Paul's assessment (1:7)

The Galatians had embraced "another gospel" (v. 6), "which," he now adds, "is not another [gospel]; but there be some that trouble you, and would pervert the gospel of Christ" (1:7). The word *another* occurs twice here. The first *another* is *heteros,* meaning another of a different kind. The second *another* is *allos,* meaning another of the same kind. The classic distinction between the two words is seen in another Pauline passage, 1 Corinthians 15:39–41, where *heteros* is used to distinguish between the glory of the heavenly and the glory of the earthly. The glory of the heavenly is a glory of a different kind than the glory of the earthly. The word *allos* is used to distinguish carefully among the flesh of men, birds, and fish. The difference is not one of genus but of species. *Allos* is also used to distinguish among the differing glories of the stars, which are differences of degree, not of kind.

Here in Galatians, Paul speaks of "a different gospel" *(heteros)* "which is not another" *(allos),* another like the one he preached. "I am astonished," he said, "that you have so soon switched to another 'gospel'—not, of course, that it is or ever could be another gospel." The "gospel" of the Judaizers differed so radically from that preached by Paul that it was not another gospel; it was no gospel at all. Paul preached salvation by grace through faith. The Judaizers preached salvation by law through works. The two were mutually exclusive. No common ground existed between the two beliefs—even though both Paul and the Judaizers appealed to the Bible to support their teaching. At the outset of his letter, Paul slams the door on any compromise.

"But there be some that trouble you, and would pervert the gospel of Christ," Paul adds. The word for "trouble" is *tarassō.* Later, when the question of law keeping, as essential to salvation, was fully aired before the leaders of the Jerusalem church, a letter was written condemning the false doctrine. The same word was used: "We have heard, that certain which went out from us have *troubled* you with words, subverting your souls . . ." (Acts 15:24).

The word for "pervert" is *metastrephō,* meaning to transform something into something of the opposite character. The Judaizers were preaching a travesty of the gospel. Paul had preached good news—salvation is full and free! It is by grace! All of the doing has been done! The Judaizers were preaching bad news—you have to keep the Law, you have to be circumcised, and you have to keep the Sabbath; you have to earn your salvation. Paul labels all such teaching as perversion.

3. Paul's assertion (1:8–10)
   a. The branded heretic (1:8–9)

Throughout the Scripture, the strongest language is reserved not for the murderer, or the adulterer, or the extortioner but for those who propagate religious error. John the Baptist called the Pharisees and the Sadducees a "generation of vipers" (Matt. 3:7). Jesus called the scribes and the Pharisees hypocrites, whited sepulchers, serpents, and a generation of vipers (Matt. 23:25, 27, 33). Now Paul pours out his own divinely inspired barrage of condemnation against the Judaizers—or anyone else, for that matter, who propagates false doctrine.

The branded heretic can be an apostle, an angel, or anyone: "But though we, or an angel from heaven, preach any other gospel unto you than that which we have preached unto you, let him be accursed. As we said before, so say I now again, If any man preach any other gospel unto you than that ye have received, let him be accursed" (1:8–9).

Some years ago, I received a phone call from a woman, a professing Christian and a member of a fundamental church in town. She asked, "Do you know where I can get a Greek Bible?"

I was astonished; the lady was no scholar. I asked, "Why do you want a Greek Bible?"

She said, "You can understand the Bible better in Greek."

I was suspicious. "Tell me," I said, calling the lady by name, "have you by any chance been talking to some Jehovah's Witnesses?" It turned out that such was the case.

I called on her husband at his place of business. He was a member in good standing in his church, one of the good churches in town. Yes, he agreed, they had been talking to some Jehovah's Witnesses. They had been having home Bible studies with some of the teachers from the local Kingdom Hall. I asked him if he would allow me to come and talk to him and his wife about the errors he was being taught. "Yes," he agreed, "you can come, but I'll have two of their teachers there as well."

"In that case," I replied, "I'll bring a friend."

I called a colleague of mine, a man whom I knew to be a skilled controversialist. The day came for the confrontation. It was a royal battle and went on for hours, but point by point the Jehovah's Witnesses were forced to reveal their true colors. Yes! They did have their own Bible. Yes! They did deny the deity of Christ! Yes! They had altered the text of John 1:1 to make the text read that Jesus was not God but only *a* god. No! They did not believe in the bodily resurrection of Christ. No! They did not believe in hell. Yes! They did believe that only 144,000 people could be born again—the rest are to be "Jonadabs," second-class citizens in the kingdom. Yes! True Jehovah's Witnesses must put in time pounding the pavement, selling *Watchtower* magazines and being obedient workers for the cause.

In the end, the Jehovah's Witnesses left, and we remained for some further counseling with our friends. It seemed that the victory was complete. However, the woman refused to give up an array of Jehovah's Witnesses books that she had bought. They seemed to exert some kind of hold upon her mind. Also, she was afraid of Armageddon. As the days passed, the fear became an obsession. I urged her to get rid of the books. She refused to do so. Prayer with her seemed to be unavailing. Efforts to put Bible prophecy into perspective, to get her back to the evangelical faith that she had once professed, met with stubborn resistance. Her husband refused to be more than a passive observer.

In the end, the woman, her husband, and their young child made their decision; they threw in their lot openly with the local Kingdom Hall, severed their connection with the local Baptist church, went to New York, and accepted baptism into the cult, manifesting a zeal for error that they had never shown for the truth.

Paul would say that the people who subverted this family are accursed. These people, now themselves active propagandists for a Christ-denying heresy, are accursed. Paul says so. The Holy Spirit says so. It is a crime in the court of heaven to subvert the true faith of Christ.

"Let him be accursed!" He might be an apostle. It might even be an angel. It could be anyone. But it makes no difference who brings the false message; it is the message, not the messenger, that matters. Just the same, the curse of God rests on the man, woman, or evil spirit who brings the message. "May the divine curse rest upon him!" Paul says.

We are so used to compromise, to tolerance of other people's beliefs, that Paul's words come almost as a shock. The problem with us, too, is that we look at the problem more or less as an academic problem, as a battle of wits between truth on this side and error on that side. It is satisfying if, in that verbal skirmish, we happen to win. It's another feather in our cap. And if we lose, well, it's too bad. We can't win them all. But God does not look upon it as an academic problem at all. The issues of all eternity hang in the balance for a human soul.

Think of the incredible, inestimable value of a soul! It was created by a direct act of God to be in His own image and in His own likeness. It is deathless. It is carved out of the very stuff of eternity. "What shall it profit a man, if he shall gain the whole world, and lose his own soul?" Jesus asked. "Or what shall a man give in exchange for his soul?" (Mark 8:36–37). Its value is so great that the Lord Jesus Himself, the second person of the Godhead, came from the mansions of glory to this sad world of woe to pay the price of our redemption. And what a price! First, He had to make that awesome stoop and be incarnated in human flesh, be born as a babe in that Bethlehem barn. He had to live a life of such stainless perfection as would win the unqualified approbation and approval of God. He had to endure the contradiction of sinners, fierce and fiery temptation, and mounting opposition and abuse. He had to go to Gethsemane, to Gabbatha, to Golgotha, and on to the grave itself. He had to give His life as a ransom for sin. And what a cruel death He died on Calvary's cross, amid the jeers and sneers of the mocking multitude! He who knew no sin was made sin for us. In the darkness that draped the horror of that final, awful torment, He cried out in agony, abandoned by God Himself. Then He had to die, descend into hades, and leave His body a lifeless corpse in a borrowed tomb for three whole days and three whole nights. Not until then did the turn in the road come, and His resurrection crowned it all in triumph. All to save us from our sins! Now we can be saved fully, freely, and forever in return for our simple faith.

As far as God is concerned, to tamper with "so great salvation" is to tamper with the eternal destiny of a soul, and that is a damnable offense. "Let him be accursed." "Anathema!" "May he be accursed!" "Let him be damned"—as one translator boldly renders it. The Holy Spirit says that He alone knows the real worth of a soul, fully comprehends the cost of our redemption, and properly appreciates the eternal horrors of hell and the endless bliss of heaven. This is no vindictive exclamation of an outraged apostle; this is God's own evaluation of the seriousness of leading another soul astray.

Paul reiterates it: "As we said before, so say I now again, If any man preach any other gospel unto you than that ye have received, let him be accursed" (v. 9). In verse 6, Paul contrasts what he calls "another gospel" with "the grace of Christ." In other words, any kind of teaching that minimizes salvation through grace alone is another gospel. Teaching that adds anything to salvation by faith through grace earns the anathema of God. "You have heard me say it before," Paul says. "Now I put it down in black-and-white—if any man preach any other gospel . . . let him be accursed."

b. The beloved herald (1:10)

"For do I now persuade men, or God? or do I seek to please men?" The word for "persuade" is *peithō,* "to prevail upon," "to win over." It seems that Paul's consistency had been called into question. Paul was willing to "made all things to all men" to win some (1 Cor. 9:22), but he never compromised a conviction or watered down a truth. His enemies would doubtless accuse him of trying to curry favor in Jerusalem by having Timothy circumcised and of trying to keep in with the Gentiles by leaving Titus uncircumcised. Paul, however, had a good reason for circumcising Timothy, who was already half a Jew by birth, and an equally good reason for leaving Titus, who was a full Gentile, uncircumcised. Paul was accused of setting his sail to match the wind and of adapting his preaching and practice to suit the occasion. This accusation Paul vigorously denies.

*Persuading* men? Yes, indeed! That was exactly what he did. That was his business. That was what he had been called to do. *Pleasing* men? Nonsense! Did it sound as though he were trying to please men—damning those who preached something contrary to the grace of Christ that he preached? "I should never have become a minister of the gospel," he says, "not if I were trying to please men." Paul knew from personal experience that popularity and preaching do not usually go hand in hand. His Galatian converts knew about the persecutions he had faced among them, especially at the hands of the Jews, for preaching boldly and without compromise the gospel of God's grace.

The faithful preacher often has to take a stand against the world's morality. He has to take an unpopular stand against drugs, abortion, sodomy, evolution, and pornography. He has to confront established error in religion and often comes into sharp conflict with entrenched religious systems that are opposed to the gospel. He has to denounce corruption and wickedness in high places. He sometimes has to deal with his own family and friends along the line of unwelcome and unwanted truth. He is called to persuade men, using every legitimate means at his disposal. But he is not called to please men.

Nor did Paul trim his sails to the changing wind. Paul reminds us of John Knox, Scotland's fearless voice. Mary, Queen of Scots, was more afraid of John Knox than of all of the armies of England. At one time in his stormy career, Knox was a galley slave, chained to an oar and under the interdiction of the court. The galleon was served by a Roman Catholic priest who came to where the prisoners were toiling at the oars and brought with him an image of the Virgin Mary. He presented the image to each of the galley slaves in turn, demanding that they, the blasphemous heretics, kiss the "Mother of God." At length, he came to John Knox. The bold preacher took the image from the priest. "Mother?" he cried, "Mother of God? This is nothing but a piece of painted wood, more fit for swimming, I think!" And before the horrified priest could stop him, he threw it overboard! Was John Knox seeking to please men? Of course not! Neither was Paul. He loved men. He gave himself wholeheartedly and unreservedly to try to win men. But compromise his message? Never!

C. The distinctives of the gospel (1:11–24)
  1. Paul's distinctive reception of the gospel (1:11–17)
    a. His claim (1:11–12)

Having thus delivered himself of his burden and made clear that there would be and could be no compromise concerning the truth. Paul now turns his attention to some personal history. He wants his Galatian friends to know just how he received the message that he preached with such passion and persuasion. We have, first, his claim. We note, first, *what Paul denied:* "But I certify you, brethren, that the gospel which was preached of me is not after man. For I neither received it of man, neither was I taught it" (1:11–12a).

The word *certify* is *gnōrizō,* "to make known." "Let me assure you," he says. Someone else did not teach him the gospel of grace that he preached. His own conversion experience gave him the clue as to how God saves men. He was saved on the Damascus road solely and simply by grace. At the time, he was himself an expert in the Law of Moses. He was a trained rabbi who was determined to carve out for himself a name, a reputation, and a career in the Jews' religion. He was a Jew, "a Hebrew of the Hebrews," indeed. He knew the Torah and was well versed in the budding Talmud. He was zealous for the Law. He was a Pharisee and committed to keeping all of the minutiae of the Law, not only the 613 commandments of the written laws but also all the endless rulings and traditions that the rabbis added over the years. On the Damascus road, however, when he was face-to-face with the risen Christ, he recognized that his Judaism actually made him an enemy of Christ. "I am Jesus whom thou persecutest!" the Lord said (Acts 9:5). The words stabbed like a sword in his soul. Yet, the Lord saved him then and there. Guilty sinner that he was, he was saved solely on the ground of grace.

No, indeed! He had not learned the gospel of men. He had not turned back to Jerusalem to seek out Peter or John to ask them to explain to him the way of salvation. He had not gone to Nicodemus to ask about the new birth or to Joseph of Arimathaea for information about the empty tomb.

Nor had he thought the gospel out for himself. It was not his as a result of natural reasoning, although his was one of the keenest minds. The gospel that he preached was no human invention.

Note *what Paul declared:* he said that he received it "by the revelation of Jesus Christ'" (1:12b). The words had come thundering into his ears. All about him had been a blaze of light that paled the very brightness of the noonday sun. The voice had spoken: "Saul, Saul, why persecutest thou me?" Smitten to the earth, he had cried, "Who art thou, Lord?" More than half convinced, he simply wanted to make sure. The face of Stephen—the face of an angel, the face of a man looking into the face of Jesus—had haunted him. "I am Jesus!" the voice had said. His instant response had been to enthrone Him. "Lord, what wilt thou have me to do?" He was already a saved man when he said that, saved and ready to serve his newfound Lord to the end. It had all been of grace. The risen Jesus had extended unmerited favor to him, the chief of sinners.

That was what had saved him! Grace and grace alone! In a flash, the light dawned. It was not law; it was grace. It was not works; it was simple faith. It was not Moses; it was Christ. It was not Sinai; it was Calvary. It was not to be earned; it was to be received. It was not trying; it was trusting. It was not by means of the rules and rituals of religion, however hedged about with both truth and tradition; it was by means of the undeserved, undiluted, undying grace of God. His gospel was received on the Damascus road "by the revelation of Jesus Christ."

b. His conversion (1:13–16b)
   (1) Paul as a religious man (1:13–14)

Paul now tells his Galatian friends how in his old unregenerate days *he zealously persecuted the Christian faith:* "For ye have heard of my conversation [manner of life] in time past in the Jews' religion, how that beyond measure I persecuted the church of God, and wasted it" (v. 13). The word rendered "the Jews' religion" is *ioudaismos,* Judaism. In secular Jewish life, the word referred to "the government, laws, institutions, and religion of the Jews." It refers not just to the religious beliefs of the Jewish people but to their religious practices as well. It is not confined to the religious practices of the Jews as enshrined in the Torah but also the religious practices of the Jews as exemplified by the scribes, rabbis, and Pharisees. This form of Judaism included what the Jews called "the oral law," as distinct from the written Law of Moses. This "oral law" was a vast and growing compilation of traditional interpretation. Some of it had turned the practice of Judaism into a denial of the faith. The aggregate became a dreadful burden to the Jewish people. The Lord denounced this rabbinic Judaism and earned the lasting hatred of the scribes and the Pharisees as a consequence.

It was Saul's devotion to "the Jews' religion" (for so the Holy Spirit calls it, disowning it as being in any way of God) that motivated him to persecute the church in his unregenerate days. He considered Jesus of Nazareth to be an impostor and a blasphemer. To his mind, Christianity was a cult of such a dangerous nature that it should be stamped out at all costs. "Beyond measure I persecuted the church," Paul says. Elsewhere, he described the persecution that he himself experienced at the hands of his enemies when he became the great Apostle to the Gentiles: "In Asia, . . . we were pressed out of measure," he says (2 Cor. 1:8), so much so, indeed, that he despaired of his very life. Conversely, he contrasts the pressure under which he lived with the superlative bliss that awaited him on the other shore. He speaks of it as "far more exceeding . . . weight of glory" (2 Cor.

4:17). The same idea of excess occurs in Paul's statement that it is the existence of the law that makes sin "exceeding sinful" (Rom. 7:13). In urging the Corinthians to seek the way of love, rather than pursue after the sign gifts, Paul calls it "a more excellent way" (1 Cor. 12:31). As Saul of Tarsus and a religious man, he had thrown himself wholeheartedly into the persecution of the church.

Indeed, he had "wasted" it. The word is *portheō,* which means "to lay waste," "to ruin," or "to devastate." We have only the barest hints in the New Testament of the fierce anti-Christian activities of the unregenerate, fanatical Saul of Tarsus. He was the accredited agent of the Sanhedrin and the archpersecutor of the church. This is one reason why Paul, in his missionary activities, was always so zealous to raise money for "the poor saints in Jerusalem." He was pursued by a memory day and night of widows and orphans in the Jerusalem church, many of whom he had made such. His behavior had been like that of a wild boar uprooting tender saplings. He was merciless. Some people he had forced to blaspheme; others had been martyred while he cheered on those who hurled the stones. Moreover, he had extended his activities to foreign cities.

Such had been his zeal in persecuting the Christian faith. Nothing but the grace of Christ could have arrested Saul of Tarsus in the fierce heat of his hatred toward the gospel. Nothing but a vision of the risen Christ could have transformed him into the great Apostle to the Gentiles, people whom he had once despised.

Next, Paul tells his Galatian friends how, in his old unregenerate days, *he zealously practiced the Jewish faith:* "And profited in the Jews' religion above many my equals in mine own nation, being more exceedingly zealous of the traditions of my fathers" (v. 14). The word for "profited" is *prokoptō,* "to advance," "to make progress." Paul had been getting on in "the Jews' religion." It was the religion that had rejected Christ, the religion of the rent veil, a religion that Calvary had rendered null and void. Jewish beliefs had been so adulterated and altered that they were no longer valid as a faith. Instead it was now called "the Jews' religion." Paul had been making great strides in it. He had been making a name for himself. He had been the fair-haired boy of the Sanhedrin; but, like the businessman who spent all of his life climbing the corporate ladder only to find when he finally reached the top that it was against the wrong wall, Paul had been climbing the wrong ladder. Paul was advancing in "the Jews' religion" but was getting nowhere. All that his religious zeal and fanaticism had done was make him a confirmed enemy of Christ.

"Above many my equals," Paul adds. The word is *sunēlikiōtēs,* "many my own age." We can well imagine that, with his brains and energy, his schoolfellows had marked him out as the classmate most likely to succeed. He had been Gamaliel's best scholar—bright and enthusiastic, a formidable thinker, and a fanatical Jew. His friends would see him striding away from class with a determined air or hear him debating some hot issue with pitiless logic and vehement passion. They would note, too, another and more attractive side of their comrade's character. He had a way with people. He had a winsome charm and personality—when he wanted to use them. They would say, "There goes the future high priest."

Paul says that he was "more exceedingly zealous." The word is *zēlōtēs.* It denotes an enthusiast, what we would call a zealot. He had been a fanatic when it came to the law. The membership of the Jerusalem church included many such people. This same word is used in connection with Paul's last disastrous visit to Jerusalem, the visit that resulted in the temple riot and his arrest. Paul, determined to be all things to all men in the cause of Christ, did his utmost to pacify the James faction in the Jerusalem church. Paul had told James and the other Jerusalem elders about the great revivals that had broken out far and wide among the Gentiles. They expressed a polite interest. Then they came to the point dearest to their narrow hearts: "When they heard it, they glorified the Lord, *and* [note the polysyndeton marking the significance of each statement] said unto him, Thou seest, brother, how many thousands of Jews there are which believe [they were not that impressed with Paul's success—after all, his successes had been with *Gentiles*]; *and* they are all *zealous of the law*" (Acts 21:20).

That was what characterized the Christianity of the Jerusalem church: many of its members were zealots for a Jewish brand of Christianity. What they represented was a kind of baptized Judaism. Note the expression "zealous of the law." Then followed that senseless suggestion, which Paul accepted to keep the peace with the Jewish Christians to his own subsequent arrest. Nor do we read that the Jerusalem church lifted a finger to help him after his arrest. On the contrary, doubtless many of them secretly were relieved that he would no longer be around to threaten their beloved Judaism. Paul's former misplaced zeal, they thought, had come home to roost.

And for what had Paul been such a zealot in his unregenerate days? "The traditions of my fathers," he says. It will help us to pause here and see what that involved.

The five books of Moses can be written out in about 350 pages. The Talmud, which first swamped and then virtually replaced it, takes up 523 books and is printed in 23 volumes. It is a wordy, rambling, and inconsistent conglomeration of songs, sermons, fables, and fancies. It has been called "the race memory" of the Jewish people. It is a motley collection of wit, wisdom, and nonsense.

It began with the *Midrash.* Around the year 443 B.C., the scribes (sometimes called the Sephardim) began to expound and interpret the Hebrew Scriptures. The later development of the *Midrash* was the work of the rabbis (*rab* originally meant "great one," and *rabbi* meant "my superior"). The Bible was their text. Their exposition consisted of simple allegories, homilies, and unsophisticated commentaries. Once begun, the *Midrash* tended to grow. It meandered more or less aimlessly through the meadows of Jewish thought from the days of the Babylonian captivity until shortly before the birth of Christ, when it underwent a radical change.

The rabbis evolved a principle that became the controlling principle in their hermeneutical system. The fact that it was based on a false premise made no difference. According to the rabbis, God had given Moses two sets of laws: the *written* law, which was inscribed on the tables of stone, and the *oral* law, which, according to them, gave specific elaboration of the Torah itself.

For instance, the fourth commandment sanctified the Sabbath as a day of rest. The rabbis explored and expanded the meaning of this simple provision of the law, adding countless rules and regulations of their own to define what constituted "work" on the Sabbath. By the time of Christ, the Sabbath (as interpreted by the rabbis) had been so hedged about with man-made rules and regulations that it had become an intolerable burden of endless dos and don'ts. The Lord brushed aside this vast accumulation of man-made restrictions.

This mythical oral law gave the rabbis great power. It was supposed to be known only by them because they were the spiritual heirs of Moses. According to the rabbis, the oral law was given to Moses at Sinai, and he passed it on to Joshua. He handed it on, in turn, to the elders, to the prophets, to the Sanhedrin, and to the men of the Great Assembly. Just before the birth of Christ, it had become the almost exclusive property of the rabbi Hillel, who handed it on to Gamaliel, Paul's former tutor. In time, it became the property of Akiba, then Maimonides, then the Vilna Gaon of Lithuania, and so on. Today, it is the property of the rabbis.

It would have been bad enough if this growing body of oral and traditional law had begun and ended with the *Midrash,* but such was not the case. The *Midrash* gave place to the *Mishna,* and that, with the advent of the *Mishna,* prepared the way for the eventual full-fledged hybrid growth of the Talmud.

The conquests of Alexander the Great changed the ancient world. In the wake of his conquests came Hellenism, the Greek system of thought, ideas, religion, art, culture, and philosophy. As a system, it was seductively alluring. The Jews tried to fight against it, but it presented them with an enormous intellectual challenge. In the end, Jewish thinkers decided that Hellenism could no longer be ignored. The naive and artless *Midrash* would no longer do; it must be harnessed to Greek thought if it were to withstand the intellectual pressures of the times—for so liberals always think when they bring their unregenerate scholarship to bear upon the things of God. It never occurred to them to bring all human philosophy, science, and religion to the bar of Scripture. To their thinking, Scripture has to be tried at the bar of human thought.

Thus, the rabbis began to add Greek reasoning to biblical revelation. This task was undertaken by a new set of scholars known as the Tannas. Instead of using the stories and sermons of the *Midrash* as supplements to Scripture, the Tannas used logic and reasoning borrowed from the Greeks to add human ideas to divine revelation. The *Mishnah* first began to make its appearance about the year 200 B.C., in both Babylonia and Palestine. It was an even more jumbled exposition than the *Midrash.* It kept on diluting the Word of God with liberal infusions of human opinion. It kept on growing for four centuries and was regarded as so sacred that it must never be written down. All of it had to be memorized, including footnotes and cited authorities. Then it had to be passed on orally to others. It was "the oral law," and mastering it called for no small feat of memory.

About the year 35 B.C., two schools of thought—one led by Shammai, a strict legalist, and the other led by Hillel, who tended to be more liberal—became popular among the Jews. In time, Hillel became the dominant Jewish theologian and was the acknowledged father of rabbinical hermeneutics. Hillel firmly established the authority of the *Mishna* among the Jews when he became the president of the Sanhedrin in Jerusalem.

Hillel was a gifted scholar, equally at home in Greek and Hebrew systems of thought. He postulated seven rules for applying logic to old ideas in order to come up with new ideas. You begin, he said, with a divine proposition—for instance, "Remember the Sabbath day to keep it holy. . . ." Then you apply the laws of reason to that divine proposition. If the resulting deductions can be demonstrated to grow logically from the proposition, then, obviously, the deduction is just as divinely inspired as the original proposition. The Pharisees, as a body, followed Hillel's teachings. Their archenemies, the Sadducees, however, rejected them. Thus, the *Midrash,* which effectively nullified the Scriptures, came into its own shortly before the birth of Christ.[2]

---

2. For further study, and to see how the *Midrash* evolved into the Talmud, see John Phillips, *Exploring the World of the Jew* (Chicago: Moody, 1981).

Because Gamaliel was the spiritual heir of Hillel, and Paul (Saul of Tarsus) had been the brightest of Gamaliel's pupils, we can see how Paul could say that he "profited in the Jews' religion above many my equals in mine own nation, being more exceedingly zealous of the traditions of my fathers." The legalizers and the Judaizers had in Paul a formidable opponent. He knew the ramifications and errors of "the Jews' religion" better than they did. He once had been a vital part of it.

### (2) Paul as a regenerated man (1:15–16b)

When Paul met Christ on the Damascus road, all of his preconceived ideas about religion were swept away; he became a new man in Christ. He now gives his Galatian friends a thumbnail sketch of his spiritual history. He tells them *how he was separated:* "it pleased God, who separated me from my mother's womb" (v. 15a). The hand of God was on the life of Paul. He tells us that God separated him at the time of his birth; he was separated by God at his conversion (Acts 9:15–16), and he was separated again at the time of his formal ordination to his lifework of world evangelism (Acts 13:2).

At no time, however, did this overruling will of God infringe on Paul's personal sovereignty and accountability as a moral human being. God persuades, but He does not push. He convicts, but He does not coerce. He does not arbitrarily impose His will on the human will. Yet, at the same time, He never loses control of human affairs. His omnipresence, omnipotence, and omniscience enable Him to gather events into His hands with the greatest ease. From our perspective, events take place in a time sequence because we live in a time sequence, but God transcends time. He lives in the eternal present tense of time. He is the I AM. From God's standpoint, all of the events of time take place simultaneously. God can call the things that are not as though they are, because He does not have to wait for the future to reveal the end of a sequence of events nor wait for a specific moment of time to come before imposing His will upon that moment.

So, then, Paul was a marked man from birth. Isaac, Jacob, Samson, Cyrus, John the Baptist, and Jesus were too. And so, in one sense, we all are. God can accept our own choices and decisions at their face value and overrule them the way a chess master imposes his will on a game. Moreover, God has His own ways of speaking to us and revealing His "good and acceptable and perfect will." He never forces us to do His will, but He does overrule the passing events of time so that all things work together according to His purpose.

So God could speak of the infant Saul, lying in his cradle in Tarsus, as being separated. It was always God's sovereign intention to send that particular human being as His ambassador to the Gentiles. Yet, as we read the book of Acts, we can see how it all worked out perfectly naturally on the human level. Saul was brought step-by-step to his confrontation with the risen Christ on the Damascus road. Thereafter, he was led step-by-step to his great lifework.

Not only was he separated but also *he was saved* because that was the key event of his crowded and eventful life: "and called me by his grace," Paul says (v. 15b). *Grace!* It was the key word in Paul's life, the key word in his testimony, and the key word in his theology. While he was in the very act of "breathing out threatenings and slaughter," Paul was arrested by the risen Christ Himself on the Damascus road. That was grace! What Paul deserved was wrath; what he received was grace.

Grace is getting something we don't deserve. Suppose that you were to look out the window of your home and see someone stealing your car. You phone the police and give a description of the person along with the make, model, and description of your car. Sometime later, the phone rings. It is the police department. "Can you come on down to the police station?" the officer inquires. "We have your car, and we have the culprit." You go down, and he is there, a woebegone-looking teenager. You inspect your car, and it is undamaged.

The officer asks, "Do you want to press charges?"

If you say, "Yes. The young man stole my car. He's a thief. He deserves to go to prison," that would be justice. If you say, "No. He seems very young. Maybe he's learned his lesson. Let him go," that would be forgiveness. But suppose that you were to say, "Let him go" and then turn to the culprit and say, "Young man, I not only forgive you but also I want to help you. Don't ever steal a car again. Here are the keys to a car I have at home. I don't use it. You can have it." That would be grace, unmerited favor, giving him something he didn't deserve. That is the basis on which God saved Saul of Tarsus, His bitterest enemy and "the chief of sinners." "He called me by his grace," Paul said.

Never to his dying day would he forget the day when he heard that call, "Saul! Saul!" ringing down from heaven! God would not have spoken to Saul like that if He had arrested him at Sinai. He would have spoken to him with a voice of thunder. There would have been lightning, the rumble of an earthquake, and the terrifying sound of the trump of God (Exod. 19:16–19; Heb. 12:18–21). Instead, God called him by his name, "Saul! Saul!" His salvation was all of grace. God's Son spoke to Saul from heaven; He spoke in tender tones and with reasoned words. He spoke in the accents of love beyond all love.

All salvation is the same. Every sinner is saved by grace. Thus, by his own testimony, Paul hammers another nail into the coffin of the legalists. They wanted to take his beloved Galatians away from Calvary and back to Sinai, but Paul's testimony responds with a resounding *No!*

But more! *He was sanctified.* He was set apart for God. He was separated and called because, as he puts it, God wanted to "reveal his Son in me" (v. 16a). Our salvation involves far more than the mere forgiveness of our sins. The Lord Jesus not only gave His life *for* us but also now gives His life *to* us. The genius of the gospel is that He who once died *for* me now, by His indwelling Holy Spirit, lives *in* me. The Lord Jesus lived here on earth for something like 12,300 days. Every one of them was a miracle of sinless perfection. He lived on earth as Man inhabited by God. The only explanation for His life—whether as a babe, as a child in that Nazareth home, as a teenager, as a young man working at the bench, or as an itinerant prophet tramping the highways and byways of His native land—was God. He "went about doing good." He spoke "as never man spake." He died in extraordinary triumph and rose again exactly as He had foretold. The only explanation for His life was God. He was Man, but He was man indwelt by God. Every moment of His life, He maintained an attitude toward His Father that said, "Lo, I come (in the volume of the book it is written of me,) to do thy will, O God" (Heb. 10:7). He was Man inhabited by God, always available to His Father. His Father, likewise, was always available to Him. That was how He lived. As a result, the Holy Spirit was able, through Him, to reveal the Father to us. When Philip said, "Show us the Father, and it sufficeth us," Jesus simply replied, "He that hath seen me hath seen the Father" (John 14:8–9).

Paul had grasped the great secret of the Christian life—he was saved so that God could reveal the Son in him just as the Holy Spirit had revealed the Father in Jesus. The regenerated believer is indwelt by the Holy Spirit, the third person of the Godhead (John 14:16–18; 1 Cor. 3:16). In other words, every born again believer is a person who is indwelt by God. The only explanation of his life should be God. The things that he does and says; the places to which he goes; and what he is in nature, character, and personality should be governed by the same principle of yieldedness to the will of God that characterized Jesus. Then the Holy Spirit will be able to "reveal the Son in us." Paul had entered into that truth. The Christian life is Christ, and He is the only One who can live it. It is a supernatural life—our humanity made available to His deity. That was Paul's concept of dynamic Christianity. It was a far cry from the goal of the legalists and

Judaizers, who wanted to marry the Galatian Christians to the Law of Moses and engage them to a system of doing their best for Jesus.

Interestingly enough, the word that Paul uses here for "reveal"—"to reveal his Son in me"—is *apokaluptō,* which means literally "to unveil" so as to be "visible to the eye." It is a kindred word to that used by John in the opening clause of the book of Revelation: "The revelation *(apokalupsis)* of Jesus Christ . . ." (Rev. 1:1). The book of Revelation is the unveiling, the revealing of the Lord Jesus in all of His glory. The good news of the gospel is not simply that the Holy Spirit wants to get me out of hell and into heaven. He wants to do that, of course; but equally important, He wants to get God out of heaven and into me! We are to be so in fellowship with the indwelling Spirit of God that God will be able to make the Lord Jesus "visible to the eye" through us.

Then, too, Paul tells us how *he was sent:* "that I might preach him among the heathen" (v. 16b). He was not sent to preach Moses but Christ. He was not sent to proclaim the bad news to the Gentiles—you must become Jews if you want to become Christians. You must keep the Law if you wish to be saved. You must be circumcised and keep the Sabbath and the Jewish dietary laws. You must saddle yourself with the burden of the Law and the intolerable burden of the rabbinical rules and regulations. That would have been bad news indeed. But Paul had not been separated, saved, sanctified, and sent to preach that. He was sent to preach the gospel, to preach Christ!

There is all the difference in the world between preaching a religious creed or a legal code and preaching Christ. It would have been gloomy enough tidings had Paul been called and commissioned to preach such a message to *Jews,* born and bred in the Law and wedded to Moses as they were. But even Peter, who had been ordained to a mission to the Jews, had not been called to preach legalism to his Jewish converts. Certainly Paul had not been called to preach legalism to the heathen. He had been commissioned to preach Christ to them. The word for heathen here is *ethnos,* the usual word for Gentiles, for nations other than Israel.

No man could have been better equipped to carry the good news of Christ to the great Gentile world. Although Paul was a Jew, he was born a Hellenist Jew. He was at home in the Greek language. By birth, he was a freeborn citizen of Rome. He had been raised in Tarsus, a pagan city that rivaled even Athens and Alexandria as a center of philosophy and education.

Tarsus was very much a Greek city. It was located near the western border of the Cilician plain where the river Cydnus flowed, cold and swift, from the snows of Taurus to the sea. It was the capital of a province and, indeed, was "no mean city," as Paul once described it (Acts 21:39). It was the Marseilles of the eastern Mediterranean. Roman soldiers and officials would have been as familiar to young Saul as were the local rabbis. Paul's active and inquiring mind, Jew though he was, could and did appreciate whatever was good and noble in the Gentile world in the midst of which he was reared. It was far easier for the thoroughly cosmopolitan Paul to appreciate Gentiles than it was for the narrow-minded, somewhat bigoted James, for instance, or even the impulsive but provincial Peter.

Paul knew better than anyone the repulsion with which the average Gentile viewed a "gospel" that demanded circumcision as its "open sesame." Paul knew better than anyone how gladly the Gentiles were willing to embrace Christ. And, blessed be God, that was the very message he was sent to preach—Christ! To the Romans, who ruled the world, Paul preached a greater King than Caesar. To the Greeks, who peopled Mount Olympus with gods made in the image and likeness of fallen men, he preached the Man, Christ Jesus, Son of the living God. To that vast and countless multitude of slaves who made up the bulk of the Roman world, he offered a new Master, One who proclaimed, "If the Son therefore shall make you free, ye shall be free indeed" (John 8:36).

So then, Paul reminds the Galatians about his conversion, and while doing so, he obliquely reminds them of theirs.

#### c. His concealment (1:16c–17)

We now have some extra light shed on what Paul did immediately after his conversion. We note *his resolve:* "Immediately I conferred not with flesh and blood: neither went I up to Jerusalem to them which were apostles before me" (vv. 16c–17a). That, of course, would have been the natural thing to do. But Paul did not do the natural thing; he did the spiritual thing.

We know the sequence of events. The light from heaven blinded Paul, so his companions had to lead him, still blind, into Damascus, where he sat in darkness somewhere in the city in a house on Straight Street for some three days. All of that time, he fasted and prayed, subject to all kinds of doubts and certainties, hopes and fears, and resolves and remorse. He was awaiting a messenger, someone who would tell him what to do next. At length, a disciple named Ananias came to him and miraculously restored his sight, told him how to be filled with the Holy Spirit, baptized him, and fed him. After this, Paul remained in Damascus "certain days," boldly preaching Christ in the synagogues, proclaiming Him to be the Son of God, and astonishing everyone—because his reputation as chief inquisitor of the Sanhedrin was well known. During this time, he "increased the more in strength," growing rapidly in his newfound faith, and "confounded the Jews which dwelt at Damascus, proving that this is very Christ" (Acts 9:8–22).

This period of witness, however, did not last long. The rising wrath of the unbelievers made evident that he would have to leave the city. But where should he go? Plenty of people, we can be sure, would advise him to go to Jerusalem to sit for a while at the feet of the apostles. The Holy Spirit, however, had a better plan, and, under His guidance, Paul came to a resolve. He did not want or need to be taught the truth of the gospel by men. He had his Bible. He had met the Christ. He had been filled with the Spirit. Why could not God teach him directly?

In light of what happened at Antioch and in Galatia, it is now obvious that it would have been disastrous for him to be in any way beholden to the apostles and to the Jerusalem church. Nothing could have been more important than for Paul to retain his moral, mental, and volitional independence from the Jerusalem church and its innate legalism. His resolve then—and it was a right one—was to stay away from Jerusalem until such time as he had sorted things out for himself. He was certainly not going to let the Jerusalem church pour him into its mold. In any case, if things were already getting hot for him at Damascus, he could well imagine the rage and fury that awaited him at Jerusalem. No! It was best to stay away from Jerusalem until things had simmered down and until he had sorted things out for himself in his own mind.

We note next *his retirement:* "But I went into Arabia," he says (v. 17b). This is taken to be a reference to the Nabataean kingdom, which was founded in the second century before Christ and had its capital at Petra. It stretched south from Damascus into the Arabian Peninsula. At the time of Paul's conversion, Aretas, the Nabataean king, was at war with Herod Antipas, tetarch of Galilee and Perea, over the insult done to his daughter, whom Herod had divorced to marry Herodias. Plenty of Gentiles were in the Nabataean kingdom, both as residents and as nomads.

Some scholars think that Paul, fleeing from Damascus, plunged immediately into his new calling of Gentile evangelism. Proof of this is seen in the incident that took place after his return to Damascus. "In Damascus," he told his Corinthian converts, his mind going back to the incident, "the governor under Aretas the king kept the city of Damascenes with a garrison, desirous to apprehend me . . ." (2 Cor. 11:32). One can assume, therefore, that Paul had done something to attract the hostile interest of the Nabataean authorities because the king's envoy in the city of Damascus wanted to kidnap and abduct him. What would Paul have done to incur such hostility but preach the gospel? On the other hand, Paul might well have done something on his way back to Damascus to provoke the ire of Aretas.

Paul most likely sought for some considerable time to enjoy the silences of Sinai for meditation, Bible study, and prayer. Perhaps he sought out the very sites hallowed of old by Moses and Elijah as their meeting place with God. As in later years, Paul said "I must see Rome," so now he seems to have said, "I must see Sinai." He desperately needed time alone with God, his Bible, the Holy Spirit, and the memory, forever imprinted on his soul, of Jesus in His glory.

So, we can well picture Paul as he headed for the place for solitude. In his bag, he had his copies of the Torah, the Psalms, and the Prophets. He found a shady spot for himself, perhaps beneath the ramparts of Mount Sinai, and there he read again Psalm 22; Psalm 69; Isaiah 53; and Genesis 22. *Ought not Christ to have suffered?* he asked himself. He reconstructed the promises of the Messiah in the Old Testament—He was to be born in Bethlehem, He was to labor in Galilee, He was to minister to the poor and oppressed, He was to do always those things that pleased the Father, He was to be crucified, and He was to be buried for three days and three nights, but His body was to be preserved from corruption. He was to rise again and ascend on high. It was all there! How could he have been so blind? The Messiah was to be the Son of David, Israel's rightful King. He was to reign from the river to the ends of the earth. How could that be? That did not fit with the story of the historical Jesus, did it? A second coming, of course! He had seen Him in His glory. That was no problem. He was coming back to fulfill the remaining prophecies of Daniel and the glowing prophecies of Isaiah and the other prophets! So far, so good.

But what about the Law? Judaism, he now knew, had degenerated into a lie. But what about the sacrifices and the feasts of the Old Testament? They were types, pictures. That was it! Even under law, there was grace. And the rent veil! How could he have forgotten that? Judaism was obsolete. What, then, was Christianity? How did the Jew fit into this change of dispensations? It could well have taken Paul the best part of three years to think through what was, in fact, the theology of the New Testament. He had gone to Sinai with his Old Testament in his pack; he came back from Sinai with Romans, Ephesians, Thessalonians, and Hebrews in his heart.

Next, Paul mentions *his return.* He "returned again unto Damascus" (v. 17c). He had been gone for three years. At this time, Paul had one of his hairbreadth escapes, narrowly evading his watchful foes by being let down over the wall of the city in a basket! However, Paul does not mention this interesting item in his Galatian letter. The Galatians knew for themselves how perilously Paul lived in his missionary career. He never flinched from danger. They knew that. Here, Paul was simply wishing to make the point that, far from rushing off to Jerusalem to get some kind of blessing, instruction, or endorsement from the apostles, he deliberately stayed away from them for three years.

2. Paul's distinctive reputation in the gospel (1:18–24)
   a. His acceptance in Jerusalem (1:18–19)

Paul had already formulated his theology and begun his apostolic ministry when he first went back to Jerusalem. He had neither sought nor needed any authorization, endorsement, or recognition from the Jerusalem church or its apostles. However, it was eminently desirable that, sooner or later, he establish some kind of relationship with the original disciples of Jesus. He tells us how that contact came about: "Then after three years I went up to Jerusalem to see Peter, and abode with him fifteen days. But other of the apostles saw I none, save James the Lord's brother."

What a meeting that must have been, the meeting between Peter, the great Apostle to the Jews, and Paul, the great Apostle to the Gentiles. There they stood, looking each other in the eye. Peter, the simple Galilean fisherman, and Paul, the onetime rabbinic scholar, liberal Hellenist, and favored son of the Sanhedrin. Outside of Christ, the two men would have had nothing in common; in Christ, however, they were brothers and fellow members of the body of Christ.

We can well imagine the hundreds of questions that Paul had to ask Peter. He had not come to discuss theology or to seek Peter's approval of his gospel. He had come to fill in the gaps in his knowledge of Christ. So, beginning at Nazareth, Peter would recount the story of Jesus that is now enshrined in the four Gospels. He would tell of the Lord's baptism, temptation, and ministry in Galilee. He would tell of the miracles that he had seen—how Jesus turned water into wine, stilled the storm, walked upon the waves, and fed the hungry multitudes. He would tell of the countless healing miracles—how He healed the sick, cleansed the leper, cast out demons, and raised the dead. Paul would want details. Then Peter would tell Paul what Jesus had taught. Paul would listen eagerly as Peter recalled the Sermon on the Mount, the parables, the Olivet discourse, and the long talk and the priestly prayer in the Upper Room.

Then Peter would take Paul on a tour of Jerusalem. "Here's the Upper Room, Paul," he would say, "where we kept the last Passover and where Jesus instituted the Lord's Supper. Here is where the church was born—I was sitting right there, Paul, by that window, when the Holy Spirit came like a rushing mighty wind and in cloven tongues of fire."

They would go out to Gethsemane. "That's where He prayed, Paul, and here's where the three of us fell asleep. That's where He stood when Judas kissed Him. Right here, I cut off the ear of Malchus. He healed him, Paul! Simply picked up the severed ear and put it on again! Just like that!"

They would go out to the Hill of Evil Counsel. "That's where they had their fire, Paul. And there I denied Him. But, oh! Blessed be His name! He sought me out after His resurrection and forgave me. Now let's go out to the tomb."

Last, they would go out to the Mount of Olives, and Peter would say, "And here He ascended into heaven. Here the two angels came with the final word: "'I shall return.'"

Paul met James, the Lord's brother, too, and what a host of questions Paul would have for him. Paul would instantly recognize, in James, the narrow legalist. He would readily understand how a man like James would hold out against Jesus for so many years. He had done so himself. "Tell me, James," Paul might well ask, "what was Jesus like at home? Tell me about Mary and Joseph. Tell me about the carpenter's shop in the years Jesus worked there."

So the two of them, Peter and James, could fill in the blanks in Paul's knowledge of the historical Jesus. Neither of them had any say in his theology.

#### b. His activities among Gentiles (1:20–21)

We note, first *what he swore:* "Now the things which I write unto you, behold, before God, I lie not" (v. 20). Paul seems to have been assailed on all sides. His enemies were saying that his gospel was of man and that, in any case, he was not being true to the gospel with which he claimed to have been entrusted. They were saying that it was incredible that he had met only Peter and James in the Jerusalem church. He must have met more than them.

Paul's integrity was at stake. The independence of his gospel and its direct divine revelation was being challenged. Paul evidently thought it imperative, at this point in his letter, to put himself under oath. He was telling the truth. He had not met the entire apostolic body. He had met only Peter and James, the Lord's brother. His gospel had been given to him by direct divine revelation. He had not received it from any man. He was true to the revelation given to him by God. It was imperative that the Galatians believe him.

We note also *where he served:* "Afterwards I came into the regions of Syria and Cilicia" (v. 21). No gaps existed in the narrative. After his brief visit to Jerusalem, Paul was escorted down to Caesarea, the Roman seaport on the coast of Palestine. From there, he took ship for his native Tarsus, where he remained, evangelizing his hometown and homeland until the time Barnabas came looking for him to solicit his help in evangelizing Syrian Antioch. Paul had nothing to hide. He had made no more trips to Jerusalem and had held no secret meetings with the apostles. His next visit to Jerusalem was the one he would mention later in this letter (2:1–10).

Paul's comment here about "the regions of Syria and Cilicia" is of interest. In 67 B.C., Pompey thrashed the pirates of the eastern Mediterranean seaboard and reduced Cilicia to the status of a Roman province. He won his resounding victory over Mithridates in 64 B.C. and turned Syria into a Roman province too. From about 25 B.C., all of eastern Cilicia, including the city of Tarsus, was administered as a single Roman province under the jurisdiction of a legate with his headquarters at Syrian Antioch.

Little is known of Paul's activities in this area, but his missionary efforts were evidently successful (Acts 15:23, 41). It is not at all unlikely that during this period Paul incurred the displeasure of his father and was disinherited (Phil. 3:8).

The fame and popularity of the heathen schools located at Tarsus would have made Paul's parents all the more careful to shield their son as much as possible, in his impressionable years, from pagan contamination. Jerome preserves a tradition that the family originally came from Giscala, a town in Galilee. Paul himself was a Hellenist, thoroughly at home in the Greek language. He was at home, too, in the Septuagint, from which he always quoted when referring to the Old Testament Scriptures. The readiness and skill with which Paul expressed himself in Greek at Athens, upon the Areopagus, proves his early training in that language. However, he could still refer to himself as "an Hebrew of the Hebrews" (Phil. 3:5), no doubt because of his strict, early training as a Jew. Doubtless, his parents, like all other devout Jews, saw to it that their son's earliest words and sentences were in Hebrew. Paul likely spoke both Greek and Hebrew with equal fluency from earliest childhood. In any case, Paul's parents, although liberal enough in some things, were no Hellenizers in theology, nor would they want their son to be too inclined to adopt Greek habits and opinions. Paul himself tells us that he was raised to be a strict Jew

(2 Cor. 11:22). He was raised in a Gentile world but in a home that was Hebrew to the core.

We can imagine what high hopes Paul's father had of his bright and eager boy and with what pride he packed him off to Jerusalem to finish his education at the feet of the renowned rabbi Gamaliel. He could envision for his son a career as a distinguished rabbi, ending up as a member of the Sanhedrin and even as the high priest of his people. He had the brains, industry, courage, charm, and drive to take him to the top.

When Paul showed up in Tarsus as a Christian, and as a totally committed one at that, it must have been a shock to his father. Perhaps rumors of Paul's activities had already reached the people back home. Perhaps Paul had visited home to tell them of his marvelous conversion on the Damascus road. Then he had disappeared into Arabia; but now he had turned up again at Tarsus, determined to spread the gospel with all of his natural drive and in the power, passion, and persuasion of the Holy Spirit. It was too much for his parents; they disinherited him.

Still, Paul, as much as he might grieve over the opposition of his family, was not the man to abandon his high calling on that account. So he labored on in "the regions of Syria and Cilicia," plowing his long, lonely furrow dead straight with his eye on the prize at the judgment seat of Christ.

### c. His acknowledgment in Judea (1:22–24)

In concluding this section of his letter, Paul mentions two things. First, he mentions *the Jewish believers and their dreaded persecutor.* He tells his Galatian friends that he was "unknown by face unto the churches of Judaea which were in Christ: but they had heard only, That he which persecuted us in times past now preacheth the faith which once he destroyed" (vv. 22–23). Many people in the Judean churches had never seen the face of Saul of Tarsus. They were not only thankful they had not seen the fierce face of the Sanhedrin's Torquemada but ensured that, if at all humanly possible, they never would see his face. It was a face to be feared. Even when the tidings had first reached Jerusalem and seeped out into all Judea that Saul of Tarsus had been saved, many people did not believe it! "It's a trick," they said. "He's as clever as a fox. He just wants to infiltrate the churches. Then, when his lists of Christians are complete, he'll throw off his mask and have us at his mercy. Saved? Saul? Not on your life!" (Acts 9:26). But suddenly, the persecutions stopped. Saul of Tarsus was no more. He vanished from the scene. Peace descended on the Judean churches.

Paul tells, finally, of *the Jewish believers and their delighted praise:* "And," he adds, "they glorified God in me" (v. 24). The time came when the stories could no longer be denied. Their archenemy was now actively preaching "the faith which once he destroyed." They kept on hearing this report. Greek scholars point to the strong imperfect of the verbs (v. 23). The news filtered in from Damascus and elsewhere. At last, there could be no more doubt. A notable miracle had taken place. The wolf had become a sheep! The persecutor had become a preacher. "They glorified God in me." They kept on finding new causes for giving glory to God in the conversion of Saul. It was not just that the persecution had stopped, although that in itself would have been sufficient to give glory to God! They could go to bed at night assured that there would not come the dread knock on the door and the demand, "Open in the name of the Sanhedrin." They could hold their meetings without having to post sentries and be afraid of spies. It was not just that the persecution had stopped; the persecutor had been saved! He was now a Christian, one of them, a believer, a brother, a fellow member of the body of Christ. And it was not just that the persecutor had been saved; he was now preaching the faith that once he destroyed. And it was not only that he was preaching the faith he had once destroyed; he was preaching it boldly and successfully. "Hallelujah! What a Savior!" "They glorified God in me," says Paul.

D. The defense of the gospel (2:1–21)
  1. Paul's unwavering challenge to the church at Jerusalem: the center of Jewish Christianity (2:1–10)
    a. The crucial test (2:1–3)
      (1) The time (2:1)

The focal centers of interest in this part of Paul's letter are Jerusalem and Antioch, the centers of Jewish and Gentile Christianity, respectively. In both places, Paul had confronted the Judaizers head-on. His keen mind had seen, right from the start, the spiritual peril to the church if the Judaizers were allowed to win. They would have made the Jerusalem church the mother church, Peter a pope, Christianity just another Jewish sect, and Gentile Christians second-class citizens in the kingdom of God. Paul was prepared to fight to the death to prevent such a tragedy from happening.

He begins this section of his letter by describing his confrontation with the Jerusalem church. He spells out for his Galatian converts, who had become the living proof of his fears, the crucial test he had forced upon the Jerusalem church.

We note first the reference to *Paul's calendar:* "Then fourteen years after I went up again to Jerusalem" (v. 1a). The word *then* can be rendered "next." Paul is assuring the Galatians that he is not suppressing or concealing any of his visits to Jerusalem in this summary of his activities.

The book of Acts records two visits of Paul to Jerusalem in company with his friend and colleague Barnabas. The first visit was in connection with famine relief (11:30; 12:25); the second visit was in connection with the Jerusalem conference, which was convened to consider the whole question of imposing Judaism on Gentile Christians (15:2–32). The incident recorded here in Galatians would seem to be connected with the first of these visits. Paul dates the event as being "fourteen years after." It is not certain whether he means fourteen years after his conversion or fourteen years after his first visit (1:18–20), which took place three years after his conversion.

Then we note *Paul's companions.* Paul made this visit with Barnabas. Paul adds that he took Titus with him too (v. 1b–c). So then, we see Paul accompanied on this visit by Barnabas the gentle and Titus the Gentile.

Barnabas was a thoroughly likeable man. He was the kind of man for whom the Bible says that other men would die. "Scarcely for a righteous man will one die," Paul wrote, "yet peradventure for a good man some would even dare to die" (Rom. 5:7). Quite possibly, he had Barnabas in mind when he wrote that verse because Barnabas was "a good man, and full of the Holy Ghost" (Acts 11:24).

Barnabas was a Levite. He was originally called Joseph but had his name changed by the apostles, who nicknamed him Barnabas, doubtless because of his Christian character. He was a true "son of consolation," or "son of comfort" (Acts 4:36). The word used to describe him is *paraklēsis,* a kindred word to that beloved name of the Holy Spirit, the *Paraklete,* "the Comforter." Barnabas was a Cyprian Jew. After his conversion, he sold property he possessed on the island of Cyprus and put the proceeds at the feet of the apostles. Barnabas introduced Paul to the apostles at a time when everyone was still suspicious of him. When the Gentile revival broke out at Antioch, and the Jerusalem apostles decided that someone should go there and inspect the work on their behalf, the apostles chose Barnabas. He was delighted at what he saw and stayed on to help. He soon realized, however, that the work was far beyond his own talents, so off he went to Tarsus to find Paul. He had long since concluded that Paul was an extraordinary person, farsighted, wholly committed, and gifted both naturally and spiritually beyond any other man he knew—a very apostle indeed.

Barnabas knew nothing of jealousy. He must have known that Paul would soon eclipse him, no matter what the enterprise or where the place. Spurgeon once wrote, "It takes more grace than I can tell, to play the second fiddle well." He could have been describing Barnabas. Barnabas and Paul became the first church-sent foreign missionaries of the gospel age. Together, they pioneered and suffered and triumphed in Cyprus and Galatia. The Galatians, of course, knew Barnabas as a good, godly, gracious, and gifted brother.

"Well," says Paul, "Barnabas and I went up to Jerusalem, and we took Titus with us." That was a Pauline touch. Barnabas was not the kind of man who would deliberately force a fight, but Paul was made of sterner stuff. It was all very well for the Jerusalem church to pay lip service to Gentile freedom from the Law. Words were cheap, especially when no Gentiles were around, clamoring for reception into the Jerusalem church. Paul was determined to force the issue and make them back up their words by deeds.

Titus was a full-blooded, uncircumcised Gentile Christian. He seems to have come from Antioch. He had qualities that Paul appreciated and later used to the full. He was a Greek, a convert from heathenism. He is not mentioned at all in the book of Acts. Professor Ramsay believed that Titus was Luke's brother and that the absence of his name from the book of Acts was in keeping with Luke's determination to keep his own name out of that narrative. Paul later used Titus as his personal envoy in his difficult and delicate negotiations with the Corinthian church. He is mentioned twice here in Galatians, nine times in 2 Corinthians, and once in 2 Timothy as well, of course, as in the pastoral letter that Paul sent to him and that bears his name.

### (2) The truth (2:2–3)

Paul now explains why he went to Jerusalem on this occasion and why he took Titus along. We note *Paul's guidance:* "And I went up by revelation," he says (v. 2a). The word is *apokalupsis.* The word is used to describe the communication of the knowledge of God to a soul (Eph. 1:17). It is likely that Barnabas was going up to Jerusalem anyway, and Paul, always eager to go to Jerusalem but warned away from the place by the Holy Spirit (Acts 22:17–21), would have liked to go with him. He now received clear guidance from God that he should go. The situation was fast coming to a head. Unless something happened, there would be two churches, a Jewish church and a Gentile church, something quite foreign to the mind of the Holy Spirit (Eph. 2:11–16). Paul wanted his Galatian friends to know that the Holy Spirit sent him to Jerusalem on this important occasion and had guided him to take Titus along. He had not gone on his own initiative. He had certainly not gone, cap in hand, to seek some kind of authorization for his ministry from the apostles and elders of the church in Jerusalem. He had gone to force the issue and to fight for Gentile independence from Judaism and the Mosaic Law.

We note also *Paul's gospel.* He says, "[I] communicated unto them that gospel which I preach among the Gentiles, but privately to them which were of reputation, lest by any means I should run, or had run, in vain" (v. 2). Paul's first concern, upon arriving in Jerusalem, had been to secure a private meeting with the acknowledged leaders of the Jerusalem church. This was simple common sense. It is far easier to arrive at a consensus when a few fair-minded and intelligent people sit down together to discuss an issue than it is to carry the day with a crowd. Paul, Barnabas, Peter, John, and James, the Lord's brother, in conference together, could pray, meditate, wait upon the Holy Spirit, reason, discuss, disagree, and seek calmly and rationally to find common ground. One cannot reason with a mob, and a crowd can easily be turned into a mob. A mob is swayed by emotion rather than by reason. Plenty of hot passions could easily have been kindled on both sides of this touchy but vital issue. Paul knew how to move a mob, if it came to that, and, indeed, he did so on one occasion (Acts 23:6–10), something he regretted afterward (Acts 24:18–21). He had no intention of deciding this vital issue by appealing to the uncertain passions of a crowd. He sought out the responsible brethren. The word for "reputation" is *dokeō,* people well thought of, people who were held in consideration.

The purpose of the meeting was to make quite clear to these men exactly what it was that he preached. He had not come to learn the gospel from them. He already knew what the gospel was. He had received it directly from the Lord. He had it firsthand on much higher authority than any they could bestow. But, because of the brewing storm, the center of which was the Jerusalem church itself, it was essential that these responsible brethren should hear from Paul himself just exactly what it was that he preached. He did not need their endorsement to preach it. Nor would he have stopped preaching it even if they had disagreed with it or even commanded him to stop preaching it. They had no authority or jurisdiction over him. Paul had absolutely no doubt that what he preached was the truth, the whole truth, and nothing but the truth. He did not need for them to tell him so. But it would be to everyone's advantage if they could be brought to see that this was so.

What does Paul mean, then, by the added statement, "lest by any means I should run, or had run, in vain"? Paul was afraid that the Judaizers, who dogged his steps and subverted his converts, would render his labors null and void. The Jerusalem elders would either have to endorse him or them on the question of Gentiles and the Mosaic Law. Paul had not the slightest shadow of doubt that he was right and that the Judaizers, who emanated from Jerusalem, were preaching a lie. Paul did not need the endorsement of the Jerusalem elders to validate his gospel. But he certainly needed for them to do something about their home-grown Judaizers who were trailing after him, rendering his ministry and his efforts vain by subverting his converts to Judaism. For the Jerusalem leaders to be able to act intelligently and spiritually in this critical situation, they would need to know, understand, and appreciate not only what he preached but also its divine source and authority. Unless the Jerusalem leaders repudiated the false teachers, it was evident that there would soon be such a breach between Jerusalem and the Gentile churches as would be irreconcilable, and that would be disastrous. It would deny the great truth of the oneness of the body of Christ and would lead to denominationalism of the very worst kind.

Well, Paul was successful. From his revelation, he had assurance from the Holy Spirit that he would be successful. Hence, the presence of Titus. He had brought him along not only as a sample of the grace of God at work in the heart and life of a former pagan but also to put the Jerusalem leaders to the test. We can be sure that Paul had well briefed Titus as to what he could expect in Jerusalem. The legalists would be sure to turn up the heat.

The time Titus spent with Paul and Barnabas in Jerusalem must have been full of interest for the young Greek. He would be able to see firsthand the scenes of the Lord's passion. We can be sure that Gethsemane, Gabbatha, Golgotha, and the graveside were as full of interest for him as for any modern Christian pilgrim—more so, perhaps, because no shrines would have yet been built over the sites, and the actual places would have been absolutely certain, not just speculative, as is often the case today. Then, too, he would meet Peter, John, and James, the Lord's brother. If Titus was, indeed, Luke's brother, we can well imagine the stories that he had to tell him when they met again.

But all of this would have been offset to some extent for Titus by the sour looks of the legalists, their slights and snubs and open hostility. He would be urged to accept circumcision as required by the Mosaic Law. They would cite the long, hallowed sanctity of the Law with its inflexible insistence on obedience to all of its commands. They would press upon him even Abraham's need for circumcision and God's displeasure with Moses for neglecting to circumcise his sons (Gen. 17:10–14; Exod. 4:24–26). They would urge him to start keeping the Sabbath, to participate in the ritual law, to offer sacrifices, and to adhere to the strict observance of the Mosaic dietary laws. And, with the tireless zeal and persistence of cultists in all ages, they would pursue him day and night, urging, badgering, and persuading. They would try to get him away from Paul, knowing they were no match for Paul. And when their persistent efforts to seduce Titus from his loyalty to Paul failed, they would whip up sentiment and prejudice against him among the rank and file of the church and put political pressure on the apostles to take their stand against allowing the Gentile any kind of fellowship either at the Lord's Table or at their own tables at home. They failed.

Paul could remember it all so well. He wrote, now, to his Galatian converts, "But neither Titus, who was with me, being a Greek, was compelled to be circumcised" (v. 3). As for the responsible leaders of the church at Jerusalem, Paul had won them over completely: "Not one of them intimated that Titus, because he was a Greek, ought to be circumcised," he said. It was a complete victory at the highest possible level of church council. The leaders of the Jerusalem church accepted Titus, at face value, as a Christian.

b. The contested truth (2:4–5)

(1) How Paul faced his foes (2:4)

Mind you, Paul says, there was a battle—but not on the apostolic level where it mattered most. The question of circumcising Titus would not have arisen at all except for "false brethren, unawares brought in, who came in privily to spy out our liberty which we have in Christ Jesus, that they might bring us into bondage." There we have *their mask removed.* They were "false brethren." The word is *pseudadelphos.* The only other place the word occurs is in 2 Corinthians 11:26, where Paul, in listing the perils that he had faced in the course of his missionary career, mentions "perils among false brethren." One translator renders the word as "pseudo-Christians." Paul contended that these people were not genuine Christians at all. We are much more tolerant than either Jesus or Paul of those who hold false doctrine. Doubtless, many people in Jerusalem considered these false teachers to be genuine believers. Paul scorns the idea. To him, they were counterfeits, and the word he uses to describe them rips off their mask. We can well imagine the short shrift that Seventh-day Adventists, Roman Catholics, liberal Protestants, and others would receive at Paul's hands were he alive today.

Then we have *their method rebuked.* "Unawares brought in," Paul says. The word is *pareisaktos.* They were smuggled in, or, as one translator puts it, "they wormed their way into our meeting." In everyday Greek, the word was used to describe enemies secretly introduced into a city by traitors within the walls. They "came in privily," Paul adds *(pareiserchomai).* The whole thing was underhanded. The mark of the serpent was betrayed in their method.

Then, too, we have *their motive revealed.* Paul bluntly calls them spies. They came "to spy out our liberty . . . in Christ Jesus," he says. The word *kataskopeō* denotes just that, "to spy out," or "to search out in order to overthrow." In the Septuagint, the word is used in exactly this sense. When David sent messengers to Hanun, the new king of Ammon, to console him over the recent death of his father, his counselors poisoned the young king's mind: "Thinkest thou that David doth honour thy father?" they said, "hath not David rather sent his servants unto thee, to search the city, and *to spy it out, and to overthrow it?*" (2 Sam. 10:3). Somehow, these false brethren to whom Paul alludes were infiltrated into the church by "them which were of the circumcision" (2:12; Acts 15:5) to "spy out our liberty which we have in Christ Jesus." Why? "That they might bring us into bondage," Paul adds. To then try to tie us up with rules and regulations. Their sole purpose was to take away the freedom that we have in Christ and exchange it for bondage. They underestimated Paul.

(2) How Paul fought his foes (2:5)

If they thought that they would deceive or intimidate Paul, they were very much mistaken: "To whom we gave place by subjection, no, not for an hour; that the truth of the gospel might continue with you." Submit? Never! Not for a moment! Paul was adamant. He knew all about "the circumcision," as he called these Jewish bigots. He had been down that road. They could tell him nothing about rules and regulations.

Paul had already tried living the Christian life on their terms.

> For we know that the law is spiritual: but I am carnal, sold under sin. . . . For I know that in me (that is, in my flesh,) dwelleth no good thing: for to will is present with me; but how to perform that which is good I find not. For the good that I would I do not: but the evil which I would not, that I do . . . I find then a law, that, when I would do good, evil is present with me. For I delight in the law of God after the inward man: but I see another law in my members, warring against the law of my mind, and

> bringing me into captivity to the law of sin which is in my members. O wretched man that I am! who shall deliver me from the body of this death? (Romans 7:14, 18–19, 21–24)

That was before he struck it rich in Christ (Rom. 7:25) and learned "the law of the Spirit of life in Christ Jesus" (Rom. 8:2).

He was not going to have a few narrow-minded, unsaved, and carnal Jews, who could not keep the Law themselves, clamp it back either on him or his converts. Their concept of the gospel was false in precept, futile in practice, and fatal in purpose. It offered no salvation for the sinner and no sanctification for the saint. They could not fool Paul. Both before and after his conversion, he had tried their recipe and tasted the bitterness and poison of its brew.

c. The crowning triumph (2:6–10)
  (1) Paul's message accepted (2:6–8)

The miniconference with the leaders of the Jerusalem conference was a resounding success. There would have to be a major conference later, but at least Paul and Barnabas had carried the men who really mattered in Jerusalem right through theologically to resurrection ground.

Paul now mentions *the big names:* "But of these who seemed to be somewhat, (whatsoever they were, it maketh no matter to me: God accepteth no man's person:) for they who seemed to be somewhat in conference added nothing to me" (v. 6). This sheds new light on the case. The Judaizers who were now storming Paul's Galatian churches were busy boosting the reputation of the Jerusalem church and the greatness and stature of the original apostles, those who for three and a half years had been the companions and disciples of Christ. "You Galatians are making so much of this Paul," they were saying. "You should see and hear the real apostles. This Paul of yours! He would not cut much of a figure in Jerusalem, let us tell you. He would be 'Mr. Little' indeed alongside Peter or John. Ah! There are men for you! You should hear Peter preach! You should hear John recount the Upper Room experience! You should hear them describe the miracles of Jesus. They were there! They saw Him turn water into wine! They saw the Master raise the dead! This Paul of yours needs to come to Jerusalem. He would soon be trimmed down to size."

When Napoleon was told that Wellington had been put in charge of the British army in Portugal, he simply sneered. He had heard of Wellington's successes in India. He called him "the *Sepoy* general." So! He had won victories over a handful of Sepoy barbarians. Well! Just wait until he faced French troops led by the genius who had brought all of Europe to its knees. Wait until he came face-to-face with Napoleon! But when at last the two men met on the field of battle, Wellington soon proved himself the master of Napoleon.

Paul went to Jerusalem to face these men whose fame was being touted throughout Galatia. With all due respect for these men, giving all honor where honor was due, Paul was not greatly impressed. The story of the life and death of Jesus might be in safekeeping with these men. But when it came to the significance of that life and death—well, they added nothing to him! Indeed, Paul was not even concerned to find out what their position was. God is not impressed by a man's office. And when it came down to the bottom line, these men had absolutely nothing to add to him. They told him nothing that he did not already know. They were certainly in no position to give him any new commission. Nor could they subtract a single word from the gospel that he had been set apart by God to preach. And, Paul might have added if grace had not stayed his pen, what had they done? They had been commissioned to begin at Jerusalem and all Judea, then to evangelize Samaria, and to reach out to the uttermost parts of the earth (Acts 1:8). Well, they had achieved success in Jerusalem and Judea. Samaria had been evangelized—but by one of the deacons, not by one of the apostles. And, as for "the uttermost parts of the earth," they had done little or nothing about that.

Paul turns now to *the big news.* The Jerusalem leaders had done one thing, and it was good news, big news for the Gentiles. "They . . . added nothing to me," Paul says. "But contrariwise, when they saw that the gospel of the uncircumcison was committed unto me, as the gospel of the circumcision was unto Peter; (For he that wrought effectually in Peter to the apostleship of the circumcision, the same was mighty in me toward the Gentiles:)" (vv. 7–8). Facts were facts. In the end, the leaders of the Jerusalem church had turned out to be fair-minded men. They recognized that the gospel for the Gentiles was as much Paul's call and commission as the gospel for the Jews was Peter's. Peter had seen some outstanding successes in his labors among the Jews. There was no denying that! Paul had seen some outstanding successes among the Gentiles. There was no denying that either! So Peter and Paul were equals!

It is not that Paul is disparaging the leaders of the Jerusalem church. Their personal stature and prestige was high, especially in the Jerusalem church. What Paul did object to was the attempt being made by the Judaizers to use their status to diminish his own. Well! The Jerusalem elders had now acknowledged Paul's status to be every bit as impressive as Peter's. Paul did not need that recognition for himself, but his beloved Gentiles needed to hear it. It would silence at least one argument of the Judaizers.

In writing the book of Acts, Luke seems to have made a special effort to show that everything Peter did, Paul did. Thus, he tells us the name of both Peter's first Gentile convert (Cornelius) and Paul's first Gentile convert (Sergius Paulus). He tells how Peter was visited by an angel and how Paul was visited by an angel. He tells how Peter healed a lame man and how Paul healed a lame man. He tells us how Peter raised someone from the dead and how Paul raised someone from the dead. He tells how Peter was miraculously released from prison and how Paul was miraculously released from prison. He gives, at length, Peter's first sermon and Paul's first sermon. He tells of the miraculous influence of Peter's shadow and the miraculous influence of Paul's handkerchief. He tells how Peter had a confrontation with a magician and how Paul had a confrontation with a magician. He tells how once Peter was worshiped by some Gentiles and his reaction, and he tells how once Paul was worshiped by some Gentiles and his reaction.[3] Yes, indeed! Paul was every bit as much an apostle as Peter was, and the elders at Jerusalem had the common sense and spiritual discernment to see it.

### (2) Paul's mission accepted (2:9–10)

Now Paul mentions by name *the pillars of the church:* "And when James, Cephas, and John, who seemed to be pillars, perceived the grace that was given unto me, they gave to me and Barnabas the right hands of fellowship; that we should go unto the heathen, and they unto the circumcision" (v. 9). That was not hard for them to do because they were not that keen on going to the heathen themselves anyway, at least at that time (Acts 10:14–20).

We tremble when we think how much swung in the balance on this occasion. But the Lord knew what He was doing years before when, walking along the seashore of Galilee, He had stopped to watch Peter and John mending their nets. Here were two ordinary, hardworking, down-to-earth individuals of quite opposite temperaments but both practical, sensible, impressionable, and teachable—indeed, just the kind of men eventually to entrust, under His Holy Sprit, with the destiny of His church. Probably, Paul and Barnabas had more trouble with James, the Lord's brother, than with the other two apostles.

---

3. See John Phillips, *Exploring Acts* (Grand Rapids: Kregel, 2001).

James comes first, although he, like Paul, was a latecomer to the ranks of the Lord's redeemed people. When Paul had gone to Jerusalem on the previous occasion, it had been to see Peter (1:18). He adds, almost as an afterthought, that he also saw James. But James was not the kind of man to remain in the background. He had a forceful personality (2:11–12), was inclined to be a legalist himself, and was known for his asceticism. He seems to have taken the lead, on Paul's final and disastrous visit to Jerusalem, in forcing upon Paul, in the name of unity among God's people, the somewhat compromising concessions that, in the end, led directly to Paul's arrest in the temple (Acts 21:18–39). He wrote the first New Testament document. Martin Luther, who thought that he detected elements of legalism in the epistle, called it "an epistle of straw." It certainly has a very Jewish texture, but if it was written that early in the history of the church, that would account for that fact. The time of its writing is often placed as before the Jerusalem council. It belongs to the Pentecostal years when the church was still Jewish and when all of their meeting places were still called "synagogues" (James 2:2). Perhaps it was the publication and circulation of this encyclical epistle that catapulted James to prominence.

In any case, by the time of Paul's second visit to Jerusalem, James had not only become increasingly influential in the church but also is named first. Doubtless, the fact that Peter was forced to flee from Jerusalem about this time because of Herod's murderous intentions (Acts 12:17) gave James an opportunity to increase his leadership role. When Peter, John, and the other apostles finally embarked on a genuine ministry abroad, James remained in Jerusalem more or less in charge of the church. Certainly none of the other elders would dispute the authority of this rather formidable individual. He was able to cow Peter (v. 12), but he did not awe Paul.

Peter and John were among the Lord's very first disciples and are almost as familiar to us, from the Gospels and the book of Acts as well as their own writings, as people we meet every day. Before their call to follow Jesus, they had been business partners. They were men of quite different temperament. Peter was bold, blustery, impulsive, and given to speaking and acting before thinking. John was more contemplative, visionary, and impressionable but not without a temper. Peter was a doer; John was a dreamer. We often find them together in the later part of the gospel story and in the book of Acts. They were a good pair and made for a well-balanced team.

Paul was willing enough to give all three men credit for being "pillars," but evidently he was not that much impressed by their position and certainly felt himself under no obligation to defer to it. So! They had known Jesus in His earthly life and ministry. What they once were made no difference to Paul now. They had their place, but that gave them no authority over him or his converts. He had received his call and commission directly from the nail-pierced hands of the risen and ascended Christ. Indeed, "the Lord from heaven" was Paul's favorite designation for the Christ of God (1 Cor. 15:47).

On the whole, then, the meeting had gone very well. The "pillars" had recognized the grace given to Paul and Barnabas. The word for "perceived" is *ginōskō,* which carries the idea of acquiring knowledge, of getting to know something by experience or effort, of learning something. We can well believe that a meeting with Paul would be a learning experience for these three Galileans! At least they were teachable. The Holy Spirit saw to that.

They sealed their mutual understanding with a hearty handshake. Or, as Paul puts it, they gave him and Barnabas "the right hands of fellowship; that we should go unto the heathen, and they unto the circumcision." The Lord had charged *them* to make disciples of all nations (Matt. 28:19), to witness for Him to earth's remotest bounds (Acts 1:8), to go, indeed, "into the world" (John 20:21), to "the end of the earth" (Luke 24:47), no less. They were willing, it seems, to settle for less. If Paul was willing to do it for them, more power to him. They were quite willing to shake hands on that deal. Eventually, they were thrust out into the wider world (1 Peter 1:1; Rev. 1:9–11), a world where Paul had already plowed, planted, and reaped the first abundant crop. Both Peter and John later addressed themselves to churches in western Asia Minor, long since evangelized by Paul.

Paul also mentions *the poor of the church:* "Only they would that we should remember the poor; the same which I also was forward to do" (v. 10). Paul and Barnabas, indeed, had brought with them, on this occasion, relief money to help victims of a prevailing famine. Paul was always zealous to raise money in his Gentile churches far and wide to relieve the poor saints in Jerusalem (Rom. 15:25–28; 1 Cor. 16:1–4; 2 Cor. 8:1–9, 15).

We can picture Paul sitting in his first church service in Jerusalem. The number of widows and orphans would impress him. The heart of the great apostle would go out to them. *Why are there so many of them?* he would ask himself. Then he would see them looking at him. He would try to read the expressions on their faces. Some of the mothers would point him out to their children. He might overhear a sibilant whisper: "That's Saul of Tarsus over there. Yes! The one who martyred your father." Suddenly, it would dawn on him. No wonder there were so many poor saints in Jerusalem! He had once wreaked havoc among them. He had made many of them poor. The tears would come to his eyes. He would get up and ask for the forgiveness of the church. "I did it in ignorance," he would say (1 Tim. 1:13). It would be his only excuse. But those faces would haunt him ever afterward. He did not need a James, a Peter, or a John to urge him to remember the Jerusalem poor. It was almost impertinence that they should do so.

2. Paul's unwavering challenge to the church at Antioch: the center of Gentile Christianity (2:11–21)
   a. Peter's conduct (2:11–13)

To the Jews, the church at Antioch posed a threat to the church at Jerusalem. At Antioch, the first genuine attempt was made to evangelize Gentiles. True, Peter had been sent to the house of Cornelius (Acts 10); but beyond formally opening the door of the church to the Gentiles, Peter had taken little or no further interest in that challenge. The revival that had broken out among the Gentiles at Antioch had brought a massive influx of Gentiles into the church.

We can well imagine how attractive Christianity must have been to the pagans of the first century. They were sickened by the utter godlessness of heathendom. They were weary to death with the theological inanities and the moral decadence of the pagan religions, and they looked longingly toward the lofty religious ideals of the Jews. They were repelled, as often as not, however, by the self-righteous arrogance of many Jews, by their hypocrisy, and by their contemptuous attitude toward all things Gentile. They were insulted by Jewish dietary laws that closed the door on all ordinary social intercourse, and the idea of circumcision as the only way to acceptance into the Jewish faith repelled them. When the Christians offered them salvation by grace through faith in Christ, free from all of the hindrances of Judaism, they flocked into the church. Soon, the Gentiles far outnumbered the Jews in the Antioch church. Soon, Gentiles would far outnumber Jews in the church everywhere.

The Jerusalem church viewed this reality with some alarm. They sent Barnabas to Antioch to see what was going on. Barnabas had been thrilled to the very core of his being and had stayed on to help. Moreover, he had brought Paul into the work. Paul's vision, zeal, drive, and anointing gave even greater impetus to the growth of the Antioch church. No wonder the Judaizers tried to curb what was going on and sought to reduce the Gentile church to subservience to the Jerusalem church. They felt threatened. Paul now recounts an incident, relevant to the whole issue of Gentile freedom from the Law, that had taken place at the church at Antioch and in which both Peter and Barnabas had been involved. He concentrates, first, on Peter's conduct.

We note *its critic:* "But when Peter was come to Antioch, I withstood him to the face, because he was to be blamed" (v. 11). As we shall see, Peter played a two-faced game at Antioch and drew down on his head the righteous indignation of the apostle Paul, who was a respecter of no man's person.

We can imagine Peter's popularity when he first arrived at Antioch. Here was the man who had spent three and a half years with Jesus. People were thrilled. They flocked to his meetings. The buildings where they met couldn't contain the crowds. Every Christian home in Antioch was open to him. People would be awed if even so much as Peter's shadow fell upon them. They hung upon his words. They couldn't hear enough from him. As soon as the service was over, instead of going home, they would flock around the warmhearted apostle with a thousand questions about Jesus, the disciples, the birthday of the church, and Peter's visit to Cornelius. And Peter loved every minute of it.

We can well imagine that, as Paul and Barnabas had said their final good-byes upon leaving Jerusalem, Paul would look Peter in the eye and grip his hand and say, "Come and see us, Peter. Come on up to Antioch. Come and see for yourself." And so Peter had come, and he had been an instant success. And how he loved that Gentile hospitality! He even developed, perhaps, a taste for Gentile food. Certainly, he did not refuse a single invitation—at first that is.

Then something had happened, and everything had turned sour. Peter compromised himself, and Paul heard about it. He "let Peter have it straight between the eyes," as we would say today. Paul, aroused, angry, and defending his beloved Gentile converts against Judaistic shibboleths, was a man to be feared. He was like a bear robbed of her whelps. We can well imagine that Peter must have quailed before the fire in Paul's eye, the blistering eloquence of his tongue, the driving force of his will, and the irresistible logic of his words. Peter's critic was Paul, and Paul was full of the Holy Spirit and fire. "He was to be blamed," Paul says. The word is *kataginōskō,* meaning "condemned." He stood accused by his own conscience and in the sight of the whole Gentile church.

Now Paul tells us what Peter had done. He reveals *its character:* "For before that certain came from James, he did eat with the Gentiles: but when they were come, he withdrew and separated himself, fearing them which were of the circumcision" (v. 12). Paul saw cowardice and compromise in Peter, probably the two things that he detested most. He also saw the old Peter, the Peter who denied the Lord before a serving maid while warming his hands at the world's fire. Paul's wrath kindled. Apostle or no apostle, Peter must be forced to face the carnality and consequences of his two-faced behavior.

Everything had been going so well. The Gentiles had lionized Peter, put him on a pedestal, hosted and dined him all over town. They had been thrilled and delighted at the wholehearted endorsement of their churches, the warmhearted good fellowship in their homes by the great Simon Peter himself. Then some newcomers had arrived in town from Jerusalem—"from James." Peter was intimidated at once, although why he, a chosen apostle, should bow and scrape to James is hard to see. James must have had a forceful personality indeed.

However Paul interpreted the agreement reached at Jerusalem, it is quite evident that the ultra-Jewish James certainly did not envision a total breakdown of Jewish dietary laws enabling such hearty fellowship in Gentile homes as Peter was now enjoying at Antioch. It is hard to escape the conclusion that, when news reached Jerusalem of Peter's wide fraternization with Gentile Christians, James immediately sent some of his followers off to Antioch to stop it.

The "certain" ones who came "from James"are represented by the word *tines.* They likely were messengers from James. We are not told what they said to Peter. They no doubt told him that the Jerusalem church was scandalized by his behavior, that his liberalism was becoming common knowledge in the city, and that it was hindering the work of Jewish evangelism. Obviously, Peter should have sent the messengers right back to James, telling him to mind his own business. Had not the Lord already taught him not to call unclean those whom He had cleansed? Peter had gone over all of this ground before (Acts 11:1–18). Nevertheless, he caved in.

He began to turn down invitations. He retreated into his shell, restricting his contacts thereafter to the fellowship of Jewish Christians. Paul bluntly says that he did it "fearing them . . . of the circumcision."

Next, we note its *consequences:* "And the other Jews dissembled likewise with him; insomuch that Barnabas also was carried away with their dissimulation" (v. 13). That, as Shakespeare would have put it, "was the most unkindest cut of all." That Peter should have been so hypocritical was disastrous. That Barnabas should have been party to it was well nigh incredible. If Paul was disappointed in Peter, he was utterly dismayed by Barnabas. Perhaps at this point he began to entertain some first small doubts about dear Barnabas; he had expected better things of him.

We can well imagine the hurt and confusion in the Gentile camp. They had virtually idolized Peter, and now their idol proved to have feet of clay. The rift between Jew and Gentile might have rapidly become "a great gulf fixed" had not Paul come striding boldly in. "I withstood him [Peter] to the face," Paul says (v. 11). "He was to be blamed." The word *dissimulation* here is *hupokrisis,* from which we get our word *hypocrite.* It simply means "playacting." Paul couldn't stand that. Peter must have spent a very uncomfortable half hour with Paul. By the time Paul was finished with him—weeping, pleading, arguing, and praying—Peter would be far more afraid of Paul than he ever was of James. It speaks volumes for both Paul's powers of persuasion and Peter's honest repentance and fair-mindedness that he never held his well-deserved chastisement at Paul's hands against him (2 Peter 3:15–16).

b. Paul's convictions (2:14–21)
   (1) Paul's discernment of the problem (2:14)

Nor was Paul's confrontation with Peter a private matter. Peter's compromise had affected the whole church, so Paul tackled him in public too: "But when I saw that they walked not uprightly according to the truth of the gospel, I said unto Peter before them all, If thou, being a Jew, livest after the manner of Gentiles, and not as do the Jews, why compellest thou the Gentiles to live as do the Jews?"

Whatever Peter's motives might have been for his behavior and whatever excuses he might have offered in self-defense, Paul saw Peter's conduct as an outright threat to the liberty of the Gentiles. The Lord Himself had taught Peter, in the matter of Cornelius, to discard the obsolete dietary laws that so separated Jews from Gentiles. That Peter had been living "after the manner of Gentiles" was evident from Peter's earlier behavior at Antioch. Indeed, that had evidently been his habit earlier when he was in Gentile communities—until he came under the influence of the Judaizers. But changing his coat and practicing social separation from the Gentiles was tantamount to telling the Gentiles that unless they formally became Jewish proselytes they would be second-class citizens in the church. It was not that Peter brought direct pressure to bear upon the Gentiles, but his example would certainly put indirect pressure on them to conform to Jewish faith and practice. The liberty of the Gentiles was at stake. Paul thought that he had laid that ghost to rest once and for all—at least so far as Peter, John, and James were concerned. It was downright hypocrisy for Peter to live like a Gentile and then to turn around and imply that Gentiles must live like Jews.

(2) Paul's discussion of the problem (2:15–21)
(a) The Law cannot bring us to redemption ground (2:15–18)
i. The Jewish Christian position (2:15–16)

The rest of this chapter is a summary of what Paul said to Peter. Note the use of the word *we*. It refers to Peter and Paul, both of whom were Jews, and, to all Jewish Christians, wedded from birth to the Law of Moses. Paul's first point is that the Law cannot redeem us. The Law *cannot* justify; the Lord *can* justify: "We who are Jews by nature, and not sinners of the Gentiles, knowing that a man is not justified by the works of the law, but by the faith of Jesus Christ, even we have believed in Jesus Christ, that we might be justified by the faith of Christ, and not by the works of the law: for by the works of the law shall no flesh be justified" (vv. 15–16).

The problem is that the Law condemns us. Elsewhere, Paul wrote, "By the law is the knowledge of sin" (Rom. 3:20). Paul's personal testimony was clear: "I had not known lust, except the law had said, Thou shalt not covet" (Rom. 7:7). He adds, "I was alive without the law once: but when the commandment came, sin revived, and I died. And the commandment, which was ordained to life, I found to be unto death . . . the law is holy . . . but I am carnal, sold under sin" (Rom. 7:9–10, 12, 14). The Law does not justify; it condemns. We cannot keep the Law—not in its letter, let alone in its spirit. So the Law cannot justify.

When a person is arraigned in court, he can leave condemned, forgiven, or justified. The Law can only condemn. The judge might issue a pardon, but, given the fact that we have all broken the Law of God, it cannot justify.

Years ago, back before the days of warranties, a wealthy Englishman purchased a Rolls Royce car and took it on his vacation to the south of France, where it broke down. He wired back to the factory, and the company flew a mechanic, long before flying was commonplace, to the south of France to diagnose the problem. After doing so, the mechanic flew back to the factory, picked up the part he needed, flew back to the south of France, repaired the car, and sent the customer on his way. The man expected to get a sizable bill, but time passed, and no bill came. He finally wrote a letter to the Rolls Royce factory, thanking them for the excellent service they had given him when his car broke down and asking them to send him his bill. After all, he was a wealthy man and could certainly afford to pay for services rendered.

He received a letter from the company, reading, "Dear Sir: We have no record of anything ever having gone wrong with your car."

That is exactly what it means to be justified. The word itself is sometimes paraphrased "just-as-if-I'd" never sinned. To be justified means that God has no record of anything having gone wrong in one's life! Justified! The Law cannot justify a guilty man, but Jesus can and does! The Law cannot bring us to redemption ground, but Jesus can and does.

Therefore, the position of the Jewish Christian was clear. The works of the Law could not save him. He was shut up to Christ for salvation. "By the works of the law shall no flesh be justified." The Jew and the Gentile stood on the same ground before God—lost and in need of Christ.

ii. The Jewish Christian problem (2:17–18)

The problem lay in the fact that Jews looked with contempt upon Gentiles. They called them "sinners of the Gentiles" and despised them. Paul scoffs at the idea that, somehow or other, Gentiles were worse sinners than are Jews. "But if, while we seek to be justified by Christ, we ourselves also are found sinners, is therefore Christ the minister of sin? God forbid. For if I build again the things which I destroyed, I make myself a transgressor." What is Paul saying here?

Well, let's listen in again on his conversation with Peter. "Now look here, Peter," we can almost hear him say, "we Jews discovered ourselves to be sinners when we sought the real truth about being justified by Christ. We discovered that we, too, had missed the mark *(hamartōlos)* just as badly as any Gentile. Now let me ask you a question. When Christ revealed to us our true condition as sinners, does that mean that He made us sinners? Nonsense! However, if I try to rebuild the whole structure of justification by law, if I put myself back under law after discovering the truth of justification through Christ, then I really do become a sinner *(parabatēs),* I really do become one who steps over the line. In other words, Peter, if I build again the things that I broke down to be justified by Christ, then I really do become a sinner. By yielding to faith in Christ as a means of salvation, we abandon law keeping as a means of being justified. We acknowledge that we are sinners, wholly dependent on God's grace. Jew and Gentile alike have no other way of being justified before God."

When a person sets about rebuilding something that he once acknowledged was useless and fit only for demolition, what is he doing? He is implying that he has made a mistake. "Is that what you want to teach, Peter?"

Paul put it to Peter thus: "Do you want to tell the world that justification by faith through grace alone is a mistake? That really the old way was right after all?

That the right way to go is by means of keeping the Law, by being circumcised, and by abstaining from certain kinds of food?" We can well imagine that Peter had no answer to that argument; he could only agree with Paul.

(b) The Law cannot bring us to resurrection ground (2:19–21)

i. A principle (2:19)

Paul now advances the argument from the Law as a means of salvation to the Law as a means of sanctification. The Law cannot bring us to *redemption* ground; it cannot *save* us. The Law cannot bring us to *resurrection* ground; it cannot *sanctify* us. First, Paul states a principle: "For I through the law am dead to the law, that I might live unto God" (v. 19). The Law ministered death.

The death penalty was attached to the breaking of every one of the Ten Commandments. The death penalty haunted every wrong act under the Old Testament law. Nowhere is this fact more evident than in Leviticus 20.

> Whosoever he be of the children of Israel, or the strangers that sojourn in Israel, that giveth any of his seed unto Molech; he shall surely be *put to death.* (v. 2)

> The soul that turneth after such as have familiar spirits, and after wizards . . . a man also or woman that hath a familiar spirit, or that is a wizard, shall surely be *put to death.* (vv. 6, 27)

> Every one that curseth his father or his mother shall be surely *put to death.* (v. 9)

> The man that lieth with his father's wife . . . both of them shall surely be *put to death.* (v. 11)

> If a man lie with his daughter-in-law, both of them shall surely be *put to death.* (v. 12)

> If a man also lie with mankind, as he lieth with a woman, both of them have committed an abomination: they shall surely be *put to death.* (v. 13)

> If a man lie with a beast, he shall surely be *put to death.* (v. 15)

> If a woman approach unto any beast, and lie down thereto, thou shalt kill the woman, and the beast: they shall surely be *put to death.* (v. 16)

Similar death sentences are handed out elsewhere in the Mosaic Law. In Exodus 21, for instance, we have another catalog of capital offenses.

> He that smiteth a man, so that he die, shall be surely *put to death.* (v. 12)

> If a man come presumptuously upon his neighbour, to slay him with guile; thou shalt take him from mine altar, *that he may die.* (v. 14)

> He that smiteth his father, or his mother, shall be surely *put to death.* (v. 15)

> He that stealeth a man, and selleth him, or if he be found in his hand, he shall surely be *put to death.* (v. 16)

> He that curseth his father, or his mother, shall surely be *put to death.* (v. 17)

> If an ox gore a man . . . if the ox were wont to push with his horn in time past, and if hath been testified to his owner, and he hath not kept him in, but that he hath killed a man or a woman; the ox shall be stoned, and his owner also shall be *put to death.* (vv. 28–29)

Similarly, we read:

> The seventh day . . . shall be to you an holy day, a sabbath of rest to the LORD: whosoever doeth work therein shall be *put to death.* (Exodus 35:2)

> When the tabernacle setteth forward, the Levites shall take it down: and when the tabernacle is to be pitched, the Levites shall set it up: and the stranger that cometh nigh shall be *put to death.* (Numbers 1:51)

> Thou shalt appoint Aaron and his sons, and they shall wait on their priest's office: and the stranger that cometh nigh shall be *put to death.* (Numbers 3:10)

> Those that encamp before the tabernacle toward the east, even before the tabernacle of the congregation eastward, shall be Moses, and Aaron and his sons . . . and the stranger that cometh nigh shall be *put to death.* (Numbers 3:38)

> And the LORD said unto Aaron, . . . thou and thy sons with thee shall keep your priest's office for every thing of the altar, and within the veil; . . . and the stranger that cometh nigh shall be *put to death.* (Numbers 18:1, 7)

> If there arise among you a prophet, or a dreamer of dreams, and giveth thee a sign or a wonder, and the sign or the wonder come to pass, whereof he spake unto thee, saying, Let us go after other gods . . . that prophet, or that dreamer of dreams, shall be *put to death.* (Deuteronomy 13:1–2, 5)

> If thy brother, the son of thy mother, or thy son, or thy daughter, or the wife of thy bosom, or thy friend, which is as thine own soul, entice thee secretly, saying, Let us go and serve other gods . . . thou shalt surely kill him: thine hand shall be first upon him to *put him to death.* (Deuteronomy 13:6, 9)

Such was the Law. It ministered death. No man had tried to keep the Law more sincerely and zealously than young Saul of Tarsus. He had tried with all of the intensity of which he was capable to keep the Law. He failed. "The commandment came," he said. "Sin revived" (*anazaō,* "sprang to life"). "I died" (Rom. 7:9). The Law slew him. "I through the law am dead to the law," he says. Once a man is dead, the Law has no more power over him. "I am dead to the law, that I might live unto God."

The believer is dead to the Law. We must distinguish between *the Law as a standard* and *the Law as a system.* Obviously, the believer is not dead to the Law as a standard. All of the commandments of the Decalogue are repeated in the New Testament as being a standard for human behavior—except the fourth commandment, that is, the commandment concerning the Sabbath. Paul says,

> He that loveth another hath fulfilled the law. For this, Thou shalt not commit adultery, Thou shalt not kill, Thou shalt not steal, Thou shalt not bear false witness, Thou shalt not covet; and if there be any other commandment, it is briefly comprehended in this saying, namely, Thou

> shalt love thy neighbour as thyself. Love worketh no ill to his neighbour: therefore love is the fulfilling of the law. (Romans 13:8–10)

The Law still exists as a standard, but it is fulfilled in another law, the law of love. Love lifts all human behavior to such high ground that it is scarcely necessary even to cite the Law as a standard.

For the Jew, however, the Law existed not only as a standard but also as a system. It is often referred to as the Mosaic covenant, a covenant established with the Hebrew people at Sinai. It was given to Israel in three parts. First were the commandments that expressed God's holiness, His righteous will, and His irreducible minimum for human behavior (Exod. 20:1–26). Second were the "judgments" that governed Israel's social life as "one nation under God with liberty and justice for all" (Exod. 21:1–24:11). And third were the "ordinances" that governed the religious life of Israel (Exod. 24:12–31:18). The whole legal system was binding upon Israel. The Jews were to govern their behavior not only by the moral law but also the ceremonial law. The ceremonial law itself comprised a considerable body of legislation covering their sacrifices and offerings, their feast days and fast days, their tithes, their tabernacle and temple, their priesthood, their Sabbaths, their initiatory rite of circumcision, and their ceremonial cleanness and uncleanness.

This was the Law as a system, a religious system given to the Jewish people. The Lord Jesus fulfilled every jot and tittle of the Law by His life and in His death. The Law as a system is now obsolete. The witness to that fact is the torn veil of the temple, which was rent by the hand of God when Christ died on the cross of Calvary (Matt. 27:5; Heb. 10:19–22). The Law as a standard is fulfilled by us in the higher law of love; the Law as a system is now null and void and of no further significance, except insofar that its types and symbols illuminate New Testament truth and reality.

"I through the law am dead to the Law, that I might live unto God," Paul says. "You see, Peter," we can hear him say as he patiently tries to explain to his erring colleague the truth of the matter, "all the law could do was condemn me to death. Very well, I accept the death sentence. Now I am dead, dead to everything, dead to myself, dead even to the Law. That is all the law can do—slay me. It brings me to the place of death, but it cannot bring me to resurrection ground. Christ can and does. So, having accepted the death that the Law administers, I now can 'live unto God.'" So, Paul states a principle.

### ii. A position (2:20)

Now that he is "in Christ," Paul steps boldly out of the death into which the Law delivered him and onto resurrection ground. There are two steps in the full realization of this new life that we have in Christ. First, we are *identified with Christ:* "I am crucified with Christ: nevertheless I live" (v. 20a). This is one of the most important truths in the New Testament. When Christ died, I died. The Lord Jesus not only died *for* me but also He died *as* me. All we have to do is reckon it to be true. Here is the eternal fact: "I am crucified with Christ." Actually, the verb is in the perfect tense: "*I have been* crucified with Christ." The Lord Jesus, though sinless, took my place and was identified with my sin. On the cross, He suffered the full penalty of the Law and was exposed to the full horror of the wrath of a holy, sin-hating God. Because death nullifies all claims and obligations, in the death of Christ, the believer has died to all of the demands and jurisdiction of the Law.

Paul adds, "Nevertheless I live. . . ." When Jesus rose from the dead, I rose from the dead. When He stepped forth from the grave to take His eternal stand on resurrection ground, in the eternal counsel of God, I stepped forth from the grave and took my stand on resurrection ground. That is the truth of identification with Christ.

But there is more to it than being identified with Christ. We are *indwelt by Christ.* We are recipients of His matchless life and matchless love: "I live; yet not I, but Christ liveth in me: and the life which I now live in the flesh I live by the faith of the Son of God, who loved me, and gave himself for me" (v. 20b–c).

We can almost see Paul beam as he takes Peter by the arm and says, "Don't you see, Peter? It's no longer the Law; it's the Lord! Did you *die* for Jesus, Peter? Of course not! He died for you, to take care of the past tense of your salvation. Do you *live* for Jesus? No! Of course not! He now lives in you, to take care of the present tense of salvation. He died on the cross to save you from your *sin;* He lives in you to save you from your *self!* The Law has nothing to do with it. The Law's day came to an end at Calvary. The whole system of circumcision, ritual cleanliness, and eating and drinking certain kinds of food is as dead as Calvary can make it. It is not even a question now of your living for the Lord, let alone your living for the Law. It is a question of Christ, having fulfilled all of the Law's demands, now living in you! You see, Peter, we do what we do because we are what we are; therefore, we need both what Christ did and what Christ is. He did what He did because we did what we did—our faith in that fact *saves* us. We are what we are; therefore, we need what He is. Because He is what He is, He can live in us. Our faith in that is what *sanctifies* us." We cannot help but wonder what Peter said to that explanation. Paul's inspired logic must have overwhelmed him. Surely the petty quibbling and shibboleths of James and the legalists must have suddenly seemed silly and the very epitome of error itself.

### iii. A perspective (2:21)

But Paul was not quite through with Peter. He had one more parting shot for not only Peter but also all of those who still think that some kind of doing one's best for Jesus is the way to go. "I do not frustrate the grace of God: for if righteousness come by the law, then Christ is dead in vain" (v. 21). In the end, it all comes down to a question of law or grace. We are saved either by law keeping or by grace. As believers, we live either by the Law, by some system of self-effort, or by grace.

The word for "frustrate" here is *atheteō*—"to disannul." Paul says that he did not act toward the grace of God as though it had been rendered null and void. That is what legalism implies. At Calvary, God established grace as the means whereby He would deal with fallen man, just as at Calvary He rent the temple veil and rendered null and void the Law and Judaism. Paul was not about to let Peter, or James, the legalist, or anyone else for that matter, get away with the kind of behavior that Peter had exhibited at Antioch, which said, in effect, that grace had been voided after all, and the Law, with its rules and rituals, was restored in its stead. "If it were possible for a man to establish righteousness by means of the Law, then Christ died for nothing. If the Law could be an instrument of salvation and sanctification, then Christ died uselessly." That was Paul's parting thrust at Peter.

PART 3

# An Exposition

## Galatians 3:1–4:31

A. How Paul interrogated the Galatians (3:1–5)

Having reviewed some pertinent facts of recent history for his Galatian converts, Paul now turns to an exposition of grace and faith, as opposed to law and works, as a means of getting right with God. He begins with a series of penetrating questions. He asks the Galatians, first, about *their seducers:* "O foolish Galatians, who hath bewitched you, that ye should not obey the truth, before whose eyes Jesus Christ hath been evidently set forth, crucified among you?" (v. 1).

The word *foolish* is *anoētos,* signifying "senseless." The Lord used the noun to describe the two disciples on the road to Emmaus who were so "slow of heart to believe all that the prophets have spoken" (Luke 24:25). They had not sufficiently reflected on the Scriptures and the significance of Calvary. Paul used the word when, in writing to the Romans, he described himself as debtor "both to the wise, and to the unwise" (Rom. 1:14). The word for "bewitched" is *baskainō,* and it occurs only here in the New Testament. It means "to fascinate," or "to hypnotize." That is how a serpent catches a bird that has wings and could easily escape from it. If the serpent can once catch the bird's eye, it can hold it spellbound until it can get within striking distance. I saw a young boa constrictor do that once to a mouse. The mouse simply stood, gazing in fascinated horror at the slowly approaching serpent. It made no attempt to get away. It simply stood still, shaking in every limb, and awaiting its doom. Similarly, the Galatians had been hypnotized by the clever arguments of the text-juggling legalists. "Who has been casting a spell on you?" Paul demands of his foolish Galatians.

The expression "evidently set forth" is *prographō.* The word means literally "proclaimed" or "placarded." When I was a boy in Britain, we would sometimes see men wearing placards, large boards covered with advertisements or announcements. The boards were joined by a couple of shoulder straps. The "sandwich board men," as they were sometimes called, wore one placard in front and one behind. Everywhere they went, they carried the message. In Bible times, a magistrate would thus "placard," or publicize, the fact that an execution had taken place. Today, the word could probably be rendered "advertised." Therefore, the Galatians were without excuse. Paul had "placarded," "proclaimed," or "advertised widely" the death of Christ on Calvary's cross and its blessed significance to lost people.

"Who hath bewitched you?" Paul demands. It had to be someone who was as fanatical as he used to be in his old unregenerate days. It had to be someone who was so wedded to Judaism that not even the death of Christ could free him from his views and vows. Something about the Law was very fascinating, bewitching, and seductive to new Gentile converts as well as to people who were newly saved from Judaism. It had the advantage of being venerable and old. It had the advantage of being God-breathed, a divine revelation, inspired of the Holy Spirit, written with the finger of God on tables of stone. The gullible Galatians could not see that God Himself had rent the temple veil, just the way Moses had once smashed the tables of stone. Judaism was dead.

Something is very subtle about appealing to the Bible itself in support of error. The unwary can easily be deceived by the glib: "This is what the Bible says: 'Remember the sabbath day, to keep it holy'" (Exod. 20:8), or "See, the Bible says, 'Forbid not to speak with tongues'" (1 Cor. 14:39), or "When you're dead, you're dead. The Bible says so. It says, 'The dead know not any thing'" (Eccl. 9:5). It is the old cultic trick of "interpreting" a Scripture without regard to its context, without regard to the scope and purpose of the book in which it is found, and without regard to the people to whom the particular passage was addressed. We must always find out under what circumstances and by whom a passage was written. We must regard the culture, the history, and the geography that form the background of the passage. We must consider the usual rules of grammar that apply and consider also the dispensation to which the passage belongs. Ever since Pentecost, with its radical change in God's administration of human affairs, any sound interpretation of Old Testament Scriptures must take into account the change of dispensations. Grace is not law (although there was grace under a dispensation of Law and although there is law under a dispensation of grace). Calvary has changed the basis of God's dealings with men. The church is not Israel, although saved Jews in the church are spoken of as "the Israel of God." Israel is a temporal nation with national hopes, goals, and destiny. The church is supranational, spiritual, heavenly, and eternal. Mount Sinai imposes a different set of principles than does Mount Calvary.

Those who are either ignorant of these things or choose to ignore them end up distorting the Scriptures. Error remains error no matter who teaches it and no matter how much Bible it quotes. The hypnotic fascination of error, indeed, lies in its seemingly authoritative but actually deceptive use of Scripture. The fact that the Judaizers could appeal to so many Old Testament Scriptures to "prove" their point is what bewitched the Galatians. The Seventh-day Adventists do the same to beguile those who heed them.

Having asked the Galatians about their seducers, Paul next asks them about *their salvation:* "This only would I learn of you, Received ye the Spirit by the works of the law, or by the hearing of faith?" (v. 2). This, indeed, is the Great Divide between the Old Testament and the New Testament. The Law said, "Do!" Grace says, "Done!" The Law said, "Try!" Grace says, "Trust!" The Law says, "Behave!" Grace says, "Believe!" Law points to the commandments; grace points to the Christ. The weakness of the Law is the flesh; the wonder of grace is the Holy Spirit.

The law of biogenesis states that there can be no life without antecedent life. The renowned scientist Louis Pasteur demonstrated that truth in his day. He held up a thoroughly sterilized and hermetically sealed flask before his audience. "It is devoid of life!" he exclaimed. "I can keep it for a hundred years, and it will still be devoid of life. I can beg and plead with it to produce a life-form, even the humblest life form, but it remains unmoved by my pleas. There is no life without antecedent life. Only life can beget life."

That was the inherent weakness with the Law. It could not produce spiritual life. The rich young ruler could say, looking Jesus in the eye when confronted with the commandments of the Law: "All these have I kept from my youth up." That did not save him—and he knew it. He was aware of a deep-seated emptiness in his soul: "What lack I yet?" he cried (Matt. 19:20). In His reply, Jesus proved to him that, although he might have kept the letter of the Law in its negative form, at least to his own satisfaction, he had never kept the spirit of the Law in its positive form (Matt. 19:21). The young man turned away sorrowful, unwilling to exchange law for life.

No amount of doing this and doing that or not doing this and not doing the other can create spiritual life. Paul tells us that the Law is "weak through the flesh" (Rom. 8:3). Jesus told Nicodemus, "that which is born of the flesh is flesh" (John 3:6). He added, "that which is born of the Spirit is Spirit." It is the law of biogenesis lifted to the spiritual plane. There can be no life without antecedent life. The Law could not give life. It could only point out a standard of behavior that God would accept but one that we are incapable of producing in the flesh. The flesh can only go on reproducing itself. It might present itself as religious flesh, as respectable flesh, as resourceful flesh, or as self-righteous flesh, but it is still flesh. God calls it "sinful flesh" (Rom. 8:3) because the flesh is never more sinful than when it is seeking to pass itself off as good. Worse still, "In me (that is, in my flesh) dwelleth no good thing" (Rom. 7:18).

No wonder Paul demands, "Received ye the Spirit by the works of the law, or by the hearing of faith?" In other words, "How did you receive the Holy Spirit, and with Him, the very life of God? Was it by trying or by trusting? by works or by faith? by seeking to keep the Law or by surrendering to the Lord?" The Holy Spirit is called "the Spirit of life" (Rom. 8:2). He, and He alone, can impart life to the soul, and He Himself cannot be acquired by works done in the flesh, even works of the Law. He can be received only by faith, "by the hearing of faith," as Paul puts it here.

This was the crucial point. When Paul appeared among them on his first missionary journey, what had he preached? Had he told them to be good and keep the Ten Commandments? Had he told them to be circumcised and keep the Sabbath? Had he told them to become proselytes of the Jewish religion and join the local synagogue? Is that how they were saved? Is that how they had received the regenerating Holy Spirit of God? Of course not! He had preached Christ to them. They had believed and had been regenerated, indwelt, baptized, sealed, and filled by the Holy Spirit. Simply to ask the question was its own answer.

Next, Paul asks the Galatians about *their sanctification:* "Are ye so foolish? having begun in the Spirit, are ye now made perfect by the flesh?" (v. 3). Does a butterfly—having emerged from its chrysalis transformed, regenerated, metamorphosed to live a new life, and equipped with gorgeous gossamer wings—continue as a caterpillar? Does it say to itself, *Well, I have been born again. I must do my best to be a butterfly. I will crawl up this stem and gnaw on these leaves!* Of course not! It spreads its wings. It catches the rising air currents. It soars from field to field seeking the nectar of the flowers. It has new life. That new life cannot be lived on the principles of the old life.

Trying to earn salvation led the Galatians nowhere. They were saved by the simple expedient of trusting Christ. They had new life in Christ. The Holy Spirit indwelt their hearts. Were they now to go back to the old, ineffective system of trying? Of course not! It didn't work when they were sinners seeking salvation, and it wouldn't work now that they were saints seeking sanctification.

The old way could be summed up thus. They were saying, "I will put all that I am as man into being good, into keeping the commandments, and into obeying the Law." It didn't work. Then they discovered the principle of faith, and they trusted Christ. They were instantly regenerated and indwelt by the Holy Spirit. The principle of obedience was exemplified by the Lord Jesus when He, in all of the wonder of His sinless humanity, put Himself at the disposal of His Father to be what His Father wanted Him to be and to do what His Father wanted Him to do.

It was the principle by which He lived when He was on earth. Similarly, we, as human beings, are to make all that we are wholly available to the Lord Jesus as God.

And that is a far cry from attempting to achieve a holy life by one's own efforts or by attempting to keep the Law as demanded by the false teachers. In his epistle to the Romans, Paul puts it thus: "For what the law could not do, in that it was weak through the flesh, God sending his own Son in the likeness of sinful flesh, and for sin, condemned sin in the flesh; that the righteousness of the law might be fulfilled in us, who walk not after the flesh, but after the Spirit" (Rom. 8:3–4). In other words, we can never succeed in producing righteousness by keeping the Law because of the weakness of our human nature. God, however, sent His Son into this world. He, in His own human nature, perfectly kept the law of God. Then He took our sins upon Himself at Calvary, enabling God to condemn and deal with our sinful nature. Now, by His indwelling Holy Spirit, the Lord Jesus can fulfill in us all of the Law's demands!

Then Paul questions the Galatians regarding *their sufferings:* "Have ye suffered so many things in vain?" he demands (v. 4). We know from the book of Acts that Paul suffered severely for the cause of Christ in Galatia on his first missionary journey. The Jews became his bitter enemies. They stirred up the Gentiles against him and, bent on mischief, chased after him from one city to another. They even stoned him and left him for dead. The book of Acts does not record any suffering on the part of Paul's converts. That does not mean, however, that the infant church did not face persecution when Paul finally left the area. Evidently the Galatians did suffer because Paul alludes to it here as a fact. It would seem, moreover, that the Jews were behind the persecution of the Christians and that some of the Galatians were about to go over to the Judaizers by means of circumcision to escape more suffering.

Paul looked upon such a move as the height of folly. What would they gain? Nothing! Judaism had nothing to offer. What would they lose? Everything! Their sufferings for Christ's sake would one day be rewarded (2 Tim. 2:12). One day, they would actually reign with Christ. If they drew back, they would forfeit their reward (Heb. 10:38), and all of their past sufferings for the Lord's sake would have been in vain. Paul earnestly hoped that they would not take that final step—"If it be yet in vain." It was another argument to add to the others, another weight tossed into the scale.

Finally, Paul questions the Galatians regarding *their signs:* "He therefore that ministereth to you the Spirit, and worketh miracles among you, doeth he it by the works of the law, or by the hearing of faith?" (v. 5). It was still the transitional age that the book of Acts covered, and the sign gifts were still in force. Paul himself had worked miracles among them, notably at Lystra, where he had healed a man who was lame from birth (Acts 14:8–10). Paul knew perfectly well that it was not by the works of the Law that the lame man had been healed. Luke also makes that clear in recording the incident. He says that Paul, "stedfastly beholding him, and perceiving that he had faith to be healed," commanded him to get up on his feet (Acts 14:9–10).

Suppose that the man had said to Paul, "Sir, you are evidently a man of God. How can I be healed of my lifelong lameness?" And suppose that Paul had replied, "Keep the commandments, worship God, avoid idolatry, do not profane God's holy name, keep the Sabbath, and honor your parents. Don't kill, commit adultery, steal, bear false witness, or covet." Would he be healed by doing those things? Of course not! It would take a miracle to heal him. It would take the Spirit of God to heal him. The only explanation for the healing of that lame man was God!

"He therefore that ministereth to you the Spirit," says Paul. The word is *epichorēgeō,* meaning "to supply." Paul uses it in 2 Corinthians 9:10, where he writes, "He that ministereth seed to the sower." The prefix *epi-* points to God's bountiful supply. Paul's phrase here can be rendered "He who supplies the Spirit to you . . . ," or "He who liberally gives His spirit to you." The reference, of course, is to God the Father. The word for "supplies" here is in the present continuous tense. The Father goes on and on ministering His Spirit to us so that we can go on and on living the supernatural life, which is ours by virtue of our faith in Christ.

Paul wants his Galatian friends to remember that the Christian life is a supernatural life. It can be explained only in terms of God. The only explanation for the Christian life is God. No such thing could be claimed about the kind of life to which the Judaizers wished to initiate the Christians in Galatia. What was supernatural about getting circumcised and observing the Sabbath and abstaining from certain kinds of food? Indeed, what was supernatural about the Judaizers themselves? Had they come to Galatia as Paul had? When pioneering a new mission field, did they habitually flood it with signs and miracles? Paul knew his enemies well enough to know that they had done nothing of the kind. All they had was a rule book, as thick as the scribes and the Pharisees could make it, of endless dos and don'ts—all to be performed in the energy of the flesh.

Thus, then, Paul interrogated the Galatians. And a thorough examination it was, one that was well calculated to give them second thoughts about the error of their ways.

B. How Paul instructed the Galatians (3:6–4:31)
   1. Believers are the seed of Abraham (3:6–29)
      a. The priority of grace (3:6–18)
         (1) The conversion of Abraham (3:6–14)
            (a) Abraham and the Seed (3:6–9)

Paul now turns his attention to an exposition of God's plan of salvation. His thoughts, at this point, center around Abraham, the great founding father of the Hebrew nation, held in such reverence by the Jews. He tells the Galatians about the *conversion* of Abraham and about God's *covenant* with Abraham. In developing his thoughts about Abraham's conversion, he draws the attention of the Galatians to *Abraham and the Seed* (vv. 6–9), *Abraham and the Scripture* (vv. 10–12), and *Abraham and the Savior* (vv. 13–14).

He begins with Abraham and the Seed (vv. 6–9): "Even as Abraham believed God, and it was accounted to him for righteousness" (v. 6). That is all Abraham had to do to be saved. Abraham's salvation was based purely and simply upon the principle of grace, which was made operationally effective in his life when he believed God. In Genesis 12, God talked to Abraham about the land. He told him to leave Ur of the Chaldees and set out for another country. Hebrews 11:9–10 tells us that "by faith he sojourned in the land of promise, as in a strange country . . . for he looked for a city which hath foundations, whose builder and maker is God." The closing chapters of the Apocalypse give us a glimpse of that glorious, heavenly city that haunted Abraham's dreams, a city with twelve foundations indeed (Rev. 21:14)! Abraham, by faith, turned his back on the old way of life in Ur of the Chaldees, set out for heaven, and became a pilgrim and a stranger in the world. But that was only preliminary. He was not counted righteous then.

In Genesis 15, God talked to Abraham about the Lord. "I have no seed!" Abraham complained. "I have no son." The Lord showed him the stars of heaven. "So shall thy seed be," He said, pointing him to the sky. "And he believed in the LORD; and he counted it to him for righteousness" (Gen. 15:6). It was when he put his faith and his trust in what God had to say about the coming "Seed"—one of the Old Testament names for the Lord—that all of the righteousness of God was transferred sovereignly to him. Then follows the remarkable story of the signing by God of the unconditional covenant with Abraham. Abraham was in "a deep sleep" at the time (Gen. 15:12). Obviously, Abraham did nothing to merit his salvation, nothing to earn being made righteous. He was sleeping soundly when the covenant was written, although spiritually he was never more awake.

The point Paul thus makes with the Galatians is clear. The Judaizers were proud of being "Abraham's seed" (John 8:33). Very well! How was Abraham saved? Simply by believing the Lord! No more, no less! That, itself, cut the ground from beneath the feet of the Judaizers. But Paul had only just begun. If that was how Abraham was saved, how are all other men saved? On the same principle exactly.

Paul now underlines for us three things. He underlines *the same faith:* "Know ye therefore that they which are of faith, the same are the children of Abraham" (v. 7). The Jews boasted to the Lord Jesus of being "Abraham's seed," the very Jews indeed, who were plotting for His life. The Lord Jesus bluntly told them that they were nothing of the kind. Sure, they were lineal, physical descendants of Abraham. But so what? That gave them no special status with God. "If ye were Abraham's *seed,*" He said, "you would do what he did" (John 8:39). And what did he do? What they refused to do—believe Him. Far from being "Abraham's seed," they were the Devil's seed (v. 44).

John the Baptist had told them much the same thing: "Think not to say within yourselves, We have Abraham to our father: for I say unto you, that God is able of these stones to raise up children unto Abraham" (Matt. 3:9). No! Being a child of Abraham, as fond as the Judaizers were of the boast, had nothing whatever to do with physical birth. It had to do with spiritual birth. They became Abraham's children when they did what Abraham did—believed in the Lord. No more! No less! It was a matter of the same faith.

Then he underlines *the sure foundation:* "And the scripture, foreseeing that God would justify the heathen through faith, preached before the gospel unto Abraham, saying, In thee shall all nations be blessed" (v. 8; Gen. 12:3). That was the good news: all nations would be brought into the spiritual blessing of Abraham. How? The same way Abraham himself was brought into blessing! That was the sure foundation.

Salvation is by faith. Paul keeps on driving the point home. It was always God's intention. Paul says to his Galatian Gentile converts that the Gentiles should be justified by faith. Therefore, in accordance with His omniscience and foreknowledge, he proclaimed the gospel two thousand years ago in the words spoken to Abraham. It was no novel idea that salvation was by faith and faith alone. That was always God's plan from the very beginning. Paul was no innovator, preaching some new and novel gospel! The gospel that he preached went back at least as far as Abraham. The Judaizers would point the Gentiles to Moses. Paul pointed them to Abraham.

Then he underlines *the simple fact:* "So then they which be of faith are blessed with faithful Abraham" (v. 9). There was not one particle of difference between the gospel that Paul preached to the Gentiles and the gospel that God preached to Abraham. The blessing bestowed on Abraham, of being counted righteous on the basis of his faith in the Lord, is the blessing now bestowed on all—the blessing of being counted righteous on the basis of our faith in the Lord.

### (b) Abraham and the Scripture (3:10–12)

Paul now draws attention to three things again. First, he mentions *a curse:* "For as many as are of the works of the law are under the curse: for it is written, Cursed is every one that continueth not in all things which are written in the book of the law to do them" (v. 10). So! The Galatians have suddenly become enamored of the Law! Have their new, fine-feathered Judaizing friends told them what is really involved in commitment to law keeping as a means of salvation? Have they told them about Deuteronomy 27:26? Have they told them about the curse of the Law?

Great and terrible were the curses of the Law, and comprehensive and far-reaching too. Deuteronomy 27 records a round dozen curses, and Deuteronomy 28 records a half dozen more, followed by a series of horrifying illustrations.

> And these shall stand upon mount Ebal to curse; Reuben, Gad, and Asher, and Zebulun, Dan, and Naphtali. And the Levites shall speak, and say unto all the men of Israel with a loud voice, Cursed be the man that maketh any graven or molten image, an abomination unto the LORD, the work of the hands of the craftsman, and putteth it in a secret place. And all the people shall answer and say, Amen. Cursed be he that setteth light by his father or his mother. And all the people shall say, Amen. Cursed be he that removeth his neighbour's landmark. And all the people shall say, Amen. Cursed be he that maketh the blind to wander out of the way. And all the people shall say, Amen. Cursed be he that perverteth the judgment of the stranger, fatherless, and widow. And all the people shall say, Amen. Cursed be he that lieth with his father's wife; because he uncovereth his father's skirt. And all the people shall say, Amen. Cursed be he that lieth with any manner of beast. And all the people shall say, Amen. Cursed be he that lieth with his sister, the daughter of his father, or the daughter of his mother. And all the people shall say, Amen. Cursed

> be he that lieth with his mother-in-law. And all the people shall say, Amen. Cursed be he that smiteth his neighbour secretly. And all the people shall say, Amen. Cursed be he that taketh reward to slay an innocent person. And all the people shall say, Amen. *Cursed be he that confirmeth not all the words of this law to do them.* And all the people shall say, Amen. (Deuteronomy 27:13–26)

> It shall come to pass, if thou wilt not hearken unto the voice of the LORD thy God, to observe to do *all his commandments and his statutes* which I command thee this day; that all these curses shall come upon thee, and overtake thee: Cursed shalt thou be in the city, and cursed shalt thou be in the field. Cursed shall be thy basket and thy store. Cursed shall be the fruit of thy body, and the fruit of thy land, the increase of thy kine, and the flocks of thy sheep. Cursed shalt thou be when thou comest in, and cursed shalt thou be when thou goes out. The LORD shall send upon thee cursing, vexation, and rebuke, in all that thou settest thine hand unto for to do. (Deuteronomy 28:15–20)

The following verses of Deuteronomy 28 expanded and illustrated these curses of the Law. The children of Israel would be pursued by disease, drought, deportation, and dread. "In the morning thou shalt say, Would God it were even! and at even thou shalt say, Would God it were morning! for the fear of thine heart wherewith thou shalt fear" (v. 67).

Such was the curse of the Law. And such has been the agelong history of the Jewish people to this very day. Scarcely a country in the world has not lifted up its hand, at one time or another, against the Jews. Even as Paul wrote his Galatian epistle, the Judaizers were themselves living under bondage to a foreign power that was occupying their land and ruling them with an unfeeling iron hand.

"How about *that?*" Paul demands. "Did your Judaizing friends tell you that? You want to put yourselves under the Law? Then make sure you keep it *all,* every jot and tittle of it, every verse and every line, every duty and every demand, every rule, every rite, every ritual, and every requirement. Don't leave out a single one for a single moment—or the curse of the Law will be upon you. There are no excuses and no exceptions." "Cursed is *every one* that continueth not in *all things* which are written in the book of the law to do them" (Gal. 3:10). What a cheerful prospect! What a thing to put in the place of God's so free, so full salvation offered to us on the basis of grace through faith!

The best disposed Jew in the world, even today, cannot keep the Mosaic Law, not even the Jew dwelling in the land of Israel. Indeed, one of the problems that the modern state of Israel had to face early in its existence was the fact that the Law was given for a nomadic, rural people, living in a temperate zone and in a simple, nonindustrialized age. As long as Jews were sojourners in Gentile lands, they could at least keep up appearances of keeping the Law, for instance, the law of the Sabbath. In a modern, industrialized society, however, certain functions have to continue regardless of high day or holy day. Public utilities have to be staffed, managed, and maintained. Water mains have to be kept open and pressure maintained. Electricity has to be supplied to consumers. Telephone services must be kept functioning. Police forces must be manned. The military must attend to matters pertaining to national security. As long as they were in Gentile lands, Jews could let the *goyim* (Gentiles) take care of those things, so they could observe the Sabbath secure in the knowledge that they did not have to profane the Sabbath by being directly involved in them. But, once the Jews had a sovereign state of their own and were responsible for their own affairs, the problem became one of instant concern. The solution has been to let nonreligious Jews break the Sabbath on behalf of the religious Jews.

Seventh-day Adventists, who come forcibly under the indictment of Galatians 3:10, have the same problem. Some years ago, when I was living in the Canadian north, I crossed verbal swords with a man who wanted to impose the Law on me. In wintertime, the temperature would frequently dip to forty-five degrees Fahrenheit below zero and would often hover at minus twenty degrees Fahrenheit. All plumbing had to be buried deep underground because in a severe winter the frost line went down some six feet into the ground. I can remember one winter when the temperature hit an arctic fifty-four degrees Fahrenheit below zero. The frost on the windowpanes was nearly an inch thick. It came through the front door and stood white and menacing on the inside panels. The doorknob was so cold that if one touched it with bare hands, the fingers stuck to it and could only be pulled away at the cost of torn skin. The furnace in our house never stopped running for days. Those who had more primitive housing had a full-time job feeding logs on the fire.

With this in mind, I said to this Seventh-day Adventist, "Tell me, what do you do in the wintertime here in Prince George, when the temperature dips below zero? How do you ever manage to keep the Law on a day like that? The Law says, 'Ye shall kindle no fire throughout your habitations upon the sabbath day'" (Exod. 35:3).

He had no answer. I continued, "What kind of suit are you wearing? Are you wearing a suit with a mixture of fabrics—wool and cotton, for instance?" Sure enough he was. "Well," I said, "even as you stand there trying to persuade me to put myself under law, you are under the curse of the Law yourself. The Law says, 'Thou shalt not wear a garment of divers sorts, as of woollen and linen together'" (Deut. 22:11).

"Indeed," I continued, "you are not even making any attempt to wear the kind of garment that the Law demands. The Law says, 'Thou shalt make thee fringes upon the four quarters of thy vesture, wherewith thou coverest thyself' (Deut. 22:12). You want me to commit myself to keep the Sabbath and take upon myself responsibility to keep the Mosaic Law when you not only do not keep it yourself but also cannot keep it; by not keeping it, you put yourself under its curse. You certainly aren't going to get me under that curse too."

Next comes *a contrast:* "But that no man is justified by the law in the sight of God, it is evident: for, the just shall live by faith" (v. 11). This verse is quoted from Habakkuk 2:4. It is quoted three times in the New Testament—here, in Romans 1:17, and in Hebrews 10:38.

Habakkuk had a problem. Indeed, his little book seems to be concerned more with solving a problem than with delivering a message. He was prophet enough to know that his people had sinned to the point where judgment was inevitable. He also knew that God had appointed the Babylonians to be the instrument in His hand for thrashing the Jewish people. But the Babylonians were worse than the Jews! How could God justify punishing a sinful people by using an even more sinful people as His tool? God's answer was very simple: "Trust Me!"

"The just shall live by faith." This text is repeated three times in the Bible. In Romans 1:17 the context places the emphasis on *"the just"*; in Galatians 3:11, the emphasis is on *"by faith."* In Habakkuk, the emphasis is on "shall live," that is, live forever, in resurrection life. In Habakkuk's prophecy, the Hebrew accents put the emphasis on the words *shall live.* It does not read "the just by his faith," but "a just one, by his faith, shall live." The word *live* points forward to the future life. The contrast is drawn, not between faith and unbelief but between the doom of the unbeliever and the prospect of the believer—perishing, or living forever. Thus, God raised the thoughts of the puzzled prophet to higher ground, raised them above the baffling tides that ebb and flow in the affairs of men, and on into the realm of the Eternal.

Paul does not lose sight of that fact. But his struggle was with those who would place the Law and works in the place of simple trust in God. So he puts the emphasis here on faith.

It was this text that revolutionized the life of Martin Luther. How hard he had tried, as a zealous and conscientious monk, to accumulate merit enough to earn his salvation! He had fasted and prayed until he was reduced to a mere skeleton. He had flagellated himself until he was a mass of cuts and sores. He had done penance and gone on pilgrimages. Then, one day, as he crawled on hands and knees up Pilate's staircase in Rome and prayed earnestly to the Virgin Mary on every step, the light dawned. The voice of God cut through his ritual prayers and thundered in his soul, "The just shall live *by faith.*" He rose from his knees, brushed off the dust of that place, marched boldly back down those stairs, and on out of the Church of Rome altogether.

That is the message that Paul keeps pounding home. Not works but faith! Not the Law but faith! Not circumcision, Sabbath keeping, observing laws of diet, and feast days and fast days but faith! No more! No less! Faith!

Now comes *a conclusion:* "And the law is not of faith: but, The man that doeth them shall live in them" (v. 12). The quotation is from Leviticus 18:5. The Law said, "This do, and thou shalt live." *Do! Do! Do!* The word runs like a refrain down through the commandments of the Law.

> Thou shalt teach them ordinances and laws, . . . and the work that they must *do.* (Exodus 18:20)
>
> Ye shall *do* of my judgments . . . I am the LORD your God . . . which if a man *do,* he shall live in them: I am the LORD. (Leviticus 18:4–5)
>
> And ye shall keep my statutes, and *do* them: I am the LORD. (Leviticus 20:8)
>
> Shall ye keep my commandments, and *do* them: I am the LORD. (Leviticus 22:31)
>
> Wherefore ye shall *do* my statutes, and keep my judgments, and *do* them. (Leviticus 25:18)
>
> [The king] shall write him a copy of this law . . . and it shall be with him, and he shall read therein all the days of his life: that he may learn to fear the LORD his God, to keep all the words of this law and these statutes, to *do* them. (Deuteronomy 17:18–19)

> This day the LORD thy God hath commanded thee to do these statutes and judgments: thou shalt therefore keep and *do* them with all thine heart, and with all thy soul. (Deuteronomy 26:16)

And so it went on! Do! The people responded, "All that the LORD hath spoken we will *do*" (Exod. 19:8). That was what they said in their folly before they knew what the Law contained. "All that the LORD hath spoken we will *do*," they said, and said again in their folly even after they knew what the Law contained (see also Exod. 24:3, 7).

"The law is not of faith," Paul says. It is of works. The emphasis is ever and always on the word *do.* "The man that *doeth* them shall live. . . ." That is why, when the young man came to Jesus, saying, "What good thing shall I *do,* that I may have eternal life?" Jesus pointed him at once to the Law and said, "If thou wilt enter into life, keep the commandments." The young man tried to hedge. "Which?" he asked. Jesus could have answered, "All!" Instead, He cited the commands of the Decalogue that dealt solely with his duty to man, including the devastating summary demand: "Thou shalt love thy neighbour as thyself." When the young man claimed to have kept these commandments always, Jesus proved to him that he never had kept them, nor could he, that he did not love his neighbor as he loved himself. Many of his neighbors were poor; he was rich, but he had no intention of giving his wealth to the poor (Matt. 19:16–22). He did not love his neighbor as he loved himself. He was a lawbreaker.

In fact, nobody loves his neighbor as he loves himself. Still less does he love God, as He demands that we love Him. When someone asked Jesus to define the first commandment, He replied, "Thou shalt love the Lord thy God with all thy heart, and with all thy soul, and with all thy mind, and with all thy strength" (quoting from Deut. 6:4–5). He added the commandment concerning loving one's neighbor as oneself and declared, "There is none other commandment greater than these." The young ruler was prepared to give mental allegiance to the Ten Commandments. The law of love, however, proved him to be a man condemned by the Law.

*"Do!"* demands the Law—"and do it from the heart." The problem is that we cannot do what is demanded. The first and greatest sinner is not a murderer, an adulterer, or a thief. The first and greatest sinner is the person who breaks the first and greatest commandment. Apart from the Lord Jesus, no man, woman, boy, or girl has ever lived who could claim to have always loved God with all of his or her heart, mind, soul, and strength. So when the Law

says, "This *do* and thou shalt live," we find ourselves confronted with the humanly impossible.

The Law says, *"Do!"* Grace says, *"Done!"* On the cross, Jesus cried, "It is finished!" All of the doing has been done. By faith we cross over from death to life, from trying to trusting, and from a system that says, "Do!" to a salvation that says, "Done!"

During one of his great campaigns, D. L. Moody was accosted by a man who had been to a number of the services and who, although convicted of his need for Christ, had kept on postponing a decision. Now the last night had come. The altar call was over, the people were going home, the work crew was busy folding up the chairs and dismantling the platform, and Mr. Moody was preparing to leave. The man finally plucked up his courage. He came to the evangelist and blurted out, "Mr. Moody, what must I do to be saved?" D. L. Moody looked at him. "I'm sorry, sir," he said, "but you're too late."

"Too late, Mr. Moody?" The man was desperate now. "Surely I'm not too late!"

"Yes, sir," said Moody. "You're too late. As a matter of fact, you're two thousand years too late if you want to *do* something to be saved. All the 'doing' has been done. But if you would like to accept Christ by faith as your personal Savior, you're just in time. You can do that right here, right now."

### (c) Abraham and the Savior (3:13–14)

So, then, Paul has spoken of Abraham and the Seed and of Abraham and the Scripture. Now he speaks of Abraham and the Savior (13–14). He has already introduced his Galatian friends to an aspect of the Law that the Judaizers downplayed—its fearful curse. Now he shows them how that *burden* was *removed by Christ:* "Christ hath redeemed us from the curse of the law, being made a curse for us: for it is written, Cursed is every one that hangeth on a tree" (v. 13). The quotation is from Deuteronomy 21:23.

In his unconverted days as Saul of Tarsus, the archpersecutor of the church, that had been the most impossible thing about Christianity—"Cursed is every one that hangeth on a tree." The Old Testament Law read, "If a man have committed a sin worthy of death, and he be to be put to death, and thou hang him on a tree: his body shall not remain all night upon the tree, but thou shalt in any wise bury him that day; (for he that is hanged is accursed of God;) . . ." (Deut. 21:22–23).

One terrible example of this punishment is recorded in the Old Testament. When Balaam, having failed to curse God's people, taught Balak, king of Moab, how to corrupt God's people, God's judgment was swift and exemplary. "You will never conquer this people with the men of Moab, my lord king," Balaam said. "I suggest you try the women of Moab." It worked.

> And Israel abode in Shittim, and the people began to commit whoredom with the daughters of Moab. And they called the people unto the sacrifices of their gods: and the people did eat, and bowed down to their gods. And Israel joined himself unto Baal-peor: and the anger of the LORD was kindled against Israel. And the LORD said unto Moses, Take all the heads [chiefs or princes] of the people, and hang them up before the LORD against the sun, that the fierce anger of the LORD may be turned away from Israel. (Numbers 25:1–4)

There must have been about a thousand of them. The incident is extraordinary, because the Jews customarily executed people by stoning, probably to avoid the special curse that rested, under the Law, upon those who were hanged.

Two other notable individuals in the Old Testament died by hanging: Ahithophel, the man who betrayed David (2 Sam. 17:23), and Absalom, the man who raised the standard of rebellion against David (2 Sam. 18:9–15). In the New Testament, we remember the traitor Judas Iscariot, who hanged himself (Matt. 27:3–5).

Saul of Tarsus was familiar with both this particular Old Testament curse and the various examples of its application. So although he might have been prepared to concede certain things about Jesus of Nazareth, it was this method of His death that, to him at any rate, made the claims of Christ false and blasphemous. He had been hanged on a tree! He had been crucified on a Roman cross. According to the Old Testament Law, therefore, He had died under the direct curse of God. Saul of Tarsus might have been willing to concede the death of Israel's Messiah. But on a tree? Never! It was the most impossible thing about Christianity. But then he met the risen and ascended Lord and saw the nail prints in His hands and feet. Thereafter, the fact that Christ had indeed died under God's curse became the most impressive thing about Christianity. He could see it now! It was necessary for Christ to die under the curse. Only thus could the curse itself be removed.

Think again of the terrible catalog of curses that were part and parcel of the

Law, aimed directly at everyone who broke the Law. When Christ died in our stead, the curses were all aimed at Him. He died on a *tree,* the very symbol of the curse of the Law, and wearing a crown of *thorns,* the very symbol of the curse from the Fall (see Gen. 3:17–19).

Thus, Christ removed the terrible burden of the Law's curse. But more! Paul points out now to his Galatian friends the tremendous *blessing* that is now *received through Christ:* "That the blessing of Abraham might come on the Gentiles through Jesus Christ; that we might receive the promise of the Spirit through faith" (v. 14). The "blessing of Abraham" was salvation by faith.

The promise of the Spirit included the *baptism* of the Spirit, which puts each believer in the Lord Jesus into the church, His mystical body; the *gift* of the Spirit, which puts all of the wisdom, love, and power of the Godhead at the disposal of the child of God; the *indwelling* of the Spirit, which puts God back in the man; the *seal* of the Spirit, which secures the believer eternally; the *earnest* of the Spirit, which guarantees the exceeding great and glorious future that awaits every believer in eternity; the *filling* of the Spirit, which enables the believer to live the life of the indwelling Christ; and the *anointing* of the Spirit, which empowers the believer for service.

Who would want to exchange all of that for the obsolete rites and impossible rules of a dead, Christ-rejecting religion? The believer in Christ can have all that Abraham had and more—salvation by faith, through grace, regardless of the Law. He can also have all that the Holy Spirit brings with Him when He enters a regenerated human heart. The Judaizers had nothing to offer that compared with that.

(2) The covenant with Abraham (3:15–18)

(a) The contract principle (3:15)

Paul is still pursuing his first major point that believers are the seed of Abraham (3:6–29). He had reviewed the *conversion* of Abraham; now he turns his attention to the *covenant* (the contract) with Abraham and begins with the contract principle: "Brethren, I speak after the manner of men; Though it be but a man's covenant, yet if it be confirmed, no man disannulleth, or addeth thereto" (v. 15). Paul draws on an everyday illustration. When a contract is drawn up in proper legal form and is duly signed, sealed, and delivered, it becomes binding on both contracting parties. It cannot be canceled or modified by someone else. That is the principle behind a contract. Even when changes are made in a contract, it has to be with the consent of both parties to the agreement. This is the working principle that enables society to function in an orderly way. God has been pleased to adopt the same principle in His dealings with men. Therefore, we can discern eight major contracts (or covenants, as they are often called) in the Bible.

1. The *Edenic* covenant governed the terms whereby Adam and Eve could live in the Garden of Eden.
2. The *Adamic* covenant detailed the new terms governing the life of sinful man on God's earth.
3. The *Noahic* covenant spelled out the new conditions that were to prevail subsequent to the Flood.
4. The *Abrahamic* covenant opened new vistas of grace and promise and is the covenant with which Paul is concerned here.
5. The *Mosaic* covenant (the Law), is also reviewed here by Paul.
6. The *Palestinian* covenant spelled out the conditions and terms under which the Hebrew people could live in the Promised Land.
7. The *Davidic* covenant established the prospect of the millennial kingdom and confirmed the promise under the Adamic covenant of a coming Kinsman-Redeemer and King.
8. The *new* covenant was foretold in the Old Testament and was ratified at Calvary in the blood of Christ.

The covenant principle is basic to all of God's dealings with men. Where a covenant is introduced and overlaps with a previous covenant, the new terms are rendered necessary by man's sin and violation of the earlier agreement. In such cases, the new provisions do not cancel the older ones. They are of a temporary nature and are sufficiently flexible to preserve inviolate the essential clauses of the original agreement. From the time of man's fall, no matter what contract is in force, the basis of man's salvation remains unchanged. God has only one way of saving men, no matter in what the age they live. He saves men by grace through faith on the basis of the finished work of Christ.

### (b) The covenant promise (3:16–18)

Paul now takes up the essential, basic agreement of the Abrahamic covenant and shows how that agreement has remained in force despite the later addition of the Mosaic covenant.

We note, first, *the supreme goal of the Abrahamic covenant.* This covenant was absolutely unconditional. It consisted of a series of contractual promises made by God to Abraham (Gen. 12:1–3; 15:1–21; 17:1–22). God promised the following:

1. To make of Abraham a great nation.
2. To bless him.
3. To make his name great.
4. To make him a blessing to the world.
5. To bless those who blessed him.
6. To curse those who cursed him.
7. To make him the one through whom all nations would be blessed. (This original contract was expanded and explained later.)
8. To give Abraham a seed as numerous as the stars of the heaven.
9. To emancipate that seed from enslavement in a foreign land after four hundred years in the fourth generation. That seed would become very wealthy. God's judgment was promised against the nation that oppressed Abraham's descendants.
10. To allow Abraham himself to live to a ripe old age and then die in peace.
11. To ensure that Abraham would inherit a land that would stretch from the Nile to the Euphrates.

Still more details, including the following, were added later:

12. Abraham would become the father of many nations and kings.
13. God's covenant was established between Him and Abraham's seed throughout their generations.
14. It was to be an everlasting covenant.
15. The land of Canaan, in particular, was the guaranteed possession of the covenant seed of Abraham.
16. The seal of the covenant, as far as Abraham's physical posterity was concerned, was circumcision. The widest application was given to this rite. Apart from this rite, no person could be counted part of Abraham's physical seed and heir to the material side of the agreement.
17. Abraham's wife's name was changed from Sarai to Sarah ("princess"). She, too, would be blessed. The promised seed would come through her. She would be a mother of nations and kings.
18. Ishmael was promised greatness. He would produce twelve princes and become a great and populous nation. But the Abrahamic covenant was not to be ratified in him.
19. Sarah would bear Abraham a son who would be the heir to the promise.
20. Abram's name was changed to Abraham ("father of a multitude").

All of these exceedingly great and precious promises were unconditional. All that God required of Abraham was his faith.

Paul now takes up the salient features of this great Abrahamic covenant by underlining, first, its supreme goal: "Now to Abraham and his seed were the promises made. He saith not, and to seeds, as of many; but as of one, And to thy seed, which is Christ" (v. 16). That was the supreme goal of the promise to Abraham. All was to be "yea and amen" in Christ.

In the beginning, the Seed was "the Seed of the woman" (Gen. 3:15). The text reads, "And I will put enmity between thee and the woman, and between thy seed and her seed; it shall bruise thy head, and thou shalt bruise his heel."[1] Thus, in this first prophecy of Scripture, God foretold the coming of Christ, both to redeem and to reign. The word for "seed" here *(zera')* is to be taken in the singular, as recognized by the translators of the Septuagint.

The Seed was next shown to be the Seed of Abraham, restricting the promise of the coming Christ to a single family of the world. The first promise shows that He would be virgin born but would be a member of the human race; this next promise makes Him a member of the Hebrew race. Later, the Seed is shown to be the Seed of David (2 Sam. 7:11–16), showing that He would be not only a member of the Hebrew racial family but also a member of the Hebrew royal family.

The appeal of Paul in Galatians 3:16 does not seem to be so much to Genesis 12:7, where the word *zera'* is indefinite as to number, or to Genesis 17:7, where it is plural as the context shows.[2] *Zera'* is a collective noun, like our English word *sheep*. Whether it is singular or plural must be determined by the context. Rather, Paul's appeal here would seem to be to Genesis 21:12. After Abraham's disastrous attempt to produce the promised Seed in the energy of the flesh, by involving himself with the Egyptian bondwoman Hagar (Gen. 16), God allowed matters to take their course. Then came the demand from Sarah: "Cast out this bondwoman and her son . . ." (Gen. 21:10). God endorsed this demand. "Hearken unto her voice," He said, "for in Isaac shall thy seed be called" (Gen. 21:12). Here again, *zera'* is in the singular sense, as shown by the word *Isaac* and because of the use of a singular verb.

---

1. The Roman Catholic *Vulgate* corrupts this text by rendering *it* as *she,* thus seeking to give scriptural warrant to Mariolatry.
2. The word *zera'* takes in both Abraham and his posterity. See F. F. Bruce, *The Epistle to the Galatians* (Grand Rapids: Eerdmans, 1982), 171–73. See also, C. F. Hogg and W. E. Vine, *The Epistle to the Galatians* (Grand Rapids: Kregel, 1921), 140–43.

Paul here seizes upon that singular word *seed.* The use of the word *seeds* as applied to human offspring would have been as unnatural and odd as using the word *sheeps* for the plural of *sheep* would be in English. Had God intended, however, to refer to only the natural descendants of Abraham, other words could have been used, such as *sons, descendants,* or *children.* He ignores, however, all such words that could have been used in a clean-cut singular. Paul tells us that the use of the word *seed* was by deliberate, divine choice to draw special attention to Christ as the designated Seed of Abraham.

Abraham's son Isaac, in whom "the Seed" was to be called, was born contrary to nature, as a miracle, and in response to Abraham's faith. Paul carries the whole thing further. The true Seed was Christ. He was the One to whom the promise pointed. All of the other promises centered in Him. Therefore, to share in the promises, one must necessarily belong to Christ. Paul nails down this point at the end of the chapter: "If ye be Christ's, then are ye Abraham's seed, and heirs according to the promise" (v. 29). At this point, however, Paul wants to underline two words: *promise* and *Christ.* Soon, he intends to use these two words with devastating force in his battle with the legalists. The supreme goal of the *promise* to Abraham regarding the Seed was the advent of *Christ.* Everything hinges on promise, not works; on Christ, not Moses; on faith, not law.

Next, Paul underlines *the sublime guarantee of the Abrahamic covenant:* "And this I say, that the covenant, that was confirmed before of God in Christ, the law, which was four hundred and thirty years after, cannot disannul, that it should make the promise of none effect" (v. 17). Abraham was seventy-five years old when he departed from Haran (Gen. 12:4). His departure from Haran was 430 years before the children of Israel departed from Egypt (Exod. 12:40). (The calculation includes the sojourning of the patriarchs in Canaan as well as the sojourning of the Hebrews in Egypt.) However, Paul is not so much concerned here with Old Testament chronology as he is with making a very telling point. The Law, given hundreds of years after the Abrahamic covenant, could not annul or weaken in any way the original contract. The Law had its place and purpose, but it was never intended to replace the original and wholly unconditional covenant with Abraham.

The word here for "disannul" is *akuroō,* to "render null and void." In no way could the Law of Moses undermine the force of God's contract with Abraham; everything is guaranteed by the Word of God pledged to Abraham with no human conditions attached.

The phrase "make the promise of none effect" is represented by the word *katargeō.* Could the Law have made the promise of none effect, it would have robbed the promise of its value. The word *katargeō* is used of the Lord, who—by means of His incarnation, crucifixion, and resurrection—was able to "*destroy (katargeō)* him that had the power of death, that is, the devil" (Heb. 2:14). The death of Christ effectively annuls the power of Satan. By contrast, the Law was unable to annul the prior promise, nor was it ever intended to do so. If the Law had the power to annul the promise, then God would have broken His Word to Abraham, and such a thought is unthinkable. Paul's dear Galatian converts had been snared by people enamored of Moses. Paul cleverly takes them back to Abraham.

He has one more thing to say in this context. He refers to *the sole ground of the Abrahamic covenant:* "For if the inheritance be of the law, it is no more of promise: but God gave it to Abraham by promise" (v. 18). Suppose that I were to give one of my children a promise—I will buy you a laptop computer for Christmas. I give a promise, no strings attached, backed by the integrity of my character and pledged by my given word. A promise is a promise. What if, a few weeks later, I were to add some conditions, some rules and laws that the child had to obey if he or she wished to get that present? I would have perjured myself, broken my word, gone back on my promise. I would have changed the ground rules. I would be making the attainment of the coveted object hinge upon works, something that had to be done to earn the reward and not my original unconditional promise. It would no longer be a gift but something to be earned. God does not behave like that. His character is such that it is impossible for Him ever to go back upon His promise once He has given it.

b. The purpose of law (3:19–29)
   (1) To probe the soul for sin (3:19–22)
      (a) The Law and its lesson (3:19a–b)

Having emphasized the priority of grace, Paul now explains the purpose of God's law. It has two chief functions: first, to probe the soul for sin, and second, to prepare the soul for salvation. The lesson of the Law was simple: "Wherefore then serveth the law? It was added because of transgressions, till the seed should come to whom the promise was made" (v. 19). The point and purpose of the Mosaic Law was to underline and emphasize the existence and extent of sin—until the One to whom the Abrahamic covenant referred came, the One who was to deal, once and for all, with the entire question of sin to God's eternal satisfaction.

The Law itself does not save. It was not given to Abraham but to Moses. Moreover, it was not given to Moses when Israel was yet in Egypt "in the house of bondage." God did not arm Moses with the tables of the Law and send him back to Egypt with the demand that Israel keep the commandments to be saved. On the contrary, He first redeemed them by the blood of the Passover lamb, then baptized them "unto Moses in the cloud and in the sea." Having first saved them, then separated them, He brought them to Sinai and gave them the Law—to show them how a saved people should live and to set before them the standard of behavior that God expects of His redeemed people.

In fact, the great purpose of the Law was to educate people in the scope and seriousness of their sin. It was "added because of transgressions," Paul says.

The people had hardly shaken the dust of Egypt off their sandals before their complaining began. They came to Marah and complained because the water was bitter. They wished themselves back in Egypt and murmured against Moses because they had nothing to eat. They came to Rephidim and were ready to stone Moses because there was no water to drink. Even as God was giving Moses His Law on Mount Sinai—making it possible, indeed, for Him to come and pitch His own tent among them—they were dancing around the golden calf. The Law was given because of sin, to state plainly, edict by edict, what a redeemed people must do and must not do. They marched on to Kadesh-barnea and then wished themselves back in Egypt when they heard about the giants in Canaan. Then, perversely, when sentenced to death in the wilderness, they as suddenly changed their minds and presumptuously voted to go on into Canaan in defiance of God. They listened to Korah, Dathan, and Abiram and raised the flag of rebellion against Moses and Aaron. Even the spectacular death of the conspirators did not silence them. They turned in fresh fury against God's anointed man. They provoked Moses at Kadesh because, again, there was no water. They went whoring after the women and the gods of Moab. They complained about the manna. No wonder the Law was added. Even so, it did not annul the promise.

All down through the long roll call of the commandments sounded the triumphant note of grace. Failure under the moral law brought severe penalties. It also brought guilt. The ceremonial law, the whole system of sacrifices and offerings, made provision for guilt in lieu of Calvary. So, the Law taught a lesson: transgressions were culpable and punishable. God does not condemn sin in the sinner and then condone it in the saint. The word for "transgression" is *parabasis,* which carries the idea of stepping aside. The word is always used of a breach of the Law.

The Law was added to give conscience a standard by which it could monitor human behavior. Conscience, although it is a reasonably efficient goad, is a very unreliable guide; the popular saying "Just let your conscience be your guide" is very bad advice.

For instance, when John Huss was burned at the stake, a widow approached the authorities carrying a fagot of wood that she wished to donate to the good cause. "Put it up close to the blasphemous heretic," she said.

John Huss, bound to the stake, heard the woman. "What have I ever done to you," he asked her, "that you should hate me so?"

The woman replied, "You are a heretic. It is a good work to burn a heretic. I am poor, and wood is scarce and expensive. I cannot afford this fagot; but to acquire merit, I wish to have a share in burning you."

Such is conscience. The conscience of John Huss said, "Give your body to be burned." The conscience of the woman said, "Give your fagot to burn him." Obviously, conscience needs an outside, authoritative, and divinely inspired standard by which it can be regulated. The Law provided such a standard.

The Law was added, not to annul the promise but to show us how helpless we are when it comes to meeting our obligations to God. It is also intended to teach us how great is our need of that Seed, who was the chief subject of God's great promise to Abraham. That is why the Law was in force from the time of Moses until Christ. Or, as Paul puts it, "till the seed should come to whom the promise was made."

### (b) The Law and its limitations (3:20–22)

First, Paul looks upon the *Law as a contract:* "And it was ordained by angels in the hand of a mediator. Now a mediator is not a mediator of one, but God is one" (vv. 19c–20). Moses mediated the Mosaic Law in the presence of angels. Paul adds that the fact an intermediary was needed to bring the Law to Israel was, in itself, proof enough that the Mosaic covenant was in no way a fulfillment of the Abrahamic covenant. The Abrahamic covenant had neither angel to witness it nor man to administer it because it depended on God and God alone.

In the Pentateuch, the only reference to angels in connection with the giving of the Mosaic Law is in Deuteronomy 33:2, which reads, "The LORD came from Sinai, and rose up from Seir unto them; he shined forth from mount Paran, and he came with ten thousands of saints [i.e., 'holy ones,' or 'angels']: from his right hand went a fiery law for them." David confirms this point: "The chariots of

God are twenty thousand, even thousands of angels: the Lord is among them, as in Sinai, in the holy place" (Ps. 68:17).

Angels were involved in the giving of the Law. Stephen mentioned the agency of angels to enhance the dignity of the Law. Paul mentions them to show the inferiority of the Law to the gospel (Acts 7:53; Heb. 2:2). Moses was its mediator. The presence of a mediator implies at least two contracting parties. A mediator cannot mediate on behalf of one party only. Moses was in every way qualified to be Israel's representative at Sinai. He acted as mediator on a number of occasions: during the emancipation, Exodus, and wilderness wanderings of the Hebrew people.

However, all of this is swept aside. The Law needed a mediator, but the promise needed nothing of the kind. God acted sovereignly and unilaterally in grace when ratifying His promise to Abraham. In Genesis 15, Abraham is shown in a deep sleep, as God walked between the divided pieces of the sacrifice in the customary way of ratifying a contract in that day and age (vv. 12–21). In Genesis 17, Abraham is shown prostrate on the ground, as God expanded on the great promise. So then, Law was a contract, but it was one inferior to the one of promise given to Abraham.

Thus, Paul continues showing *the Law as a contrast* (vv. 21–22). In the first place, the Law magnifies God's promise by its very *failure:* "Is the law then against the promises of God? God forbid: for if there had been a law given which could have given life, verily righteousness should have been by the law" (v. 21). Paul puts an unerring finger on the inherent weakness of the Law, as both a system and a standard; in no way could the Law give life because no amount of doing can generate spiritual life in a dead human soul.

There is no great rivalry between the Law and the promise—not when the different *function* of each is understood. How could there be when God was the Author of both? What was the great purpose of the Law? To make us aware of what righteousness is all about. What was the great purpose of the promise? To provide that needed righteousness in the Person and work of Christ (the Seed). There was no contradiction, no rivalry, and no inconsistency. The goal of both was righteousness for fallen man. The Law was given to *prove* something—our utter inability to attain a standard of righteousness acceptable to a holy God by any amount of law keeping and the fact that no law exists that can give life. The Law underlines death. The promise was given to *provide* something—the life and the righteousness that we need, both of which are found in Christ alone.

In the second place, the Law magnifies God's promise by its very *function:*

"But the scripture hath concluded all under sin, that the promise by faith of Jesus Christ might be given to them that believe" (v. 22). In effect, far from being an instrument of salvation, as the legalizers were telling Paul's Gentile converts, the Law was an instrument of condemnation. It arrests and arraigns all of Adam's ruined race. It locks them up in prison because of their sins. The only way out of that prison was to be found in the promise—Christ!

So then, one great purpose of the Law was to probe the soul for sin. It had another function:

(2) To prepare the soul for salvation (3:23–29)
(a) The Law (3:23–25)

Paul now introduces two illustrations. He speaks of *the Law as a taskmaster:* "But before faith came, we were kept under the law, shut up unto the faith which should afterwards be revealed" (v. 23).

The word for "shut up" is *sunkleiō.* It shows us men trapped as fish are trapped in a net, with no possibility of escape. Our utter inability to keep the laws of God only proved our sinful condition. God knew all about this way back when he wrote His unconditional covenant or promise with Abraham. It was necessary, however, for God to bring home to us our need of a Savior by proving to us our inability to keep His law. The Law caught us as fish in a net. Our only hope was "the faith which should afterwards be revealed."

The verb used is *mello,* meaning "about to be" revealed. The revelation of Christ was viewed as being imminent. Although the age of the Law actually lasted a long time, some fifteen hundred years, the promise of the Seed was always to be regarded as "about to be revealed." It might have taken place at any time. It hung over the entire age of the Law. At any moment, God could have broken into history. But, until the revelation was made, there was no escape from the stern eye of the Law and its unrelenting disapproval of every infraction of its commands.

The Law was a taskmaster. It constantly demanded, "Do this! Don't do that! Set aside this day, this week, and this year. Pay your tithes. Bring your offerings." The children of Israel had escaped from all of that kind of thing once. Their history as a nation begins, indeed, with them in the land of Egypt in what the Holy Spirit calls "the house of bondage." Moses had first appeared as a liberator, an emancipator, a veritable messiah. It was grace, not law, that brought them out of that house of bondage where they had labored long, suffered greatly, known no freedom, and tasted daily the taskmaster's lash.

They had exchanged one taskmaster for another—the Law. Certainly the new taskmaster was "holy, just, and good." Certainly his demands were reasonable and righteous. Doubtless, his authority, although absolute and dictatorial, was divine. But he was a taskmaster just the same, and he carried a taskmaster's lash. Stripes and imprisonment were at his beck. "An eye for an eye, a tooth for a tooth" was his call. Death was the ultimate whip in his hand. His eyes were everywhere, our tasks endless, our bondage complete. And all the while, "the faith which was about to be revealed" tarried because Israel was so slow to learn the lesson that the Law, after all, was a taskmaster, one that was impossible to please. The Jews came to kiss the hand that smote them. They were not content with the tasks it set; they sought to please the taskmaster by embellishing its edicts and by multiplying endlessly its bare demands. Then, worst of all, unable to satisfy this taskmaster, they wished to clamp his chains on Paul's freeborn Gentile converts—although "the faith about to be revealed" had been revealed indeed.

Paul has another illustration. He speaks of the *Law as a schoolmaster:* "Wherefore the law was our schoolmaster to bring us unto Christ, that we might be justified by faith. But after that faith is come, we are no longer under a schoolmaster" (vv. 24–25). The word for "schoolmaster" is *paidagōgos,* from which we derive our English word *pedagogy*. However, the thought behind the biblical use of the word is not so much that of a teacher or an instructor, in our modern sense, as that of a pastor or guide. The *paidagōgos* was often a trustworthy slave who had the guardianship of the boys of a family. He was in charge of the family's son and heir. He exercised general supervision over him, saw to it that he went to school, waited for him until his lessons were done, escorted him home, disciplined him, and kept him out of mischief and up to the mark. He had to teach the boy good manners, review his lessons with him by asking him questions, and making him recite what he had learned. Throughout the boy's childhood and youth, the pedagogue imposed necessary restraint upon him, although he was himself only a slave. But once the boy reached the age of maturity and accountability, the pedagogue's duties were over. The boy was free of his "schoolmaster."

It was in this sense that "the law was our schoolmaster to bring us unto Christ." The role of the Law was never intended to be an end in itself. It was necessary that Israel should know the restrictions and restraints of the Law. Only thus would they be able fully to appreciate all that they had in Christ. Now, however, the schoolmaster is not needed. "Faith is come!" exclaims Paul. We are put back on the ground of faith, the ground on which Abraham stood when he "believed God and it was counted unto him for righteousness." Like Abraham, we are "justified by faith." What folly, then, to want to go back to the old days of the taskmaster and the schoolmaster!

### (b) The Lord (3:26–29)

In closing this part of his argument, Paul sets forth four glorious contrasts between what we now have in Christ and what the Jews had under Law. We must consider *a new freedom:* "For ye are all the children of God by faith in Christ Jesus" (v. 26). The word *huios* refers to believers as the legitimate offspring of God with reference to origin and nature, including that of relationship to the father. We are now "sons of God." Paul is drawing here a deliberate contrast between the state of an adolescent, who is still under the restraints and restrictions of the Mosaic Law, and the believer's emancipation by virtue of his sonship in Christ. Who in his right mind would want to go back to the old bondage of the Law? It would be like a grown man sucking his thumb!

We must consider *a new factor*: "For as many of you as have been baptized into Christ have put on Christ" (v. 27). Water baptism does not put us into Christ. Paul had already thoroughly learned the lesson that an outward rite, such as circumcision, conferred no spiritual benefit. He was not about to substitute one external rite (circumcision) for another one (water baptism). Water baptism, of course, has its proper place in the Christian experience. The Lord Himself ordained it (Matt. 28:19), and it is the customary way for a new believer publicly to identify himself with Christ and confess his faith in Christ. Paul himself was baptized. The normal practice in the New Testament church was to baptize converts by immersion (Acts 8:35–38; 9:17–18). Water baptism, however, has no virtue in itself. Paul would never have pointed to his baptism as the time when he was placed "in Christ." Rather, he would have pointed to the moment of his conversion on the Damascus road.

However, water baptism is significant. It is the outward expression of an inward experience. In baptism, a believer first takes his stand in water, an element that spells death to all that he is as a natural man. If a person falls overboard at sea and is not quickly rescued, he drowns. So, then, by taking his stand in water, the believer confesses, "When Christ died, I died. I participated in His death on Calvary's cross. He died not only *for* me but also *as* me. I am identified with His death." The believer is then immersed in the water, as the word *baptizō* so clearly implies. Thus, he proclaims his burial with Christ. He is put completely out of sight beneath the water, as Christ was put completely out of sight within the tomb. Thus, the believer is buried illustratively in a watery grave. But he is not left there. He is raised up from that foreign element by the power of another's arm. Thus, he proclaims pictorially, "When Christ arose, I arose. I now stand in Him on resurrection ground. I live in Him. I am identified with Him in His resurrection. I live on the other side of death to walk in newness of life."

All of this is very important and significant. But, when all is said and done, it is only a picture. That is all that water baptism is. No more, no less. Behind the picture, however, is a spiritual reality—Spirit baptism. It is the work of the Holy Spirit to put the believer "in Christ" and to establish the mystical relationship to which Paul here refers and of which water baptism is a symbol and a type. "For by one Spirit," Paul says, "are we all baptized into one body, whether we be Jews or Gentiles, whether we be bond or free; and have been all made to drink into one Spirit" (1 Cor. 12:13). The Holy Spirit puts the believer in Christ and Christ into the believer.

So, then, Paul reminds his Galatian converts of this fact. The Law could do no such thing. In Old Testament times, the Holy Spirit sometimes inspired people. They knew at times what it was to be empowered by the Spirit, to have the Holy Spirit come upon them for some great task. But nobody in the Old Testament, nobody under Law, ever knew what it was to be baptized by the Holy Spirit and made a member of the mystical body of Christ. Nobody knew what it was to be indwelt permanently and sealed by the Holy Spirit. The Law of Moses not only was unable to confer such a benefit but also did not even contemplate such a thing. This is a new factor in the equation of God's dealings with mankind. What folly, then, to go back to the Law.

"For as many of you as have been baptized into Christ have put on Christ" (3:27). Now, instead of trying vainly to clothe ourselves with the righteousness of the Law, we have "put on Christ." That means that when God looks at us, He sees Jesus and is satisfied because He sees Christ's righteousness, not ours.

We must consider also *a new fellowship:* "There is neither Jew nor Greek, there is neither bond nor free, there is neither male nor female: for ye are all one in Christ Jesus" (v. 28). Gone forever was the old Jewish monopoly on the things of God! Paul uses the same words here as he uses in 1 Corinthians 12:13 to describe the baptizing ministry of the Holy Spirit. This fact strengthens the argument that it is Spirit baptism to which he is referring in verse 27. The baptism of the Spirit sweeps away all of the old, entrenched differences. It abolishes the *spiritual* difference—in Christ, "there is neither Jew nor Greek." In Christ, all are equal. There is not a Jewish church and a Gentile church; there is just the church, a company of born again, blood-washed, Spirit-baptized called-out ones. What the legalists were teaching was nonsense. They had no concept whatsoever of the radical change that had been wrought by Calvary and Pentecost. There was no longer any spiritual difference between Jew and Greek. The Law—with its demands for circumcision and the sanctification of certain days, with its dietary restrictions, with its ordained exclusive priesthood, and with its endless round of sacrifices—was wholly inimical to Christianity. The baptism of the Spirit abolished the difference between Jew and Greek.

It abolishes also the *social* difference. There is neither bond nor free in Christ. All are set free! All are His bond slaves! Master and man alike, mistress and handmaid, employer and employee, humblest artisan and the man with the bluest blood and purest pedigree—are all now simply members of the body of Christ. The moment they take their place before Him as lost sinners, they become heirs together of the grace of life.

It abolishes the *sexual* difference. In Christ, there is neither "male nor female." In Bible times, Jewish life and society discriminated against women. The devout rabbi would thank God every day that he had not been born a woman. But the Lord Jesus emancipated and ennobled womanhood. He was born of a woman. Women often ministered to His material needs during His earthly ministry. No woman ever hurt Him. He cast evil spirits out of Mary Magdalene, forgave the woman taken in adultery, blessed the woman who washed His feet with her tears, and honored Mary of Bethany for her magnificent faith. Women lingered to the last at the cross. They were first at the tomb. The glorious news, "He is risen!" was first proclaimed to a woman, and it was a woman who carried the tidings first to others. Women were in the Upper Room on the Day of Pentecost when the Holy Spirit came to baptize that handful of believers into the mystical body of Christ and thus to give birth to the church. Paul's first convert in Europe was a woman. It was a woman to whom he entrusted his priceless epistle to the Romans. It was a woman whom Peter raised from the dead. Yes, indeed! Once "in Christ," all of the old barriers are dissolved, "for ye are all one in Christ."

Finally, we must consider *a new future:* "And if ye be Christ's, then are ye Abraham's seed, and heirs according to the promise" (v. 29). Besides the Seed (Christ), we can trace three other types of seed to Abraham. He was to have a seed that God compared with the sand of the sea. That was his natural posterity, the descendants of Isaac and Jacob, the children of Israel, the Hebrew people, to whom God made many great and precious promises. These promises were connected with a land and look forward to a coming millennial age when Jerusalem will be the messianic capital of a global empire under the personal sway of Christ Himself.

Abraham was to have a seed likened to "the dust of the earth." His plea, "O that Ishmael might live before thee" (Gen. 17:18–21), did not go unheeded. The power, wealth, and influence of the Arab states bear abundant proof of that. But the countless descendants of Abraham through Ishmael were not counted as children of the covenant.

But then, too, Abraham was to have a seed likened to the stars of heaven. That is his spiritual seed. It is a seed made up of all of those who are linked with Abraham as "the father of all them that believe" (Rom. 4:11). This vast multitude is Abraham's spiritual posterity. We are his heirs of all of the spiritual blessings made good by God to all of those who exercise the faith in Christ that Abraham exercised.

Thus, Paul shows the abysmal folly of the Judaizers who wanted to put believers back under the Law of Moses. We are the seed of Abraham, he says. The Law has nothing to do with us at all. It has no more relevance to us than it had to Abraham, who was brought into the blessing of God on the basis of his faith in God's promise concerning the Seed, long centuries before Sinai cast its shadow over everyone. Paul now lifts the discussion to even higher ground.

2. Believers are the sons of God (4:1–31)
   a. Their birthright is declared (4:1–7)
      (1) The past: acceptance of spiritual minority (4:1–3)

It is a great thing to be the seed of Abraham; it is an even greater thing to be a son of God. This is the theme of Paul's closing argument in the doctrinal section of his letter. His discussion revolves around three facts that are closely connected to what had happened to his Galatian friends. He speaks to them of *their birthright* as sons of God and shows them the difference between being a minor and being mature. Then he speaks to them of *their betrayal* (vv. 8–20) and finally of *their bondage* (vv. 21–31).

To be counted as a son of God is the birthright of every believer. In dealing with believers as minors, Paul is looking at the past and has the Jewish believers particularly in mind. He wants to draw the contrast between the spiritual immaturity of the past and the full maturity and freedom that we have in Christ. He has already shown the Law, in its roles as taskmaster, schoolmaster, prison guard, and chaperon. He now compares it to a legal guardian. Under the old economy, the believer was a ward of the state, so to speak. His property and his inheritance were in the care of another. All of that is changed in Christ.

Paul begins with *the analogy:* "Now I say, That the heir, as long as he is a child, differeth nothing from a servant, though he be lord of all; but is under tutors and governors until the time appointed of the father" (vv. 1–2). Some scholars have seen here an appeal to that all-pervasive Roman law, under which, of course, the Galatians lived. Until he was fourteen, an heir was placed under the authority of a *tutor,* nominated by his father in his will. At the age of fourteen, the boy came of age, but he was still not free to do what he liked because the *paetor urbanus* then placed him under the control of a *curator* until he was twenty-five. Only then did he come into his full inheritance. That was the analogy. A minor—although heir to a noble name, great expectations, wealth, honor, position, and power—was still a minor and, for all practical purposes, no better than a slave.

Now comes *the application:* "Even so we, when we were children, were in bondage under the elements of the world" (v. 3). The word for "children" is *nēpios,* which implies a small child, one not old enough to speak. The Law treated people as infants. Everything has to be spelled out for an infant. A child must be told when to go to bed, when to get up, what to eat, and what to wear. From the time it gets up to the time it goes to bed, it is told what to do and where to go. Nearly all of its decisions are made for it. Such was the Law, and such was the state of spiritual infancy of those under the Law.

Indeed, here is the very essence of legalism. In the New Testament, God sets before us general principles. Legalism lays down the law. It says, "You must not do this, that, or the other thing; you must not go here, there, or the other place. You must not wear that or style your hair like that; you must wear this. You must give this amount, support these meetings or those programs, restrict yourself to this circle of fellowship, and boycott that group there. You can believe only what we tell you to believe, and you are to attack everyone who dares to differ. You may read these books, but you mustn't read those books." The result is bondage. It is grown-up childishness. Christ has freed us from all such man-made rules and regulations. We are not allowed, however, to do as we please. We are to master the principles that God has given and govern ourselves, as mature adults, by those principles.

Paul here describes the condition of those people who are under law, governed by legalism, as being "under the elements of the world." The word for "elements" is *stoicheion,* which means "elementary rules." Being governed by legalism is suitable only for a child. The word comes from *stoichos,* which signifies a row or a rank. The verb *stoicheō* signifies "to walk or march in rank." That is the heart and soul of legalism. The legalist likes to line everybody up, give orders, and make them march in step to the beat of his drum. Something about that is very intoxicating—to the one giving the orders, that is. It gives him a sense of power. Elsewhere, *stoicheion* is used of the letters of the alphabet, as elements of speech. Such was the Law. It was for people who were learning their ABCs.

But that is all past. Now Paul turns to:

### (2) The present: access to spiritual maturity (4:4–7)

The coming of Christ has changed everything. So Paul speaks next of *the advent of the Son of God:* "But when the fulness of the time was come, God sent forth his Son, made of a woman, made under the law, to redeem them that were under the law . . ." (vv. 4–5a). If we accept the Old Testament chronology as complete, then the human race lived for two thousand years under a curse brought by a woman, then for two thousand years under a curse brought by the Law. Christ has redeemed us from both the curse inherent in the Fall and from the curse inherent in the Law.

"When the fulness of the time was come," God sent forth His Son. He was in no hurry. From Adam to Noah, God allowed men to be controlled by conscience, the knowledge of good and evil, the one legacy that was rescued from the Garden of Eden. The result was a world of such appalling wickedness that the only answer was the Flood.

After the Flood, an age of government was inaugurated, and God put the sword of the magistrate into the hands of Noah and instituted capital punishment for capital crime. The age ran from Noah to Nimrod, when it again climaxed in a further crescendo of lawlessness and a further response of judgment. The human race, scattering far and wide from Babel and jabbering in countless tongues, carried with it the curse of idolatry as Nimrod's legacy.

Then God broke in again, determined to begin all over again with another man, Abraham. The age of promise began, and God's focal point of interest was the patriarchal family. Then came the migration to Egypt and the general, slow decline of the Hebrew people into slavery to and compromise with Egypt's government and gods.

The coming of Moses marked the beginning of a new day. Israel was liberated from Egypt but soon degenerated into idolatry of its own. God gave the Law and wrote a catalog of curses into its codes. The human family had failed. Now the Hebrew family failed. We trace the long history of the children of Israel under law. We mark their dreadful degeneracy, apostasy, and immorality in the days of the judges, the partial revival under Samuel, the dismal failure of King Saul, and the bright era of hope under David. All of these events followed in sequence. Then came Solomon, whose disastrous policies and dreadful compromise with idolatry brought down upon the nation the judgment of God. The kingdom was divided. The northern tribes plunged deeper and deeper into idolatry and immorality until, at length, they were uprooted one and all under the judgment of God and marched away into the oblivion of the Assyrian captivity. The southern kingdom of Judah rocked back and forth between good and bad kings and between compliance with God's law and open apostasy. In the end, it, too, followed its sister kingdom into captivity.

Seventy years later, God gave the Jews another chance. A succession of godly leaders was able to get the reborn nation off to a good start. Then the decline set in again. Formalism and hypocrisy succeeded idolatry as the nation's prevailing sin. By the time of Christ, the Jewish religion was bankrupt. The Sadducees, the Pharisees, and the Herodians were the representatives of Jewish religious thought. They had little enough in common except a determination to pay mere lip service to God and go their own ways.

When the "fulness of the time" came, Judaism was a dead religion, a religion of rite and ritual, of form and ceremony, of tradition and crushing legalism. The Gentiles, weary to death of their own bankrupt religions, turned hopefully toward Judaism only to be repelled by Jewish hostility and hypocrisy and by its bitter exclusiveness and rigid bondage to dead forms and narrow views.

The great Gentile world was equally bankrupt. The Greeks had come and gone and left their indelible mark on the world. The golden age of Greece had dazzled the world. Art, science, and government flourished. Then Alexander the Great conquered the world. Greek philosophy, culture, and religion challenged all realms of thought, and Hellenism rose and flourished. It was all, however, just a hollow promise. Greek religion was able to offer men only a pantheon of ridiculous, warring, lusting gods made in the image and likeness of warring, lusting men.

Then the Romans had their day. They sent their legions far and wide, hammered down all who stood before them, and imposed a Roman peace on the world. They brought with them iron-fisted law. They built magnificent roads and ruled over an empire of slaves. However, the Romans built no hospitals, no orphanages, and no public schools. The Roman idea of a holiday was to assemble in the amphitheater to watch gladiators fight to the death or wretched prisoners fight with bare hands against wild beasts to the accompaniment of the howls and cheers of a blood-maddened populace.

Such was "the fulness of the time." The world was morally and spiritually bankrupt. It was ripe for the coming of Christ. Because Paul's focus was on the situation in Galatia, where Jewish legalists were trying zealously to clamp the chains of the Law on the Gentile converts to Christianity, he concentrates on "them that were under the law." When it came to man's need for redemption, the Law was bankrupt. All it could do was sweep that need under the rug of ritual. The blood of bulls and goats could neither remove the stain nor loose the chain of sin.

So "God sent forth his Son, made of a woman, made under the law, to redeem them that were under the law." He came to be the promised Seed of the woman (Gen. 3:15). He came to fulfill every claim and demand of the Law (Matt. 5:17). He fulfilled the moral law in His life and the ceremonial law in His death. Thus, He could do something that the Law could not do—redeem.

Paul turns now to *the adoption of the sons of God:* "That we might receive the adoption of sons. And because ye are sons, God hath sent forth the Spirit of his Son into your hearts, crying, Abba, Father" (vv. 5b–6). That was something that a millennium and a half of law could not do for a lost son of Adam's ruined race—constitute him a son of God. The regenerating work of the Holy Spirit is what puts the believer into the family of God (John 1:11–13; 3:5–6).

It was always God's intention that man should have a unique relationship with God, which is why Adam is called "the son of God" (Luke 3:38). When God created the animals, He gave each of them a governing principle that we call instinct. However, God did not make man to be governed by instinct. Man has a body similar to that of the animals. He has senses that enable him to hear, speak, smell, see, and feel. He also has a soul and the ability to think, feel, and decide. But God gave Adam something that He gave to no animal; He gave him a spirit. The human race was to be governed, not by instinct, which would have made him nothing but a superior animal, but by his spirit. Moreover, the human spirit was to be indwelt by the Holy Spirit, making man, in very truth, "a son of God." The human spirit, in cooperation with the Holy Spirit, would govern the faculties of the soul and the members and senses of the body. As a result, man would behave in a way that was pleasing to God.

When sin entered, the Holy Spirit vacated the human spirit, leaving men with no governing principle outside their own senses, emotions, intellect, and will. When a person accepts Christ as his personal Savior from sin, he is cleansed from his sin by the blood of Christ, and the Holy Spirit takes up residence in his human spirit. "God hath sent forth the Spirit of his Son into your hearts," Paul says. Because the Law was powerless to do anything to remove sin, everything was thrown back on God's grace, back on His Son. Paul continues to bring the Galatians back to that truth.

And how real is this new love relationship that we have, so gloriously different from the old law relationship? The Holy Spirit teaches the believer to cry, "Abba, Father." *Abba* is an Aramaic word found only here, in Mark 14:36, and in Romans 8:15. It was a word forbidden to household slaves, as an acceptable form of address directed to the head of the family. Remember, that is what the Law constituted us—slaves. *Abba!* It is the word that rises to the lips of a small child. It was the Old World equivalent of our English word *Daddy.*

*Father!* That is the Greek word *patēr,* which comes from a root signifying one who provides, protects, and supports. It is the word of an adult son in the family. It was the Lord's favorite word for God. It is preeminently, although not solely, the New Testament word for God. It was a word that is constantly on the lips of the Son of God. It was a word that He taught us, as members of His family through the miracle of the new birth, to use for God. Observe, however, that the Lord never associated Himself with His disciples by using the word *our*. He always employed the singular *my*. He taught the disciples to say, "our Father"; He Himself said, "My Father."

Abba! Father! The Holy Spirit, "sent forth into our hearts," teaches us to use these two words. Jesus used them in Gethsemane. As He gazed into the dark depths of that dreadful cup, He cried, "Abba! Father!" It was the cry of One who had always enjoyed the closest intimacy with the Father but whose eternal relationship was momentarily threatened by our sin. "Abba!" It was the cry of One horror-struck by what he saw in that cup, the instinctive, agonizing cry that we would associate with a little one. The word must have torn open the Father's heart. "Abba!" Then follows the other word: *Father*. In all of the full manhood and maturity of an eternal relationship, worked out on human terms in a lifetime of unbroken love, trust, communion, and obedience, He said, "Father!" He fully understood, fully acquiesced, and fully cooperated with that good and acceptable and perfect will of His Father, which pointed so inexorably to Calvary.

The amazing fact is that we, too, can now use the same two words to express our relationship with God that Jesus used to express His own relationship with God. Moreover, the Holy Spirit teaches us to do so. Such is the magnificence of grace over law. Whoever would want to go back to a dead legalistic system of dos and don'ts? Who would want to go back to endless rules, rituals, and regulations as a means of trying to please God when, instead of an empty religion, they can have an amazing relationship? For instance, imagine one of Paul's Galatian converts sitting down, trying to memorize all of the countless petty rules with which the Jews had hedged in the Sabbath, when all that he needs is Christ! "I do always those things that please the Father," Jesus could say (John 8:29). "Abba! Father!" It is the greatest of all arguments against legalism. This is not law! This is love! And love instinctively seeks to please the Beloved. "Love," says Paul, "is the fulfilling of the law" (Rom. 13:10).

Thus, *their birthright is declared.* The Galatians, just like the Jews, are by the principle of faith Abraham's seed! But they are much more than that. They are God's sons. By referring to them as Abraham's seed, Paul takes them back beyond the giving of the Law. By referring to them as God's sons, he takes them on beyond the guidelines of the Law.

b. Their betrayal is described (4:8–20)
(1) Liberty surrendered (4:8–11)

Paul is now in a position to expose fully the peril of the Galatians and their abysmal folly in listening to the blandishments of the legalistic Judaizers who had invaded their churches. He will now show them how their *liberty has been surrendered* (vv. 8–11), how their *love* has been suppressed (vv. 12–16), and how their *loyalty has been subverted* (vv. 17–20).

He begins by showing how their liberty has been surrendered. He talks, first, of *their past bondage:* "Howbeit then, when ye knew not God, ye did service unto them which by nature are no gods" (v. 8). He takes them back to the raw paganism of their unconverted days. Perhaps he had in mind the events at Lystra, where he and Barnabas had been hailed as "the gods . . . come down to us in the likeness of men" (Acts 14:11). Barnabas, perhaps because of his venerable appearance, had been regarded as Jupiter (Zeus), the father of the gods, and Paul had been hailed as Mercury (Hermes), the messenger of the gods, evidently because of his eloquence.

Paul, as a devout Jew, had always looked with horror and disgust on pagan religions. On Mars Hill, he spoke with barely concealed scorn of the folly of idolatry (Acts 17:16, 22–23). He wrote passionately to the Romans about the abysmal folly of idolatry and the terrible insult that it presents to the awesome majesty of the true and living God (Rom. 1:19–23).

Yet, to this day, idolatry continues to have a dreadful fascination for lost people. Most Oriental lands grovel in the worst forms of idolatry. Even in Christendom, people light candles to graven images, bow down before them, venerate them, and pray to them. Various forms of idolatrous Hinduism have taken root among us.

Those who worship idols become slaves to the idols. Often, they serve them with fanatical devotion and zeal. They are held in the grip of gross superstition, bound mind and heart by evil spirits, which ever lurk behind the man-made images. "There was a time," Paul now says to his Galatian converts, "when you had no knowledge whatsoever of God. You had gods, sure enough, and you were bound by them, but they were no gods at all; they had no real existence." That was their past bondage.

By listening to the legalists, all they had done was exchange one form of bondage for another. So Paul speaks of *their present bondage* (vv. 9–11). He contrasts their *enlightenment* (v. 9a) with their new *enslavement* (vv. 9b–11). "But now, after that ye have known God, or rather are known of God, how turn ye again to the weak and beggarly elements, whereunto ye desire again to be in bondage?" (v. 9).

Such was Paul's scathing denunciation of that very Judaism of which he had once been the most zealous ambassador. He calls it the "elements" *(stoicheion),* the mere rudiments of revealed truth; the bare, elementary stage of God's dealings with men; the first lispings of the divine alphabet. To go back to that kind of thing would be like a strong, grown man, who was accustomed to eating prime rib and roast beef, going back to mush, mashed peas, and baby food.

Judaism and its legalism were now so completely obsolete that Paul turns to contemptuous adjectives in describing it. He calls it "weak and beggarly." The word for "weak" is *asthenēs.* It carries the idea of impotence. It is used to describe the lame man, sitting at the gates of a dead religion, powerless to help himself, and passed by constantly by the priests and servants of the Jewish religion (Acts 4:9). It is translated "feeble" (1 Cor. 12:22) and "sick" (Matt. 25:43). Well did Paul know the utter impotence of Judaistic legalism to make a person righteous and holy and its complete inability to give life, joy, and peace to the soul. No wonder! It was sick itself.

Not only so! Paul describes it as "beggarly." The word is *ptōchos.* It means to be destitute, in want. It is usually translated "poor." The Lord used the word to describe the wretched condition of Lazarus, whom He depicted as a "beggar" *(ptōchos),* full of sores, and eagerly but vainly desiring to be fed with the crumbs that fell from the rich man's table (Luke 16:20). Such was legalistic Judaism. Far from being able to enrich anyone, it was a beggar itself, utterly impoverished and destitute of any means whatsoever of imparting spiritual life and godliness to a human soul.

And this is what the Galatians were willing to exchange for that "adoption of sons" that set them in the royal family of heaven! Paul would have laughed in their faces if the situation had not been so tragic and serious.

"Turn ye again," he said, recording *their decision.* The verb is in the present, continuous tense. "How are ye turning?" They were in the very act of turning back to a bondage that was just as enslaving and unsatisfying as the pagan bondage that they had abandoned when they turned to Christ.

"Ye desire again to be in bondage?" he demands, underlining *their desire.* The word he uses is *thelō,* a word that emphasizes the emotional element in a decision. It focuses on the natural impulse that, as we know from experience, is usually stronger than the reasoned resolve. Paul was astonished at the great desire of his Galatian friends to put themselves back under bondage.

Many people do not like freedom. They find it difficult to make decisions for themselves. They like to be told what to believe and what to do. That is why leaders with charm and charisma can so easily find a following no matter how weird and outrageous their cause. People, after all, tend to be like sheep, following anyone who will take the lead.

Undoubtedly, the Judaizing legalizers who had invaded Galatia were convinced and determined men. It took more than ordinary zeal to send these misguided missionaries up through the Cilician Gates into Galatia simply to bring Paul's Gentile converts into the narrow Jewish fold. They were persuasive men, too, armed with telling arguments and with a battery of Old Testament texts with which to back them up. For people who were fascinated by forceful personalities and who were themselves unskilled in biblical hermeneutics, the legalizers offered something that many people found desirable—determined leadership and no-nonsense rules by which to live.

"Ye observe days, and months and times, and years," Paul says, underlining their *deeds* (v. 10). Such things regulated the Old Testament faith. The Galatians, it seems, were taking up the Jewish religious calendar as a guide to godliness. The Jews observed annual feast and fast days. They observed the Feasts of Passover, Unleavened Bread, Firstfruits, Pentecost, Trumpets, Tabernacles, and Purim. They observed all kinds of Sabbaths: the weekly Sabbath, the Sabbatic years, and the Years of jubilee. All such things have nothing whatsoever to do with Christianity.

Heedless of this fact, major segments of the professing church had thoroughly Judaized themselves. They adopted their own religious calendars and their own feast days and fast days. All that this well-meaning organization does, however, is blur the sharp edges of vital Christianity and convert it into a religion, something it was never intended to be.

Even worse is the cultic teaching of Seventh-day Adventists, who throw aside pretense and unblushingly invite us to go back to Judaism and keep the Jewish Sabbath; the Jewish Sabbath is obsolete. As we have seen elsewhere, even the Jews in Israel cannot keep it. The efforts of the narrow religious block in the Knesset to clamp rigid Sabbath laws on the state of Israel are a source of constant irritation, friction, and inconvenience to the rest of the population.

The Sabbath was for the nation of Israel before the resurrection of Christ. It was mandated as part of the Mosaic Law (Exod. 20:8–11), and severe penalties were attached to the Law for those who violated it. The idea of the Sabbath was inherent in God's creation activity (Gen. 2:1) for, having worked for six days, God "rested on the seventh day from all his work which he had made" (Gen. 2:2). Moreover, "God blessed the seventh day, and sanctified it" (Gen. 2:3). The provision of a day of rest each week was wise and benevolent for the well-being of mankind. Its incorporation into the Mosaic Law was a landmark and helped to set Israel apart from the secular Gentile nations of the world. The Jewish rabbis, not content with the simple and beneficial provision of a weekly Sabbath, succeeded in turning the whole thing into a weekly nightmare by adding to it countless petty rules and regulations, the keeping of which made the Sabbath a burden rather than a blessing.

The Lord Jesus refused to observe the rabbinic Sabbath rules. Consequently, they accused Him of breaking the Sabbath. This affront more than anything else fueled the fires of their hatred toward Him. When they challenged Him because He healed on the Sabbath, He said, "My Father worketh hitherto, and I work" (John 5:17). God's Sabbath rest had been broken by Adam's fall and human sin. It was necessary, therefore, for Him to go to work on His great plan of redemption. It was this great work that the Lord had come to earth to consummate on the cross of Calvary. The Lord, indeed, lay in Joseph's tomb on the Jewish Sabbath, a sad commentary on the total failure of Judaism.

The Lord rose from the dead on a new day, the first day of the week. Something is most significant about the way Matthew, in his "Jewish" gospel, introduces the story of the Resurrection. He says, "In the end of the sabbath, as it began to dawn toward the first day of the week" (Matt. 28:1), the women came to the tomb. The end of the Sabbath! That was more than a date mark; it was a commentary. "It began to dawn toward the first day of the week." That was more than a date mark too; it was a statement of fact. By the time Matthew wrote his gospel, the church had adopted the first day of the week, the day on which Christ rose in triumph from the tomb, as its weekly day of worship (Acts 20:7; 1 Cor. 16:1–2). But even the observance of the first day of the week is not a mandatory rule. The Old Testament believer found his rest in a day; the New Testament believer finds his rest in Christ. God rests in Christ, and so do we (Matt. 11:28–29; Heb. 4:1).

So, then, Paul rejected out of hand the infatuation of the Galatians with Judaistic notions of keeping holy days. But he was also alarmed: "I am afraid of you, lest I have bestowed upon you labour in vain" (v. 11). He underlines *their danger*, showing the seriousness of the error that was seducing the Galatians. Paul was afraid that all of his efforts over them had been wasted.

It had been a long, dangerous trip from the coast to Galatia. Some of the perils that he later recounted to the Corinthians he doubtless encountered on that enterprise (2 Cor. 11:26). Revival fires had been kindled in one city after another in Galatia. Many souls had been saved, churches had been founded, and elders had been ordained. Age-old bastions of Satan had crumbled before the preaching of the cross. His labor had not been in vain in the Lord.

But he had made many bitter enemies. The synagogues of the area were virile centers of hatred and animosity toward him and the churches that he had left behind. He himself had faced martyrdom in Galatia. He could well imagine the sardonic satisfaction that the unconverted Jews would take in seeing his Gentile churches subverted and his converts converted into proselytes. We can catch the note of desperation in Paul's words: "You astound me! You make me think it possible that all of my efforts among you have been wasted efforts."

They were in danger but not in danger of losing their salvation. Not those who were genuinely saved, that is. The eternal security of the believer is written boldly into the New Testament (John 3:16; 10:26–30; Rom. 6:23; 8:33–39). Some people in Galatia, however, were in danger of apostasy. Apostasy is the sin of knowing the truth and deliberately turning away from it to embrace a lie. No possibility of recovery exists for such people (Heb. 6:4–6). Other people were also in danger of being deceived and, although not losing their salvation, of being trapped in a life of defeat, discouragement, and disappointment (Heb. 4:1–10).

(2) Love suppressed (4:12–16)

Paul was prepared to use every weapon in his arsenal to rescue his beloved converts from their peril. So he did not hesitate to make his appeal on the personal level. He will use doctrine, reproof, sarcasm, divine logic, and Scripture. He will also make a personal appeal to the love they had for him.

We notice next *Paul's plea:* "Brethren, I beseech you, be as I am; for I am as ye are: ye have not injured me at all" (v. 12). Paul was harboring no resentment against his loved ones in Galatia. He had not taken their defection personally. He knew only too well their spiritual immaturity and how impressionable they were. When he was among them, they had wanted to worship him one moment and to stone him the next (Acts 14:11–13, 19). He made every allowance for their national character. Paul knew from where the trouble was coming—not from his volatile converts but from his cunning Jewish enemies. That was from whence most of Paul's troubles came.

"Be as I am; for I am as ye are," or, as some translators have rendered that phrase, "Become as I am because I became as ye were." Paul had been raised a Pharisee, a zealous Jew, a "Hebrew of the Hebrews." He had been trained to be a rabbi. Before he met Christ, he had been devoted to Jewish legalism. Then, receiving his ordination at the hands of Jesus to become the Apostle to the Gentiles, he had become as one of them, suffering, indeed, the loss of all things (Phil. 3:7–8) to make good his call. He had laid aside all of his advantages of birth and background. He had abandoned beckoning promotion among the ranks of his peers. He had taken his place among the Gentiles as one of them, and it had earned him the scorn and active hatred of the Jews.

"Become as I am," Paul pleads. He was free now from the Law, free from its rites and rituals, and free from its rules and requirements. He was free from all of the endless legalistic teachings and traditions of the rabbis. He was free from bondage to circumcision, Sabbath keeping, and dietary laws. He was free from all of the burdensome baggage that he had once hauled around with him and that he had once tried, as zealously as the men now sowing error in Galatia, to fasten on other people. "Be as I am! I'm free!" he cried. "If the Son therefore shall make you free, ye shall be free indeed" (John 8:36).

Paul would have identified himself, we can be sure, with John Bunyan's burdened pilgrim. In the opening scenes of Bunyan's classic, *The Pilgrim's Progress*, everything revolves around a burden and a Book. The more that the poor pilgrim (Graceless, as he was called in those early days) read in that Book, the greater his burden became. But Evangelist set his feet on the right path.

At length, Graceless came to Mount Calvary. He saw in a vision One who had died there to free him from his sin. Behind him was an open sepulcher, an empty tomb. He saw the risen Christ. The light dawned, and his burden was loosed from his back. He turned to see it rolling down a steep place until it vanished forever in the sepulcher, the grave of all of his sins. Free at last, Christian (as he is known from that point) stepped out upon the path before him, on his way at last to the Celstial City. He had a spring in his step and a song in his soul.

Such, too, had been Paul's experience. He had met the risen Christ on the Damascus road. His burden was as great as—no, it was greater than—that of Graceless. He had added to it all of the enormous weight of the Mosaic Law and all of the endless, onerous demands and dictates of rabbinical tradition. But one glimpse of Jesus, and it had all rolled away! He was free! "Be as I am," Paul urged. He would have appreciated Bunyan, and he would have identified himself with Bunyan's pilgrim.

Next, we have *Paul's preaching:* "Ye know how through infirmity of the flesh I preached the gospel unto you at the first" (v. 13). Paul reminds the Galatians that when he first ventured among them with the gospel, he had been greatly handicapped by illness. All kinds of suggestions have been given as to what Paul's infirmity was. Ramsay thought that it was malaria that Paul had contracted in the lowlands of Pamphylia. Other scholars have suggested ophthalmia and even epilepsy. Whatever it was, we do know that Paul was not a well man. As time passed, he needed the constant services of a physician, a role that Luke filled.

Paul's expression here—"Ye know how through [because of] infirmity of the flesh I preached . . . unto you at the first"—leaves room for the supposition that Paul had not originally planned a Galatian itinerary on his first missionary journey. For some reason connected with his illness, he had sought the highlands around Pisidian Antioch. But, well or ill, Paul never lost sight of his goal: to evangelize the lost. The Galatian churches were the fruit of Paul's determination not to allow physical infirmity to stop him from fulfilling his commission.

We note, too, *Paul's person* (vv. 14–15). Here we have one of those revealing autobiographical notes that crop up from time to time in Paul's letters. Such notes help us to see him as a real person and to picture him in our minds: "And my temptation which was in my flesh ye despised not," Paul says. Other translators have rendered the passage thus: "That which was a temptation to you in my flesh" (W. E. Vine); "You did not despise me or reject me with abhorrence because of the trial that my bodily condition must have caused you" (F. F. Bruce);

"You did not shrink from me or let yourselves be revolted at the disease which was such a trial to you" (J. B. Phillips); or "And your temptation which was in my flesh ye despised not, nor loathed" (R. Govett). The language certainly suggests that whatever afflicted Paul physically at that time not only was a sore trial to him but also of such a nature as would cause natural repugnance in them.

But, far from being repelled by Paul's physical appearance, they welcomed him with open arms. The message that he proclaimed more than compensated for a mere physical infirmity, however unpleasant. "[Ye] received me as an angel of God, even as Christ Jesus," he said (v. 14). He had come to set them free. They had received him as though he were a messenger from another world. We know that this was literally so at Lystra, where they hailed him as Mercury, the messenger of the gods (Acts 14:12). And, when the glorious truth about Christ dawned on their hearts, they could not have received the Lord Himself any more kindly or enthusiastically than they had received him.

It was a telling argument in the context of this epistle. The Galatians were about to trade their glorious freedom in Christ for a mess of pottage concocted from them by the legalists—a poisonous brew of self-effort, dos and don'ts, religious requirements, and man-made laws. Had they forgotten the joy of their salvation so soon, a joy so unspeakable and full of glory that not even the repulsive physical appearance of its herald had stopped them from embracing both the message and the messenger?

"Where is then the blessedness ye spake of?" Paul demands. Oh, how happy they had been! How blissful in their newfound faith and freedom! "What has happened to your joy in the Lord that you want to shackle yourselves with the iron chains of legalism and law?" Paul exclaims.

Their joy in their life and liberty in Christ had been not only ecstatic but also emphatic. "For I bear you record," Paul cries, "that, if it had been possible, ye would have plucked out your own eyes, and have given them to me" (v. 15), a statement that lends credence to the belief that Paul, at the time of his visit to Galatia, was suffering from some disfiguring form of eye disease. He might have been suffering from other things, too, of course, but it certainly seems as though an eye problem of some sort was at least part of his physical infirmity.

Oh! How they had loved him for the freedom and joy he had brought them! "Ye would have *plucked out* your own eyes, and given them to me," Paul says, reminding them. The word that he used was *exorussō,* meaning "to dig out." It is a vigorous word. The only other place it occurs is in the story of the palsied man whose four friends brought him to Christ. They found that access to Jesus was cut off by the crowd. Undaunted, they hauled their needy friend up onto the roof of the house. They then proceeded to uncover the roof. And when they had "broken it up" *(exoryssō),* they lowered him to where Jesus was (Mark 2:4). So eagerly would the Galatians have given Paul their very eyes in their honeymoon days with Christ. Paul reminds them of that fact. He will leave no stone unturned in his efforts to bring them back to their earlier faith. "You would even have given me your *eyes,*" he reminds them. He had been God's instrument to open their spiritual eyes. They wished that they could have repaid him by giving him their physical eyes. Such was the overwhelming sense of gratitude.

Then, too, we note *Paul's perception:* "Am I therefore become your enemy, because I tell you the truth?" (v. 16). Paul valued their friendship. He would do anything to cultivate their continued regard and goodwill. But he was not prepared to compromise the truth just to keep on their good side. We can well believe that the Galatians, now giving heed to doctrine that Paul vigorously opposed, would begin to feel a degree of uneasiness toward him. Their former ardor had cooled perceptibly. We can be sure that the legalists would not hesitate to do everything in their power to undermine both Paul's character and his convictions. If, by now, the Galatians were entertaining evil thoughts about Paul, that fact would add to their coolness. Paul was a wonderful friend to have. He could also be a formidable foe, as Peter had discovered at Antioch (2:11–21).

But Paul had not become the foe of his dear Galatian converts. He was foe indeed to their false teachers, but foe to the Galatians? Nonsense! Just because he told them the truth did not make him their enemy. People, however, who entertain evil thoughts about someone often tend to transfer similar thoughts to them. They think evil of someone and imagine, in return, that that person thinks evil of them. "Oh no!" Paul assures them, "I am not your enemy. I tell you the truth, but I am not your enemy." Their love for him was being suppressed, but his love for them was as bright as ever. A lesser man than Paul, hearing what people whom he had thought to be his friends were now saying about him, might react against them. Paul had long since died to all of that kind of thing.

(3) Loyalty subverted (4:17–20)

(a) The deceivers and their goal (4:17)

Paul now pauses for a moment to take a brief look at the people who were doing all of this damage: "They zealously affect you, but not well; yea, they would exclude you, that ye might affect them" (v. 17). The expression "zealously affect" is *zēloō.* It carries the idea of being zealous, or of courting someone. The action can be either good or bad, depending on the context. The word comes from a root meaning "to boil." In a good sense, it can mean "to desire earnestly" (1 Cor. 12:31); in a bad sense, it can mean "to envy" (1 Cor. 13:4) or to be jealous (Acts 7:9). Here the motives of the Judaizers are exposed as being evil. Paul knew what these people were like, knew how mean-spirited they were, and knew their narrow bigotry and evil motives. They were courting the Galatians and seeking to win them over to their views for their own ends, not because they loved them. Paul had long since proved his own genuine, disinterested, personal love for them, but these men had done nothing of the kind. He had come to evangelize; they had come to proselytize. Paul had come to win them to a Person; they had come to join them to a party. The Galatians would be a star in Paul's crown, no doubt about that. All that the Judaizers wanted, however, was to make them a feather in their cap.

### (b) The deceived and their good (4:18–20)

Let the Galatians make no mistake. Paul sought only their good. He mentions *his teaching:* "But it is good to be zealously affected always in a good thing, and not only when I am present with you" (v. 18). Nothing about Paul was mean-spirited or jealous. He had no objection to people coming to court them, even in his absence, as long as it was for the truth. But Paul could see through the legalizers; they wanted to come between Paul and the Galatians. They wanted to "exclude" them *(ekkleiō).* The word means "to shut out." They wanted to slam the door of salvation and shut people out from all that was available to them in Christ. That was their evil goal as far as the unsaved were concerned. As for those who were already saved, they wanted to exclude them from the fellowship of other believers.

When I was in my early twenties, I left Britain and went overseas. I found myself far from home; in a strange land; all alone; and far from family, friends, and fellowship. One who has not experienced it can have no idea of what a terrible thing loneliness is. I hungered for news from home and haunted the mailbox looking for letters from loved ones whom I had left behind.

I looked for a church. I was working for a bank, and in those days wages were so low that I lived almost on the poverty line. I could not afford to travel far to go to church. I found a small fellowship of believers who met not far from my lodgings, and I sought their acceptance. It did not take me long to realize that I had fallen among those who were rigid legalists.

They were good people. They treated me well during the year that I was with them. Their order of service was very distinctive, their singing was unaccompanied, their sincerity was real, and their preaching was impromptu ("as the Lord leads") because they did not consider it proper to invite speakers or to arrange an order of service. Nonetheless, from time to time, I heard gifted men and learned much.

When the year I was with them had passed, the bank moved me to another city. I approached the leaders of the church and asked if they could recommend a church in the new area, many miles from where I had been. They looked grave. "Dear brother," they said, "there are no churches at all in that part of the country." Actually, a large number of churches were there, and I ventured to say so. "Oh no!" they said, "those are not churches. We cannot have fellowship with places like that."

"What would you suggest I do?" I asked, curious by now to see how far such "separation" would go. One of the elders advised me to resign my position with the bank. "The Lord will provide," he assured me when I raised the obvious question as to how I would live in a strange land without work. I told the man that I could not resign because I had signed a contract with the bank while I was still in Britain, and the contract had not yet expired.

"Then, dear brother," he said, "we suggest that when you get to your new location, since there are no churches in the area that we can recognize, that you sit at home on Sundays and read your Bible." He said that, in all seriousness, to a young fellow in his twenties. It was the most foolish piece of advice I ever had in my life, and given in all sincereity. Fortunately, I had enough sense to reject it. The brother, however, was not yet finished. He looked me straight in the eye and warned, "If you go to any of those places there, that you call churches, don't you ever come back here."

It was my introduction to Galatianism. These men wanted to shut me out from fellowship within the vast circle of the mystical body of Christ. They wanted me to be a proselyte to their brand of Christianity, a brand of belief that was concerned more with dos and don'ts than with anything else. "They desire to shut you out!" Paul warned his Galatian converts, who were in danger of being overtaken by the siren voice of legalism.

Next, we have *Paul's travail:* "My little children, of whom I travail in birth again until Christ be formed in you" (v. 19). The gospel is not merely a set of precepts to be believed; it is a Person to be received. It is not a question of changing some pagan religion or philosophy in favor of Christianity; it is an introduction to a new life in Christ. Law and grace are mutually exclusive as a ground of salvation. Law says, "Do!" Grace says, "Done!" Law says, "Try!" Grace says, "Trust!" Law says, "It's up to you!" Grace says, "It's up to Him!" Law takes us to Mount Sinai; grace takes us to Mount Calvary. Grace provides not only for the believer to become a child of God but also for the child of God to become a man of God. The one grows out of the other as the oak tree grows out of the acorn. Growth is the evidence of life. Paul had travailed in birth once when he first brought his beloved Galatian converts to faith in Christ. Now he has to travail all over again to bring them to maturity, to save them from legalism. Any wholehearted surrender to what the legalists wanted of them—circumcision, Sabbath keeping, conformity to dietary laws, and all of the rest of it—would, of course, constitute such a denial of Christianity as would prove that those who embraced that could not have been genuinely saved at all in the first place. For them, too, Paul would need to travail in birth again because their first "birth" would have been no genuine birth at all but a miscarriage.

Which brings us to *Paul's trouble:* "I desire to be present with you now, and to change my voice; for I stand in doubt of you" (v. 20). That is what we now call "body language." One's posture, facial expression, and tone of voice speak, sometimes adding force to what we say and sometimes giving it the lie. Every child learns, early in life, to read this body language from parents and peers.

The tone of Paul's letter to the Galatians was severe, uncompromising, and full of threats and thunder. He wished with all of his heart that he could have been with them. The trouble is that letters are often cold and formal and fail to convey the twinkle in the author's eye, the twitch of his mouth, the sudden furrow between the brows, or the sudden blush or blanching of the cheek. Neither can letters convey the tone of a person's voice. We can be sure that, even as Paul wrote the stern words that comprise so much of this letter, his great heart beat with love for his converts. Here and there that love breaks through, even in such a letter as this. But the subject was too serious and the issues at stake too far-reaching, to allow full play to the heart. This was a matter for a cool head and an inflexible will. This was a time for stern rebuke and warnings and iron resolve. Paul had all of that, and they come through in this letter.

But, oh, how Paul wished that he could have been there in person. They would have seen the legalists cower and tremble before the lash of his tongue, the cold logic of his mind, and the passion of his soul. They would have seen a lion defending its young, all wrath for those who would do them harm and all yearning for those in peril of their very souls. As it was, he could only write and pray that God would make up what was lacking in tenderness of tone.

c. Their bondage is depicted (4:21–31)
(1) The approach (4:21)

Paul looks around for another way to approach the subject. He has tried warnings, threats, sarcasm, logic, and appeal. He has taken them to Sinai and to Calvary. He has reviewed pertinent matters of history. Now he tries allegory: "Tell me, ye that desire to be under the law, do ye not hear the law?" (v. 21). Because of their appeal to the Law of Moses, the legalizers infatuated the Galatians. What they said seemed to make sense. After all, a considerable part of the Bible was taken up with law. Failure to divide rightly the word of truth, failure to discern God's dispensational dealings with the human race, failure to apply sound hermeneutical principles to God's Word and to make a difference where God makes a difference could lead the unwary to think that the Law still applied not only as a standard but also as a system. Paul could well understand that. He himself could have parroted the kind of arguments that the Judaizers would use. Anyone who was steeped in Old Testament theology could make out a *prima facie* case for keeping the Law. We have the same thing today with those who try to persuade us that the church is spiritual Israel, that God is through with the nation of Israel, and that all of the exceeding great and precious promises of God to Israel in the Old Testament are now being fulfilled spiritually in the church.

"Very well!" says Paul to his Galatian friends. "You fancy yourselves to be at home in the Scriptures. You cannot discern, however, between law and grace. You seem eager to saddle yourselves with Moses and the Law. Let me give you an illustration of what you are doing. Let me take you back to an old Bible story, one with which you are familiar. Let me take you back to Genesis 16:1–16; 21:1–21. Let me tell you a story that you know by heart. And let me draw a spiritual lesson from it, one that is very much to the point in view of what you are proposing to do."

(2) The appeal (4:22–27)
a. The text (4:22–23)

Paul's treatment of this text is highly allegorical, a fact that he himself acknowledges (v. 24). In an allegory, the various entities that make up the story, whether imaginary or historical, stand for something else beyond the actual story itself. The most famous secular allegory in English literature is *Gulliver's Travels,* written by Jonathan Swift as a satire of the political absurdities of his day. The most famous spiritual allegory is *The Pilgrim's Progress,* written by John Bunyan to depict the journey that the believer undertakes when he sets out for heaven, turning his back on his old way of life.

Paul, of course, was far too experienced an expositor of the Scriptures to make a habit of allegorizing them. He does recognize the inherent typology of the Old Testament (1 Cor. 10:1–11; Heb. 9:1–14). The kind of allegorizing that he does here is drastic, but he did have the Holy Spirit's inspiration for the parallels and conclusions that he draws.

In Genesis, Moses contents himself with giving us the bare facts of the story of Abraham. That God's hand was on the details of Abraham's life and that His Spirit inspired Moses as to what details he should include in his narrative is evident. That Abraham, up to the marriage of Isaac, should have two wives and just one son by each was no accident. Neither was it an accident that they came from such different backgrounds, that Abraham married them in the order he did or under the circumstances he did, and that the sons turned out the way they did. Moses knew nothing of the deep spiritual lesson embedded deep within the story he was inspired to record. But the Holy Spirit did. The same Holy Spirit who inspired Moses to write the history inspired Paul to write the allegory. We do not have Paul's warrant, however, for allegorizing the way he did here.

Appealing, then, to the Old Testament text, Paul draws attention to *the two sons:* "For it is written, that Abraham had two sons, the one by a bondmaid, the other by a freewoman" (v. 22). The Old Testament story is graphic. Abraham's wife, Sarah, was infertile and unable to give Abraham the son for which he craved and which indeed God had more than once promised him. Sarah had a bond slave, an Egyptian woman named Hagar. Canaan was governed at that time under laws by which it was both socially acceptable and legally valid for a barren woman to marry her bond slave to her husband and then, when the bond slave's son was born, to regard it as hers by proxy. This Sarah did. As a result, Ishmael was born. However, the moment it dawned on Hagar that she was pregnant, she could not resist the temptation to look down her nose at Sarah and put on airs and graces that Sarah found insufferable.

Hagar's son, when born, quickly endeared himself to Abraham. Indeed, Abraham would have been content if God had endorsed this dubious escapade and accepted Ishmael as the child of promise, but it was not to be (Gen. 17:18–21). In due course, Sarah, long past the age of ever having children, miraculously conceived and gave birth to Isaac, the true child of promise. The typological lessons in this incident are easy enough to discern. Paul simply takes them further than we would and applies them to the situation in Galatia.

Our attention is drawn next to *the two situations:* "But he who was of the bondwoman was born after the flesh; but he of the freewoman was by promise" (v. 23). Paul skillfully identifies the main point of the story. Abraham acted in the flesh to produce Ishmael. The birth of Ishmael involved nothing of faith. He was the product of fleshly activity and worldly policy. Nor did Ismael's birth involve anything of the supernatural; Ishmael was produced in the energy of the flesh according to the ordinary working of the laws of nature. Anyone can produce an Ishmael. Our churches are full of them.

With the birth of Isaac, however, everything was quite different. Both Abraham and Sarah were too old to have children. The birth of Isaac was supernatural. Faith believed God, and God wrought the miracle. Isaac was born of faith and was the child of promise. Elsewhere, Paul puts it thus: "And being not weak in faith, he [Abraham] considered not his own body now dead, when he was about an hundred years old, neither yet the deadness of Sarah's womb: he staggered not at the promise of God through unbelief; but was strong in faith, giving glory to God; and being fully persuaded that, what he had promised, he was able also to perform. And therefore it was imputed to him for righteousness" (Rom. 4:19–22).

### b. The type (4:24–27)

Paul, having sketched in the historical facts, now draws the parallel. He looks at *the first covenant.* He sees that it can be summarized in one word—*enslavement.* He relates it all to *Mount Sinai* and to the *earthly Jerusalem:* "Which things are an allegory: for these [i.e., the two women] are the two covenants; the one from the mount Sinai, which gendereth [*gennaō,* "beareth children"] to bondage, which is Agar [Hagar]. For this Agar is mount Sinai in Arabia, and answereth to Jerusalem which now is, and is in bondage with her children" (vv. 24–25). This kind of treatment of the biblical text is unparalleled elsewhere in the New Testament. It is not at all unlikely that the legalizers in Galatia had used the two sons of Abraham to bolster their arguments and that Paul felt obliged to turn the tables on them by using the story the way he does here.

Paul sees here a parallel between legalism (and the bondage that it engenders) and the birth of Ishmael (the son of the bondwoman). Hagar, he says, represents Mount Sinai, where the Mosaic covenant was enacted. The earthly Jerusalem, from whence the legalists had come—or, at least, from whence they drew their authority—was the world center of Judaism, rabbinism, and legalism. Well did Paul know it! He had once been part of it and had been bound and blinded by it. Hagar, Mount Sinai, Jerusalem, bondage, the flesh—Paul ties them all together.

Then Paul looks at *the final covenant.* He sees that it, too, can be summarized in one word—*emancipation!* He relates it all to *Mount Zion* and to the *heavenly Jerusalem:* "But Jerusalem which is above is free, which is the mother of us all. For it is written, Rejoice, thou barren that bearest not; break forth and cry, thou that travailest not: for the desolate hath many more children than she which hath an husband" (vv. 26–27). When we accept Christ, we are delivered from the power of darkness and are "translated . . . into the kingdom of [God's] dear Son" (Col. 1:13). The earthly Jerusalem was where He was rejected and crucified. In the Apocalypse, it is called "Sodom and Egypt" because of its end-times apostasy and its covenant with the Antichrist (Rev. 11:8). The Lord now reigns in the heavenly Jerusalem, the theme of a rapturous passage, also in the Apocalypse (Rev. 21:2–22:5). A further description of the heavenly Jerusalem is given in the epistle to the Hebrews, also in contrast with Sinai:

> For ye are not come unto the mount that might be touched, and that burned with fire, nor unto blackness, and darkness, and temptest, and the sound of a trumpet, and the voice of words; which voice they that heard entreated that the word should not be spoken to them any more: [all indications that the Mosaic covenant inflicted terror in sinful people by reason of its holiness] . . . But ye are come unto mount Sion, and unto the city of the living God, the heavenly Jerusalem, and to an innumerable company of angels, to the general assembly and church of the firstborn, which are written in heaven, and to God the Judge of all, and to the spirits of just men made perfect, and to Jesus the mediator of the new covenant, and to the blood of sprinkling, that speaketh better things than that of Abel. (Hebrews 12:18–19, 22–24)[3]

In Galatians, Paul sees a parallel between the freedom that we have in Christ and the birth of Isaac, the son of the freewoman. Just as Hagar symbolically represented Mount Sinai, so Sarah, the freewoman, represents Mount Zion, where all of the redeemed ultimately will come into the full blessing of the messianic new covenant.

---

3. For an exposition of this wonderful passage, see John Phillips, *Exploring Hebrews* (Grand Rapids: Kregel, 2002), 183–186.

The heavenly Jerusalem—to which all of the saved are on the way and from whence they draw their citizenship, joy, and power—is the eternal center of freedom and bliss. Well did Paul know it! He had once been there (2 Cor. 12:1–4), and he had been awed and dazzled by it. Sarah! Mount Zion! The heavenly Jerusalem! Freedom! Faith! Paul ties all of those together too.

He called upon the Galatians to decide once and for all, as we must decide, what they wanted. They could not have both. Hagar, Mount Sinai, and bondage or Sarah, Mount Zion, and freedom! Paul cites the ultimate triumph of the once-barren wife over the intruder in a quotation from Isaiah 54:1. He quotes it to show the exuberant joy of those who have Christ "formed in them" (v. 19) by faith.

### (3) The application (4:28–31)

In four quick, stabbing statements, Paul drives home his point. First, there is *the outlook:* "Now we, brethren, as Isaac was, are the children of promise" (v. 28). How was Isaac born? By faith! How are we born again? By faith! How was Isaac formed in Sarah's womb? By faith! How is Christ formed in our hearts? By faith! Did the Law have anything to do with Isaac's birth? Of course not! Does the Law have anything to do with our rebirth? No! On what principle, then, was Isaac born? Was it through some kind of effort on his parents' part? No! Both Abraham and Sarah were dead in that area of their lives (Rom. 4:19); besides, previous self-efforts had produced not an Isaac but an Ishmael.

If it was not based on *performance,* then on what was it based? *Promise!* And, Isaac being the child of promise, what were his prospects? He became heir to all of the glorious promises that God made to Abraham (Gen. 17:19).

And what about Ishmael? What about that which was the result of fleshly activity and worldly policy? Did Ishmael become heir to the covenant? No! That which is born of flesh is flesh (John 3:6) and can never be anything else. God does not bless the flesh. Ishmael prospered, but only in carnal, material, and worldly things (Gen. 17:18–21).

Trying to keep the Law in the energy of the flesh cannot produce anything that God can bless (Rom. 8:3–4). Trusting God to keep His promise makes us heirs of all things. We are "heirs of God, joint-heirs with Christ" (Rom. 8:17). The outlook for those people who are trying to keep the Law is miserable; the outlook for those who are children of promise is marvelous.

Next, Paul underlines *the outrage:* "But as then he that was born after the flesh persecuted him that was born after the Spirit, even so it is now" (v. 29). We can well imagine the jealousy with which Ishmael eyed Isaac. For thirteen years, he had been Abraham's pride and joy. Although he was the product of the flesh, he was dear to Abraham. We always cherish religious projects of our own, even though, as admirable as they might be in many ways, they are the products of our own natural activity and not the work of the Holy Spirit. God, however, will never spiritually bless such activity. It can be nourished and developed, it can grow and flourish, and it can look like the real thing, but God can never bless it. He sees what it really is—flesh.

When Isaac was weaned, Ishmael mocked him. In that mocking laughter resided the Arab hatred of the Jew today. That laughter revealed a heart that was estranged from God, a heart that despised the Abrahamic covenant, that felt itself estranged from the promise, which had no use for Isaac and no use for Christ. Persecution of the children of the promise lurked in that laugh. Ishmael stood revealed in that laugh. The principle "that which is born of the flesh" was revealed in that laugh. Paul says that Ishmael "persecuted" Isaac. Ishmael would have harmed Isaac if he had dared. He would have killed him if he could. He was the enemy of the one who was born of God.

It is always so: "Even so it is now," Paul said (v. 29). He was writing from personal experience. He had once been the leading legalist in the land and had constituted himself the archpersecutor of the church. Then he himself had become not merely a believer but the champion of the faith. At once, his former colleagues turned against him. His bitterest enemies were Jewish legalists. They dogged his steps, subverted his converts, spread lies about him, and stirred up the authorities against him in city after city. In the end, they would whip up the mob against him in the very courts of the temple. They would plot his death and force him to appeal to Caesar to escape the dangerous conspiracy that they had formed to kill him. Down through the ages, organized religion has persecuted the Spirit-born children of God.

Paul takes another look at the Old Testament story. He points us now to *the outlaw:* "Nevertheless what saith the scripture? Cast out the bondwoman and her son: for the son of the bondwoman shall not be heir with the son of the freewoman" (v. 30). When Sarah saw Ishmael mocking Isaac, she demanded the immediate expulsion of Hagar and her son. Her mother's intuition taught her where that mocking would end once it was full grown. Reluctantly and under God's direct command, Abraham did what Sarah desired. Henceforth, Ishmael was an outlaw, banished by divine decree from the place of promise.

Thus, God will have no compromise with the flesh. One must deal with it severely. What it produces must be recognized for what it is—the enemy of God, His people, His promise, and His purposes. "For I know," Paul says, "that in me (that is, in my flesh,) dwelleth no good thing: for to will is present with me; but how to perform that which is good I find not" (Rom. 7:18). How hopeless was the legalists' claim that the Galatians could please God by keeping the Law. "They that are after the flesh do mind the things of the flesh; but they that are after the Spirit the things of the Spirit. . . . the carnal mind is enmity against God: for it is not subject to the law of God, neither indeed can be" (Rom. 8:5, 7).

The flesh is an outlaw. The flesh cannot keep God's law. It is God's enemy. Yet, all that the legalists were offering the Galatians was an invitation to saddle themselves with not only the Law of Moses but also the endless rules of the rabbis—all of which were to be "kept" in the energy of the flesh.

"Away with such a thing!" cries Paul. "Cast out the bondwoman and her son." The "son of the bondwoman [fleshly efforts to please God] shall not be heir with the son of the freewoman" (inheriting all things by faith in Christ).

Finally, we have *the outcome:* "So then, brethren, we are not children of the bondwoman, but of the free" (v. 31). Thus, Paul brings his Galatian converts back to their true place. They had not been saved by the Law but by the Lord, not by works but by faith.

Now, let us summarize Paul's teaching here. Abraham, acting in conjunction with Hagar, in the energy of the flesh, can produce only an Ishmael. Abraham, acting in cooperation with Sarah, in the power of the Spirit, however, can ultimately produce an Isaac.

Ishmael represents "that which is born of the flesh." He is utterly devoid of spiritual life. He lives on, year after year, petted and pampered, fooling himself into believing that God can bless the "believer's life" he has produced by his own efforts. In the end, however, he betrays his origin, nature, and enmity toward Christ. Isaac represents "that which is born of the Spirit." He is the product of faith in the promise. Everything about him points to Christ. He represents the Christ-life that only the Holy Spirit can impart. In the end, the future belongs to him.

For many years, Abraham was satisfied with Ishmael and all that Ishmael stood for in his life. He became attached to this, the fruit of his own self-effort. In the end, however, he came to see what a dangerous substitute he had produced for that which God had really planned. He learned that only drastic measures would do. There could be no further compromise between the flesh and the Spirit, between the work of the flesh and the fruit of the Spirit. God's demand was drastic: Ishmael must be cast out. God's answer to the flesh is the cross. The crisis came when Isaac was weaned, when he had grown to full, robust, independent life. The crisis comes when our new life in Christ can no longer coexist peaceably with the Ishmael life of the flesh.

In terms of the Galatian error, Paul refines the allegory. Hagar represents law keeping, and Ishmael represents its sorry results. The Law, as a means of salvation and sanctification, might offer the soul something, but it will be counterfeit. Sarah represents faith and the promises of God in Christ as a means of salvation and sanctification. This is the real thing.

So, then, let his Galatians, and all legalists since, decide which it is to be—Hagar or Sarah, Sinai or Zion, the earthly Jerusalem or the heavenly Jerusalem, law or grace, faith or works, carnality or Christ. Let them decide! There can be no compromise. Let them decide at once. They must cast out the legalists and all that they stand for. They are the enemies of God.

PART 4

# An Exhortation

## Galatians 5:1–6:10

A. The law of liberty in Christ (5:1–15)
1. The foundation of our liberty (5:1–6)
a. That liberty attested (5:1)

Did the Galatians want to put themselves under law? Well! Paul had some laws that they could consider. In these next two very practical chapters, he will discuss the law of *liberty* in Christ (5:1–15), the law of *likeness* to Christ (5:16–26), the law of *love* for Christ (6:1–6), and the law of *life* in Christ (6:7–10). If law there must be, then here is law, not law in terms of precepts but law in terms of principles. That is the great difference between the Old Testament and the New. The Old Testament gave rules and regulations; the New Testament gives principles by which to live. When a believer starts laying down the law for another believer ("You can't go here, you must go there, you can't eat that, you can't drink that, you must not wear this, you must wear that, don't have fellowship with this person, don't read that person's books"), then we have legalism.

Paul then begins this section of his letter, which is devoted mostly to exhortation, with a discussion of our liberty in Christ. He will be occupied with three things—the *foundation* of our liberty (5:1–6), the *foes* of our liberty, and the *frontiers* of our liberty (5:13–15). He begins with the foundation. Note how that foundation is *attested:* "Stand fast therefore in the liberty wherewith Christ hath made us free, and be not entangled again with the yoke of bondage" (v. 1).

Free! "If the Son therefore shall make you free, ye shall be free indeed," Jesus said to men who thought that they were free but who were the hopeless slaves of sin (John 8:33–36).

Free! Paul was writing mostly to slaves. Rome's iron heel ground most men into the mud. Even as he penned these words, armor-clad Roman soldiers clanked past his door. The harsh commands of a centurion could be heard above the tramp of marching men. Most of Paul's converts were slaves. Christianity took its first, firmest, and fastest root among slaves. If millions of people in those days shared one great, common desire, it was the desire to be *free.*

During the long years of their bondage in Egypt, the Hebrews had but one desire—to be free! In Babylon, fifty thousand Jews rose up as a single man at the chance to be free once Cyrus gave the word. The Maccabees fought the Syrians to a standstill to be free. In Paul's day, the Zealots fought until Jerusalem was reduced to rubble and the temple was a heap of smoking ruins in order to be free.

Beaten, they would rise and fight again, hopelessly but gloriously, at Masada, defying Rome to the very last man. They fought again under the pseudomessiah Bar Chochba until the exasperated Romans banished every last Jew from the land and changed its name to Palestine in scornful honor of their Philistine foes.

The same desire for freedom beats within each breast. Sir Francis Drake took a handful of tiny ships to fight Spain's mighty armada because Englishmen were determined to remain free. The American colonies fought against their motherland to be free. During the American Civil War, brother fought brother over the right of men to be free. Although people sneer at it today, Harriet Beecher Stowe's classic *Uncle Tom's Cabin* once had an honored place in many American homes, alongside the Bible and Bunyan's *The Pilgrim's Progress.* Its appeal? It championed the right of the black man to be free. Alex Haley's book *Roots* took the publishing world by storm because it appealed to that same deep human need—the need to be free.

Paul struck a powerful note: "Stand fast therefore in the liberty wherewith Christ hath made us free!" he said. Free! Paul was writing to people most of whom had been ground into the mud by Rome. He was writing to people who, whatever their physical and material state, had been set free spiritually by Christ. The very word that he used, *eleutheria,* spoke volumes. It spoke of manumission from slavery. The Greeks had a roundabout way of securing freedom for a slave. A god supposedly purchased the manumitted slave. The slave provided the money, but, because slaves had no legal standing, he could not purchase himself. So his master paid the appropriate amount into the temple treasury on the slave's behalf. A document bearing the words *for freedom* was executed. Then, because the slave was now the property of a god, nobody could enslave him again!

"Free!" says Paul. You have been purchased! You are the property of the Son of God. Nobody has any right to enslave you again. Which, of course, was just what the legalists were trying to do. They were trying to shackle Christ's freemen with the chains of the Law with their silly man-made rules and regulations of religion.

"Stand!" he cries, "Stand fast!" It is one of Paul's great rallying cries in his epistles (1 Cor. 16:13; Phil. 1:27; 4:1; 1 Thess. 3:8; 2 Thess. 2:15). "Stand firm! Plant your feet!" It would bring to mind the Roman way of waging war. When faced by wild, undisciplined enemy hordes, the Romans simply locked their shields together, planted their feet firmly on the ground, and presented to the charging enemy an iron wall of steel and resolution. That is the kind of stand that we must take against error. We must not yield a single point. Truth is truth; error is error. The two are at war. There must be no giving in on a single issue where error is involved. Paul, the most conciliatory of men, would never compromise when it came to truth.

"Be not entangled," Paul warns. The word is *enechō.* Herodias, the stolen wife of Herod Antipas, had a "quarrel against *(enechō)* [John the Baptist]" (Mark 6:19). She would have killed him had she been able. Until such time as her plots could find their focus, she "kept cherishing a grudge" against him. This is what the legalists were doing at Galatia. They cherished a grudge against Paul's converts. They had a quarrel with them because they were free. Similarly, the Pharisees nursed a hatred toward the Lord Jesus because He both refused to be bound by rabbinical traditions and denounced their hypocrisy. "The scribes and the Pharisees," Luke says, "began *to urge (enechō)* him vehemently, and to provoke him to speak of many things" (Luke 11:53). The Galatians were up against the same thing. The legalists were putting on the heat, using all of the pressure they could muster to capture them. "Stand fast!" Paul pleads. "Don't give in!"

He reminds them of the foundation of their liberty: "Christ hath made us free." What folly it would be to go back to the old system of the Law! Surely, they did not want to be children of the bondwoman. The chapter division here might make us forget the context. We are not of Sinai but of Zion, not slaves but sons, not disinherited and disowned but heirs and jointheirs, the aristocracy and nobility of heaven.

b. That liberty attacked (5:2–6)
   (1) The seriousness of the attack exposed (5:2)

"Behold, I Paul say unto you, that if ye be circumcised, Christ shall profit you nothing." That was the ultimate battleground. Circumcision was the seal of the Abrahamic covenant (Gen. 17:9–14) for the natural seed of Abraham. Moses confirmed it as necessary for all aliens who wanted to share in the religious blessings of Israel (Exod. 12:48). It was, of course, for all Jews. Moses included all who wished to keep the Passover. "Moses therefore gave unto you circumcision," Jesus told the Jews (John 7:22), refering, no doubt, to Leviticus 12:1–3, where the seal given to Abraham for the Hebrew people was formally mandated as a requirement under the Law. By the time of Christ, circumcision was as much an identification mark of the Jewish religion as keeping the Sabbath and observing the dietary laws. The Gentiles looked upon it with scorn. It was the one stumbling block, indeed, that kept many God-fearing male Gentiles, who were greatly attracted to Jewish monotheism, from actually becoming Jewish proselytes. It was far easier for a Gentile woman to become a proselyte than it was for a Jewish man. A woman did not have to cross this particularly unpleasant barrier. The fact that Paul saw no need whatsoever for Gentiles to be circumcised to become Christians made the gospel he preached attractive to spiritually awakened Gentile men. No wonder so many of them flocked into the church. Christianity offered them far more than Judaism did—and with no strings attached.

Now the Judaizers were telling Paul's converts that they had to be circumcised after all. Paul warned them in no uncertain terms against taking any such step. The attitude of the legalists was that both the Law and the gospel came from God. One could not have the gospel without the Law because both came from God. It was needful to accept the gospel; it was equally needful to accept circumcision. The Gentiles, like the Jews, needed both. On the surface, it was a plausible argument. But all error is superficially plausible.

The point, however, is that circumcision and the gospel represent opposite principles. We must remember that Paul has just demonstrated this fact in his illustration of Sarah and Hagar. You cannot be both Ishmael and Isaac. You cannot stake your claim to both Sinai and Zion. Calvary marks a giant fork in the road. It is to be one or the other, either all that is summarized in Christ or all that is summarized in circumcision. It is either to be a life commitment to the *Law* or a life commitment to the *Lord.* You cannot get to heaven on a principle of trying and on a principle of trusting.

Paul affirms this point solemnly: "Behold, I Paul say unto you . . ." I, Paul! The apostle, your apostle, the Apostle to the Gentiles, the apostle who won you to Christ! I, Paul, your spiritual father, your benefactor, your friend. I, Paul. Not some other man purporting to speak in my name, not someone else claiming to tell you what I think and believe but I, Paul, someone you know, your very own Paul. Let there be no doubt at all as to where I, Paul, stand on this crucial matter of circumcision.

"If ye be circumcised, Christ shall profit you nothing." Strong language indeed! The *if* here is followed by the subjunctive mood, and it expresses a hypothetical but possible condition, one that is contingent on circumstances that the future will show. In 1 Corinthians 7:18, Gentiles are expressly forbidden to submit to this initiatory rite. In Acts 15, the Jerusalem Council endorsed the Pauline position that circumcision was not to be imposed on Gentiles. Of course, this does not mean that no circumcised person can be saved, for such an extreme position would make it impossible for Jews to be saved. The warning here does not apply to those who were circumcised in infancy or to a case such as that of

Timothy, who was already a half Jew and who voluntarily accepted circumcision at Paul's hand (Acts 16:3) to increase the effectiveness of his ministry among Jews.

What Paul prohibits is the acceptance of circumcision as a religious rite, to acknowledge it as binding on Christians, and to endorse all for which it stands in the mind of a Jew. "Christ shall profit you nothing," Paul warns. The Lord can, will, and does save to the uttermost all those who come unto God by Him (Heb. 7:25). Those who want to come to God on the ground of circumcision, however, cut themselves off from Christ. They prove that they never knew Him. Those who trust in circumcision negate trust in Christ. They circumvent His saving work, and Christ will be of no use to them. He did not need to die if circumcision could secure for them a place in heaven.

Obviously, then, the challenge that the legalists and the Judaizers posed was very serious indeed.

(2) The seriousness of the attack explained (5:3–6)

(a) Terrible warnings (5:3–4)

Paul sets before his Galatian friends two terrible warnings (vv. 3–4). The first one has to do with *falling into debt:* "For I testify again to every man that is circumcised, that he is a debtor to do the whole law" (v. 3). This verse repeats and underlines the warning of the previous verse and explains why circumcision and Christianity are opposite and exclusive poles of the same magnet. Ever since Pentecost, to be circumcised, as a matter of religious significance, carries both an implication and an obligation. It implies a deliberate choosing of Mount Sinai over Mount Calvary. A person could conceivably drift unconsciously into some errors. Nobody could drift carelessly into circumcision. That would call for a definite, conscious decision. The whole operation is distasteful, radical, and extremely painful. A person no more drifts into circumcision than he drifts into having his tonsils or appendix removed. A case has to be made, a decision reached, a surrender accepted, an operation performed, and, in the Gentile world of Paul's day, a stigma accepted. A person might drift into slovenly habits of body or mind, but a person did not drift into waking up suddenly to find himself circumcised. That was the result of thought and action. It was deliberate. The implication is that for a Gentile convert to accept circumcision means that he has thought about it and made a choice. Paul wants his Galatian friends to understand the seriousness of the choice. It is the choice of law over grace, of works over faith, of a legal system over a living Savior. The person who knowledgeably makes such a choice repudiates Christ. He not only proves himself never to have been genuinely saved in the first place but also puts himself forever beyond the pale of salvation in the second place. A fuller discussion of this implication is found in Hebrews 6:4–8.

Not only an implication but also an obligation exists to keep the whole Law. Circumcision was the way a Gentile became a Jew under the Mosaic covenant (Exod. 12:44, 48). It was an initiatory rite, and it carried with it the obligation to accept all of the tenets of the Jewish religion. Whatever else that might or might not have embraced, it certainly involved a commitment to keep the Mosaic Law, as not only a standard but also a system. All 613 commandments of Sinai became immediately obligatory. Moreover, the Judaizers would have added all of the countless rules and regulations of the rabbis. What was being offered to the Gentiles was not only bondage but hopeless, heartbreaking bondage. They were being offered the bondage of promising to keep the Law without having power to keep the Law. What was offered was the heartbreak of knowing with ever-increasing certainty that now this particular law had been broken, now that this violation was added to the debt, now this other failure compounded the debt. Until, ultimately, the person ended up a ten thousand-talent debtor, bankrupt and with nothing to pay before a law that was adamant and inflexible, the accusing prosecutor, witness, and judge all in one. One might have had Christ and not only a free pardon but also justification, and that by faith alone.

Falling into debt! That was the first of the two terrible warnings. The second warning was a warning against *falling from grace:* "Christ is become of no effect unto you, whosoever of you are justified by the law; ye are fallen from grace" (v. 4). That does not mean that a person who chooses justification by law loses his salvation; such a person never had a salvation to lose in the first place. All he had was a false profession.

"Christ is become of no effect to you." That phrase might be rendered, "Ye are severed from Christ," or "You automatically cut yourself from the power of Christ," or "You have become estranged from Christ." The words point to a moment when the decision was made to embrace Judaism. A decision to embrace Judaism, a Christ-rejecting religion, meant a decision to renounce Christ. At that fateful moment of decision, people cut themselves off from Christ as a sawn branch is cut from a tree. All of the initial convicting work of the Holy Spirit is of no avail to such a person. All such professions of faith in Christ are shown to be mere worthless words.

Why? Because, by deliberate choice, they now seek to be "justified by the law," something that is wholly alien to the gospel in principle and utterly impossible in practice. No man, except Jesus, ever lived who could keep the law of God in the letter and the spirit. The Judaizer cuts himself off from Him.

No wonder Paul adds the following clinching, devastating comment: "Ye are fallen from grace," or, as it may be rendered, "You put yourself outside the range of His grace." The tense used points again to that fateful moment of decision when they repudiated the gospel of God's grace, which Paul preached to them with such seeming success, in favor of the Judaizers' system of keeping the Law. The moment they submitted themselves to circumcision, not as a mere minor surgical procedure but as a voluntary commitment to Judaism, they cut themselves off from grace as a means of salvation.

The word for "fallen" here is *ekpiptō.* It is used of the withering of grass beneath the burning rays of the sun: "As the flower of the grass he shall pass away. For the sun is no sooner risen with a burning heat, but it withereth the grass, and the flower thereof falleth [*ekpiptō*], and the grace of the fashion of it perisheth" (James 1:10–11). Peter uses the same illustration and the same word (1 Peter 1:24). When Paul was on that stricken ship, being driven out of control before the storm, he sought to hearten his fellow passengers by describing the visit that he had received by an angel. He had the assurance that not a single life would be lost. "Howbeit," he said, "we must be cast [*ekpiptō*] upon a certain island" (Acts 27:26). The same word is used of the fear that the sailors had when they undergirded the ship "fearing lest they should fall [*ekpiptō*] into the quicksands" (Acts 27:17) and of their fear of falling upon rocks (Acts 17:29). It is used to describe chains falling from a person's wrists (Acts 12:7) and of stars falling from heaven (Mark 13:25). Evidently, it is a serious thing to fall from grace. It is only by the grace of the Lord Jesus that anyone can be saved (Eph. 2:8). To turn from grace to law, from faith to works, from Jesus to Judaism, and from Calvary to circumcision is a fall indeed.

Paul cannot emphasize enough the seriousness of it all. Look at the words and phrases that he uses: "Christ shall profit you nothing" . . . "Debtor to do the whole law" . . . "Christ is become of no effect unto you" . . . "Ye are fallen from grace."

Paul piles up the words to underline the terrible spiritual peril in which people stood who were willing to sell the birthright offered to them in Christ for a dish of Jewish pottage. The very word he uses for falling from grace summons its own series of scenes. It pictures the flower of hope and promise fading and falling before it is ever brought to fruit; the quicksands; the foam-lashed rocks of an iron-bound shore, looming ahead in the darkness amid the fury of a storm at sea; Christ and His cross, His grace, and His finished work spurned for the very system of religion most responsible for His death. Bankruptcy! Debt! What more could Paul say? Terrible warnings indeed!

### (b) Triumphant waiting (5:5)

But, then, by way of contrast, there is triumphant waiting: "For we through the Spirit wait for the hope of righteousness by faith." The Law was deceptive because it seemed to offer some kind of immediate return for the sinner's investment. It offered, at least to some people, a kind of smug satisfaction in not having stolen, sworn, seduced another man's wife, slain someone, or succumbed to idolatry. It ministered, in some people, to a false pride in having kept the feasts and fasts, in having tendered one's tithe, or in having sanctified the Sabbath. It offered a false complacency—of having signed the covenant by means of circumcision, of having done something for one's salvation.

This, of course, is the very essence of all false religion. It is a way as old as Cain. However great the delusion, those who look to baptism, confession, penance, good works, Sabbath keeping, and the like do get a false sense of having done something to win the approval of God. The reward, although quite worthless, is immediate and does last sometimes for some time. But the price always goes up. A daylong fast must be exceeded the next time by a weeklong fast. A pilgrimage to some local shrine must be surpassed the next time by a pilgrimage to Mecca or to Rome. A hair shirt this week must be augmented the next week with flagellations; ten stripes today must be upped to twenty stripes the next time. The demands are incessant and increasing and can never be met. The feeling of accomplishment gives way to a sense of failure. The goal is absolute perfection, something that is impossible outside of Christ. So hope fades, despair moves in, and conscience awakes. Sinai thunders, failure reigns, death comes, and a lost eternity yawns. And, for this, the Galatians were prepared to abandon Christ.

But for those who cleave to Him, there is hope indeed. For the believer there is the Holy Spirit, hope, and righteousness by faith. The Holy Spirit indwells every true-born child of God. Indeed, He is "the earnest of our inheritance" (Eph. 1:14). All of the righteousness of Christ is ours the moment we put our trust in Him. We might stumble and fall, but we have the unquestioning hope that we shall yet see Christ's righteousness wrought in us, fully and forever in terms of our state as it already is in terms of our standing.

"We wait" for it, Paul says. The word means that we look forward to it. The word is often used in connection with the second coming of Christ (1 Cor. 1:7; Phil. 3:20; Heb. 9:28). One day, we shall be like Him for all eternity. John Nelson Darby has expressed it thus in his hymn "And Is It So?":

And is it so—I shall be like Thy Son?
Is this the grace which He for me has won?
Father of glory (thought beyond all thought!)
In glory, to His own blest likeness brought.

Yet it must be! Thy love had not its rest
Were Thy redeemed not with Thee fully blest,
That love that gives not as the world, but shares
All it possesses with its loved co-heirs.

Whoever in his right mind would want to exchange that hope for the loveless laws of the legalist?

(c) True working (5:6)

But what about works? Do we who are content to rest all on Christ have no works to perform? Paul speaks next of the true work that results from faith in Christ: "For in Jesus Christ neither circumcision availeth any thing, nor uncircumcision; but faith which worketh by love" (v. 6). Here, the words *circumcision* and *uncircumcision* refer to Jews and Gentiles. The Jews made the distinction between circumcised and uncircumcised a matter of prime importance. The tradition went back a long time. When David offered to fight the great Philistine giant, Goliath of Gath, King Saul remonstrated with him. David at once began to speak of secret victories. "Thy servant slew both the lion and the bear," he said, "and this uncircumcised Philistine shall be as one of them" (1 Sam. 17:36).

It was common in Paul's day for the Jews to speak complacently of themselves as "the circumcision" and to speak contemptuously of the Gentiles as "the uncircumcison." In Christ, however, the old barrier between Jew and Gentile, emphasized and focused by circumcision, was abolished. The whole question of circumcision was so trivial an issue in Paul's eyes that he would never have raised the subject at all if the Judaizers hadn't made it an issue and a mandatory requirement for salvation.

But the issue had been raised. Paul dealt with it (vv. 2–4), and now he summarily dismissed it. Because it made no difference, in Christ, whether a man was a Jew or a Gentile, what did matter? Faith! Hope! Love! These three. In Christ, everything boils down to simple faith and sublime hope that are manifested, not in law but in love. That is what works! If works there are to be, let love take over their operation. Let love fill the believer's heart, let the love of Christ overflow all of its banks to touch everyone we meet, every situation we face, and every issue of life. Whatever love suggests, that is what we have to do!

2. The foes of our liberty (5:7–12)
   a. Their doctrine revealed (5:7–9)

Having discussed the foundation of our liberty in Christ, Paul now turns his attention to its foes. He describes both their doctrine and their doom. He begins by showing *how their doctrine spoils:* "Ye did run well; who did hinder you that ye should not obey the truth? This persuasion cometh not of him that calleth you" (vv. 7–8). They had been off to a good start. Paul could remember the dynamic days he had spent among them and how eagerly they had embraced the gospel. They were off and running when he had left them.

But someone had raised a roadblock in the way. The word for "hinder" is *enkoptō,* which was used of people breaking up a road or putting an obstacle in the path. "Who broke up the road along which you were making such good progress?" Paul demands.

Often in my travels along the American highways, I will encounter a sign that reads, "Roadwork Ahead". Sure enough, around the next bend in the road, traffic is stalled. The caterpillar tractors, heavy earthmoving equipment, and big shovels are there. There are the workmen in their hard hats. There's the man with the flag, waving the traffic ahead into a single lane. And there ahead is the improvised traffic light, glaring red, bringing all vehicles to a stop. It means both danger and delay. It is bad enough when warnings are posted, when every effort is made to clear the road and let the impatient traffic through. But what if there were no signs? What if the obstructions were deliberate? What if they were set up maliciously, not to improve the highway but as traps for the unwary motorist? That was what Paul was asking. He knew only too well the natural dangers and difficulties of the Christian life. But what of those men who were deliberately obstructing the way? "Who are they?" he demands. Paul had no patience with false teachers who would do such a thing.

Somebody had been persuading them. Whoever it was, the arguments had not come from God. The Devil can quote the Bible. He dared to quote it (or, rather, deliberately to misquote it) to the Lord Himself. Nearly all cultists appeal to the Bible to give credence to their errors. The Judaizers had the whole Mosaic Law to which to appeal. But they quoted Scripture without any regard for that monumental dispensational change effected by Calvary and Pentecost that had rendered Judaism null and void. As Paul would put it, they did not "rightly [divide] the word of truth" (2 Tim. 2:15).

So the Judaizers were spoilers. They put their hindrances in the way of those who were making progress in the truth. But the false doctrine did something else. Paul showed the Galatians *how their doctrine spreads:* "A little leaven leaveneth the whole lump" (v. 9). Throughout the Scripture, leaven is used as a symbol of corruption that spreads furtively, secretly, and unseen until it permeates everything. It usually symbolizes false doctrine at work within the corporate body of the people of God. Leaven was sourdough. It was introduced into the dough of a new loaf, which was then left to stand in a warm spot until the fermenting, spreading influence of the old had thoroughly taken hold of all parts of the new. The only way to stop the action of the leaven, once it had been insinuated into the new loaf, was to put the loaf in the oven. The action of the fire stopped the action of the leaven.

That is the trouble with false doctrine! That is why the Old Testament prophets, the Lord Himself, His apostles, and discerning, Spirit-filled men in all ages have been so vigorous in exposing error and in denouncing those who propagate it. It spreads. It does its corrupting work until it has taken over the whole. Not a major denomination in Christendom has not eventually been taken over by liberalism, legalism, fanaticism, formalism, ritualism, or some other such corrupting influence.

By its third generation, every new movement, born of revival by the Spirit of God, needs a fresh moving of the Holy Spirit if it is to survive. With the first generation, freshly discovered truth is *a conviction;* those who see it and embrace it propagate it with zeal. They would willingly die for it. They will give up all they have for it. "Buy the truth, and sell it not," advised the wise man (Prov. 23:23). That is the motto of the first generation.

By the time the second generation takes over, what was once a conviction has become *a belief.* The second generation has been taught these truths. They have heard the first generation tell tales of battle, fire and sword, of persecution and pioneering, of the high price that was paid for these truths. They have been brought up in them, drilled in them, made to memorize them, and urged to accept them for themselves. And so they do, but not with the same fire and fervor of the first generation. But they believe them. They can give chapter and verse for their beliefs. The zeal to spread them has cooled, but they still hold to them and defend them and still rear their children to believe them.

By the time the third generation is in charge, what was first a conviction and then a belief has become *an opinion.* The truths are now lightly held. Compromise is acceptable. Things are watered down, distinctives disappear, and an accommodation is reached with dissenters and other groups who hold some things in common. First, the sharp edges are blurred, then new ideas are introduced; things that would have made the first generation turn over in its grave the third generation tolerates with smiling ease. The power has gone; the drive has gone. There is talk of renewal. New methods are tried. More money is poured in. Projects are announced. Doctrines are tinkered with. The emphasis is on education. The Holy Spirit moves out. Error moves in. But revival is needed, not renewal. When revival does not come, people drift away or some kind of phony, counterfeit revival is accepted. The lump is now thoroughly leavened. People might continue to "play church" for a very long time, but "Ichabod" can be written over what remains. The glory is departed. The Holy Spirit has moved on elsewhere. History furnishes us with countless examples.

Paul could see the deadly leaven at work in Galatia. It was spreading. It wasn't even the third generation; yet, this particularly virulent heresy already was permeating the Galatian churches. Paul was alarmed. All he could do was write, warn, and pray.

### b. Their doom revealed (5:10–12)

Paul can think of no argument that he will not use in his battle for the souls of his Galatian friends. We note *his confidence:* "I have confidence in you through the Lord, that ye will be none otherwise minded . . ." (v. 10a). He appeals to them. He expresses his faith in them. "I'm sure," he says, "that you will not take that final, fatal step." Paul knew that no genuinely born again believer could repudiate the gospel in the way the Judaizers were demanding. The majority in the Galatian church seems to have been still wavering at the time Paul wrote this letter. Certainly anyone who took the final step into the Judaizing apostasy, after reading Paul's letter, could never have been genuinely saved in the first place. This view is reinforced by a careful analysis of the two major warning passages in Hebrews (5:11–6:21; 10:26–30).

Apostasy is not the same as backsliding. Only a genuine believer can backslide. There is restoration for the backslider. The Holy Spirit convicts the backslider, and the Father chastens the backslider. The backslider might die in his sinful condition, but he will still go to heaven. He will be "saved, so as by fire" (1 Cor. 3:15). Only an unbeliever can become an apostate. An apostate is a person who has been enlightened to the truth but who turns away from it. He repudiates it and embraces some kind of error. The apostate crucifies afresh the Son of God and puts Him to an open shame. It is impossible to renew this kind of person to repentance. God abandons him to his false beliefs. He has despised the Spirit of grace.

Paul was confident that not a single truly Spirit-born Galatian believer would apostatize into the Judaistic heresy being so zealously propagated in their midst. Anyone who took that final, fatal step would prove, by that very action, that the root of the matter was never in him at all.

We note also *his conviction:* "but he that troubleth you shall bear his judgment, whosoever he be" (v. 10b). Paul held out no hope to the Judaizers themselves. They were wedded to their ways. He was sure that they would not receive his letter in any good spirit at all.

The word for "troubleth" is *tarassō.* It is used of the agitation of the water at the pool of Bethesda (John 5:7). It is used of the Lord's inner anguish as He accompanied His dear friends, Martha and Mary, to the tomb of their brother, Lazarus (John 11:33). It is used to describe the consternation of the disciples as they faced the fact that Jesus was soon to leave them (John 14:1). It is used of the agitators who tried to foment trouble for Paul at Thessalonica (Acts 17:8). This is what the Judaizers were doing at Galatia. They were upsetting the faith of Paul's converts. Paul hands them over to judgment. It made no difference who they were, although Paul probably had a good idea who they were. They would face a serious charge one day. Paul was a firm believer in God's sovereign control over human affairs and in His holding men accountable for their actions.

We note also *his condition:* "And I, brethren, if I yet preach circumcision, why do I yet suffer persecution? then is the offence of the cross ceased" (v. 11). Paul knew the pressure that was being brought to bear on his beloved Galatians. He knew the kind of persecution that some of them were facing. He was experiencing the same pressure and persecution himself. Some of the Judaizers seem to have been trying to persuade Paul's converts to accept their views by saying that the apostle himself still advocated circumcision. Paul indignantly disassociates himself from any such story. Advocate circumcision indeed! Why, if he were to advocate that rite, his troubles would cease! It was precisely because he refused any compromise with legalism that he was the constant target for persecution.

The legalists might have found some ground for their charge in that Paul advocated circumcision in the case of Timothy. That Paul had circumcised Timothy would be a well-known fact in Galatia because Timothy had come from the area (Acts 16:1–3). Timothy's, however, was a special case. The Holy Spirit makes Paul's motive clear: "Him would Paul have to go forth with him; and took and circumcised him because of the Jews which were in those quarters: for they knew all that his father was a Greek" (Acts 16:3). The Galatians also knew that his mother was a Jewess. So Timothy was already half Jewish. It made sense to Paul to make Timothy wholly Jewish if by doing so would increase Timothy's usefulness in evangelizing Jews. However, Paul certainly did not circumcise Timothy because he thought that circumcision was essential to salvation. Perhaps, had he known how his action would be misrepresented, he would not have circumcised Timothy in the first place. In any case, if Paul made a mistake, he learned from it. He soon saw that any attempt to win the goodwill of the Judaizers was never going to work. As for preaching circumcision, such a charge was nonsense. He did nothing of the kind, and he paid dearly for not doing so. Of course, he had once preached circumcision ("if I yet [still] preach circumcision . . ."), but that was before his conversion.

The real reason Paul suffered persecution was "the offence of the cross" (v. 11). Everything about Christ scandalized the Jews. He was born poor and lowly in a Bethlehem stable, surrounded by cattle, the son of a peasant woman, the adopted son of a laborer from the despised Galilean town of Nazareth. The Jews never recognized that He was the rightful heir to David's throne. His life and teaching cut cleanly across theirs. He refused to pay any respect to their rabbinical rules and regulations, openly defying their man-made Sabbath shibboleths. They could not deny His miracles, but the more reckless of them had a ready explanation. They attributed them to Satan, just as they attributed His mysterious birth to fornication. They argued with Him incessantly about the Law and about Moses and the commandments. They hated Him because He refused to endorse their traditions. They were outraged by His love for publicans and sinners. They wanted a militant messiah, not a meek Messiah, a sovereign, not a Savior. They wanted someone who would smash the power of Rome and make Jerusalem the capital of a new world empire, someone who would confirm them in their seats of power. Above all, they were scandalized by His cross. That someone claiming to be their Messiah should end up on a Roman gallows was the last straw, although they themselves were responsible for putting Him there. The mocking title that Pilate gave Him—"This is Jesus of Nazareth, the King of the Jews"—still rankled in their souls. As for His resurrection, they had a ready enough explanation for that: there was no resurrection; the disciples stole the body.

The cross! To preach the cross was an offense to the Jews, and it was nonsense to the Romans and the Greeks. Yet, Paul knew that Calvary enshrined the greatest truth in the world. He knew that the preaching of the cross was the message for lost mankind. In the preaching of the cross resided "the power of God unto salvation." The gospel was God's high explosive, the divine dynamite to convict, convert, and consecrate sinners willing to believe it. So, although such preaching might be offensive to the unregenerate human heart, no other message existed. For preaching that message, Paul was mobbed in Jerusalem, mocked at Athens, and murdered at Rome. No indeed! The cross's offense had not ceased. If the Galatians thought that they could mitigate their own sufferings by being circumcised, they were wrong. All they would get in return for that ritual would be the pall of spiritual death upon their souls.

"I would they were even cut off which trouble you!" Paul exclaims (v. 12). This is a strong expression. The word *apokoptō* means "to amputate" (Mark 9:43, 45). It is used of the cutting off of Malchus's ear by Simon Peter (John 18:10, 26). The Judaizers wanted Paul's converts to be circumcised, to submit to a minor amputation to enhance their religious standing. Scornfully, Paul says in effect, "What they need is to go all the way and emasculate themselves." That is literally what he means. They should emasculate themselves, make eunuchs of themselves.[1] That would put an end to their pernicious teaching, for then, according to the Law itself, they would be cut off from "the congregation of the LORD" (Deut. 23:1). We might think such an exclamation to be radical and not what we would expect from a great apostle. But it was precisely because he was an apostle, the very apostle to the Gentiles, indeed, that Paul did make such a statement. What the Judaizers were trying to effect was the cutting off of those Gentile believers from the body of Christ. No wonder Paul does not hesitate to call a spade a spade. Paul had no false modesty. He was as fierce as a tiger defending its cubs when it came to defending his converts from cultists.

1. See F. F. Bruce, *The Epistle to the Galatians: A Commentary on the Greek Text* (Grand Rapids: Eerdmans, 1982), 238.

3. The frontiers of our liberty (5:13–15)
    a. We are not free to indulge in carnality (5:13)

We are free! The Law has no claim upon us. But love does. Therefore, free though we might be, we cannot do certain things. Love for the Lord will make us draw the line for ourselves at certain things. Love for others will ensure that other things are equally impossible. Indeed, we are not free to cross certain frontiers. We are not free, for instance, to indulge in carnality: "For, brethren, ye have been called unto liberty; only use not liberty for an occasion to the flesh, but by love serve one another" (v. 13). To abuse our freedom to indulge the flesh would not be liberty but license. As Paul puts it in Romans 6, we are not free *to* sin; we are free *from* sin. We are no longer dead *in* sin; we are now dead *to* sin. Jews were in bondage to the Law, Gentiles were in bondage to idols, and all of us are in bondage to sin. The Lord sets us free at the infinite cost of Calvary. Our grateful hearts should acknowledge the incalculable debt we owe Him. How ungrateful it is to use our newfound liberty as an excuse for self-indulgence.

We are not to use our freedom for "an occasion to the flesh." The word is *aphormē,* which carries with it the idea of a base of operations in war. Paul saw the Law as providing sin, for example, with a base of operations for its attack upon the sinner. The Law has a tendency to stimulate sin into action. A sign reads "Do Not Touch," and at once we want to touch the forbidden article although, perhaps, the thought of touching it had never entered our minds until we saw the sign. The prohibition stirs the latent lawlessness of the soul into action. It becomes its base of operations (Rom. 7:8, 11).

An example of this concept of "a base of operations" is provided in Paul's attitude toward money. Paul refused to receive financial remuneration, for instance, from his converts at Corinth. Later, when his enemies were looking for something to use against him, they found themselves deprived of this base of operations by Paul's wise precaution.

Now Paul warns us not to let our very liberty in Christ be seized upon by the flesh as a base of operations against us. If we allow that to happen, we shall soon find that we have lost our testimony and brought ourselves into bondage to our lower nature.

Far from allowing anything to happen like this, we should use our newfound liberty in Christ as a base of operations from which love can reach out to serve other people. The word for "serve" is *douleuō,* which means to serve as a bondman or a slave. All that a slave does is serve other people. That is Paul's summation of the Christian life: we are saved to serve, and the Lord Jesus has set the pace.

The whole gospel of Mark is a portrait of the Lord Jesus as the perfect Servant of Jehovah (Isa. 52:13). The key verse in Mark's gospel says, "The Son of man came not to be ministered unto [i.e., not to be served], but to minister [i.e., to serve], and to give his life a ransom for many" (Mark 10:45). The gospel of Mark divides on that verse. First, we see the Lord Jesus giving His life in service, then we see Him giving His life in sacrifice. If that was what He did with His life, how can we do any less with ours? Love moved Him to lay aside the boundless freedom that He had as the eternal, uncreated, self-existing second person of the Godhead to "take upon him the form of a servant" (Phil. 2:7). Love should motivate us to emulate the supreme example that we have in Him.

### b. We are not free to indulge in conflict (5:14–15)

Paul continues. We have, first, *the single word:* "For all the law is fulfilled in one word, even in this; Thou shalt love thy neighbour as thyself" (v. 14). Very well, then! The Galatians wanted to keep the Law? Well, let them! Let them keep it as reduced to that single word—*love!* Love is the fulfilling of the Law. To love one's neighbor as one loves oneself means that the whole legal code can be abolished. Love will not commit murder or adultery. Love will not steal, bear false witness, or even covet. On the contrary, love will transform the Law's negatives into life's positives. Love, far from murdering, will pick up the wayfarer on the Jericho road; pour oil and wine into his wounds; put him on his own mule; take him to the nearest hospice; pay for his meals, medicine, nurse, and shelter; and then pledge whatever balance might still be due. Love will build a hedge of sanctity around his neighbor's home, wife, and children. Love will be ever ready to pour the oil of gladness on his neighbor's family; be quick to mediate when needed; and be swift to help, encourage, and bless. Love will anticipate the poor man's needs. It will open its treasure store to provide quick, generous, and practical aid—all without charge. Love will speak well of the man who is accused, ever looking for something good to commend him and something positive, helpful, and honorable to say. Love will rejoice at the other man's prosperity, will seek to further it, and will put helpful opportunities in his way. "Law?" asks Paul. "Who needs law when there's love?

"Love your neighbor as yourself," says Paul to the Galatians. That's all the law you will ever need.

Then comes *the sarcastic warning:* "But if ye bite and devour one another, take heed that ye be not consumed one of another" (v. 15). Paul adds a warning that sprang directly out of his love for the Galatians. To love a person does not mean that it will never be necessary to confront that person with a sharp warning. The Galatian churches seem to have been not only facing a seductive error from without but also were being torn apart from within. The believers were quarreling with one another, probably over the whole question of law keeping. This was one of the sad side effects of the teaching of the Judaizers. Even if the majority was delivered from the delusion, the squabbles that this insidious teaching engendered among the believers threatened to destroy the fellowship altogether. Fighting among themselves was no way to combat the error. The enemy would triumph if the churches split into warring factions, even if he never succeeded in snaring the believers in error. Paul uses very graphic language here. He pictures a pack of wild animals tearing and devouring one another. We find a touch of sarcasm in his words.

B. The law of likeness to Christ (5:16–26)
   1. The provision for Christlikeness (5:16–18)

All of Paul's letters deal with belief and behavior, with principles and practice. Teaching that emphasizes only our beliefs can become hard and cold; teaching that emphasizes only our behavior can become merely an exercise in psychology. Paul's letters maintain a proper balance between faith and practice. He has now made the full transition in Galatians to the practical side of his teaching.

We are to be like Jesus! That is the substance of his practical teaching. He shows, first, the provision that God has made to make it possible for redeemed sinners to be like Jesus. First, we have *a command:* "This I say then, Walk in the Spirit, and ye shall not fulfil the lust of the flesh" (v. 16). The Holy Spirit is God's answer to the flesh. Man in sin is not man as God intended him to be. Man in sin is a monstrosity. He is the product of a diabolical graft, wrought upon his nature, person, and personality by the Evil One. The product of this graft is what the Bible calls "the flesh." It is wholly evil. Paul says, "In me (that is, in my flesh,) dwelleth no good thing" (Rom. 7:18). It is totally beyond redemption. God will not bless it or have dealings with it. All He will do with it is put it to death (Rom. 6:6, 11). That is why trying to keep God's law does not work. Paul says that the weakness of the Law was the flesh (Rom. 8:3). Any attempt on our part to keep God's law is bound to fail because man in sin is incapable of doing so. "They that are in the flesh cannot please God," Paul adds (Rom. 8:8). Indeed, "the carnal mind is enmity against God: for it is not subject to the law of God, neither indeed can be" (Rom. 8:7).

As we have already seen, God made man to be indwelt by Him. The human spirit was to be the home of the Holy Spirit. The human spirit, in harmony with the indwelling Holy Spirit, was to control the soul, mind, emotions, will, as well as the senses, functions, and needs of the body. Man, inhabited thus by God, would exhibit to the universe God, manifest and magnified in a human body. Once sin entered, the Holy Spirit departed. The flesh took over. The flesh controls the mind, the heart, the will, and the senses of man in sin. Before regeneration, such an individual is known in Scripture as *a natural man.* He simply behaves according to the dictates of his fallen Adamic nature. The portrait of the natural man is found in Romans 7:7–14. All of his efforts to please God are doomed to failure. All false religion displays fallen man's utter inability to know God in the flesh or to understand God's Word. Jesus said to Nicodemus, "Marvel not that I say unto thee, Ye must be born again" (John 3:6–7). We are born spiritually dead, cut off, that is, from God. We need to be born again, born of the Spirit, born from above (John 3:3).

When a person accepts Christ as personal Savior from sin (John 1:11–13), various miracles take place. His inner man is cleansed by the precious blood of Christ. He becomes "an habitation of God through the Spirit" (Eph. 2:22), for the Holy Spirit takes up permanent residence in that person's body (John 14:16; 1 Cor. 3:16; 6:19) and quickens to life again the human spirit within.

Every born again believer has two natures. He has the old, unregenerate nature with which he was born, "the flesh," or "the old man" as it is called. This nature can do nothing right. He also has the new nature, the divine nature, the nature wrought in him by the Holy Spirit. This nature is incapable of sin (1 Peter 1:23; 1 John 3:9; 5:1, 18). The two natures are at war, as Paul so graphically describes in Romans 7. When a believer allows the old, flesh nature to have its way in his life, he is known as *a carnal man.* The portrait of the carnal man is found in Romans 7:15–25. When he allows the indwelling Holy Spirit to have His way in his life, he is known as *a spiritual man.* The portrait of the spiritual man is given in Romans 7:1–6.

The Holy Spirit's command here is blunt and to the point: "Walk in the Spirit, and ye shall not fulfil the lust of the flesh." It is one or the other, and it is up to us. The potential for living a holy life is now ours because of the cleansing power of the blood of Christ and the permanent residency of the Holy Spirit. It all becomes a matter of obedience, of yielding to the Holy Spirit, of making ourselves available to Him, moment by moment, situation by situation, and decision by decision. Paul does not see this as optional but as mandatory. It is the only way the Christian life can be lived.

It was the way Jesus lived. He did what He did because He was who He was: God manifest in the flesh. He was never anything less than God. He was God overall, blessed forevermore, Creator of the universe, second person of the Godhead, upholding all things by the word of His power. The demonstration of deity in humanity on those terms, however, would have been awesome and spectacular, frightening and not much help to us. So Jesus came to live here as Man—not as an ordinary man, and not as a fallen man, but as Man indwelt by God. So, He did what He did because He was who He was. We cannot draw the line between His deity and His humanity. We cannot say, "Now He is behaving as God; now He is behaving as Man." He was both God and man, all of the time and in every situation. Filled, ever and always, with the Holy Spirit (John 3:34). So it was that moment by moment, situation by situation, the Lord Jesus set before a lost world a full-color, three-dimensional, tangible, and audiovisual demonstration of what God intended man to be. That is why He is called "the second man" (1 Cor. 15:47). Adam failed; Jesus never did. At one and the same time, He showed the world what God is like ("He that hath seen me hath seen the Father"—John 14:9) and demonstrated what God intended man to be like. God is like Jesus. We are to be like Jesus, which, of course, is exactly what God intended Adam to be like (Gen. 1:26). Now that we are regenerated and indwelt by the Holy Spirit, the potential of being like Jesus is restored to us. We are to make ourselves available as He makes Himself available to us.

The key to all of this is obedience, availability, a willingness to let God be God in us. The only things that hinder us from wholly demonstrating to a lost world what God is like are our inbred disobedience and self-will. All too often, we are simply not available. We resist and grieve the Holy Spirit.

There is still another limiting factor, however, even when we are most available and most fully obedient. Our bodies have not yet been redeemed (Rom. 8:23). But one day we are going to have bodies "like unto his glorious body" (Phil. 3:21). "We shall be like him; for we shall see him as he is" (1 John 3:2). Then redemption will be complete, and we shall be like Him for all eternity.

Meanwhile, Paul says, "Walk in the Spirit, and ye shall not fulfil the lust of the flesh." We are commanded to let the Holy Spirit, now indwelling us, to have His way in our spirit, soul, and body. All of His resources will then be available to us, giving us victory over the old nature and its ways.

The word *walk* is *peripateō*. It embraces the whole round of our human activities, whether as lost sinners (Eph. 4:17) or as regenerated children of God (1 Cor. 7:17; Col. 2:6). It refers to our outward life, which people all around us can see. "Let your conduct be controlled by the Spirit," is one way of rendering the Word here. "Live your whole life in the Spirit," is another way of putting it. Inherent in the concept of "walk" is the idea of making progress. We walk one step at a time. Our progress might not be fast, but it should be steady. We might stumble and fall, but we get up, seek cleansing, and keep moving forward.

Next comes *a contrast:* "For the flesh lusteth against the Spirit, and the Spirit against the flesh: and these are contrary the one to the other: so that ye cannot do the things that ye would" (v. 17). In the Scriptures we find that the Father, the Son, and the Holy Spirit are paired off against the world, the flesh, and the Devil.

God the Father and the world are diametrically opposed. All of the way through the Lord's Prayer in John 17, this conflict is revealed and emphasized. The Lord speaks of "the men which *thou* gavest me out of the world" (John 17:6). "I am no more in the world," He said, "but these are in the world. . . . Holy Father, keep through thine own name those whom thou hast given me" (John 17:11). "As thou hast sent me into the world, even so have I also sent them into the world" (John 17:18). He prays that "the world may know that *thou* hast sent me" (John 17:23). He said, "O righteous Father, the world hath not known thee" (John 17:25). When He promised to send the Holy Spirit, He said, "I will pray the Father, and he shall give you another Comforter . . . whom the world cannot receive" (John 14:16–17). In summarizing His mission, Jesus said, "I came forth from the Father, and am come into the world: again, I leave the world, and go to the Father" (John 16:28). James said, "Ye adulterers and adulteresses, know ye not that the friendship of the world is enmity with God? whosoever therefore will be a friend of the world is the enemy of God" (James 4:4). Along the same line, John wrote, "If any man love the world, the love of the Father is not in him. For all that is in the world . . . is not of the Father, but is of the world" (1 John 2:15–16). He said, "The world knoweth us not, because it knew him [i.e., the Father] not" (1 John 3:1).

In the same way, the Son is the special adversary of the Devil. Throughout the entire Old Testament, Satan's great goal was to prevent the birth of Christ by so corrupting the Hebrew people and the Davidic line that it almost needed to be destroyed. On one occasion, he almost succeeded (Exod. 32:7–14). The enmity began with God's judgment on the serpent at the time of the Fall: "And I will put enmity between thee and the woman, and between *thy seed* and *her seed;* it shall bruise thy head, and thou shalt bruise his heel" (Gen. 3:15). In the Apocalypse, John summarizes what happened when Herod massacred the babies of Bethlehem. (It was a deliberate attempt by Satan to get rid of Christ.) John tells us that "the dragon stood before the woman which was ready to be delivered, for to devour her child as soon as it was born" (Rev. 12:4). The Devil did his best to overthrow Christ in the Temptation and failed dismally (Matt. 4:1–11). He tried to have Him murdered at Nazareth (Luke 4:28–29). Anticipating Calvary, Jesus said: "The prince of this world cometh, and hath nothing in me" (John 14:30). John says, "For this purpose the Son of God was manifested, that he might destroy the works of the devil" (1 John 3:8).

Along the same line, the Holy Spirit is seen as the special divine adversary of the flesh. We see this fact as far back as the Flood: "And the Lord said, My spirit shall not always strive with man, for that he also is flesh" (Gen. 6:3). In explaining to Nicodemus the need for the new birth, Jesus said, "That which is born of the flesh is flesh; and that which is born of the Spirit is spirit" (John 3:6). Paul wrote, "They that are in the flesh cannot please God. But ye are not in the flesh, but in the Spirit, if so be that the Spirit of God dwell in you" (Rom. 8:8–9). So we come back to our text: "The flesh lusteth against the Spirit, and the Spirit against the flesh: and these are contrary the one to the other: so that ye cannot do the things that ye would."

The war has been going on for a long time, but we are on the winning side. All of the infinite resources of the Godhead are available to us. In our struggle with the flesh, the Holy Spirit is our special Helper. He knows all of the subtle wiles of the flesh. He knows where it lurks, knows its deceits and disguises, knows its incorrigible wickedness, and knows its pretended virtues. The Holy Spirit is on our side. He is our ally against this subtle foe. He dwells within, where the battle is to be fought. We are not left helpless in this battle, nor are we simply the battleground between these two foes. We are to "walk in the Spirit." That calls for a deliberate choice. We yield either to the flesh or to the Spirit.

"Ye cannot do the things that ye would," Paul says. We must deny our natural desires. We are to do the things that the Holy Spirit wants us to do. That is the whole point and purpose of our human spirit being indwelt by the Holy Spirit. Instead of giving in to the lust of the flesh, we are to give in to the desires of the Holy Spirit.

So, there is to be *a commitment:* "But if ye be led of the Spirit, ye are not under the law" (v. 18). Paul wants to emphasize that living a holy life is not achieved by self-effort or by trying to keep the Law. It is achieved by responding to the leading of the Holy Spirit. The specter of the Law keeps making its appearance because of the subtlety of the flesh. If the flesh is not allowed to indulge its repulsive side, it will indulge its religious side. It will dress up in its Sunday best and go to church. It will walk the aisle, submit to baptism, sing in the choir, teach a Sunday school class, and indulge in good works. It will sing, pray, and take Communion. It will wear a hair shirt, fast, and deprive itself. It will carry a Bible and go on visitation. It will go to Bible school and seminary and get ordained to the ministry. It will write articles for Christian magazines and review books. It will even become a missionary. There is nothing that the flesh will not do. It is a great doer. It will persuade us that all of this "doing" is just what God wants. It is just another way of putting us under law.

Holy living, however, is not to be achieved by doing but by being. The only way we can be what God wants us to be is to cooperate with the Holy Spirit. The Holy Spirit never coerces, never compels, never puts on the pressure, and never bullies. He does not drive; He leads. He leads; we follow. He leads us into all truth. He leads us in the paths of righteousness. He leads us step-by-step. He leads gently, understandingly, and unerringly. He leads us in our daily quiet time. He leads us by the godly counsel of Spirit-taught men. He leads through the circumstances of life. He leads by gently witnessing with our spirit in the innermost recesses of our being. He leads by quickening our conscience. He leads by encouraging us or by restraining us, by assuring us or by reproving us. He leads, but He never drives. He never gives us that "now-or-never" feeling or that "do-this-or-else" urging. He leads. We follow one step at a time.

2. The proofs of Christlikeness (5:19–23)
    a. The sinful man revealed (5:19–21)

Now comes one of those lists that are so common in the writings of Paul. He piles up word after word to expose the evil nature of man for what it is. All of these sins—seventeen of them—he simply classifies as "the works of the flesh." "The lust of the flesh" (v. 16) shows the *source* of man's natural wickedness; the "works of the flesh" trace the *course* of man's wickedness. The one is inward; the other is outward. Every one of the sins cataloged here is abhorrent to the Holy Spirit. For convenience, we can categorize them in three ways.

First there are *sexual sins:* "Now the works of the flesh are manifest, which are these; Adultery, fornication, uncleanness, lasciviousness" (v. 19). All of the sins listed here are "manifest," that is, they are open, obvious, and well known. The word is *phaneros,* "open to view" or "visible."

The first sin in the list is "adultery." The word used is *porneia,* the general word for illicit sexual intercourse. It includes adultery, although in some places it is distinguished from it (Matt. 15:19; Mark 7:21). It is akin to the word *porne,* the word for a harlot, and often signifies liaison with a prostitute. The word is also used to signify sexual activities within degrees prohibited by God's Word or frowned on by society, as, for instance, the man whom Paul told the Corinthian church to excommunicate because he was committing incest with his father's wife (1 Cor. 5:1). The word was commonly used for all kinds of sexual misbehavior.

In the Greco-Roman world of Paul's day, casual and promiscuous sex was as common as it is today. People thought nothing of it. At Corinth, in particular, immorality was so widely practiced that (like Sodom in the Old Testament) the name of the city became a synonym for vice. To "Corinthianize" was to practice debauchery. In the days of the regency, profligate young sprigs of the British aristocracy were called "Corinthians." In cities where sexual immorality was rampant, Paul's converts had trouble throwing off promiscuity as an accepted lifestyle, even once they were saved and added to the church. A similar situation exists today. Young people, often members of a sound local church, experiment with premarital sex. Extramarital sex is common. People who profess to be saved think that it is still permissible to continue living together as man and wife although they have never been married. The Holy Spirit exposes all such behavior as one of "the works of the flesh" against which He militates.

Next comes "fornication." This time the word is *akatharsia.* It means "impurity." It is the negative form of *katharos,* which means "pure" and was often used in pagan society to denote that degree of ceremonial cleanliness that enabled a devotee to approach his god. *Akatharsia,* then, suggests those things that are permitted in life that make a person unfit to approach God. The word has a wider meaning than does *porneia,* which relates to specific sexual sins, and it signifies a general state of mental impurity. People who watch dirty movies, read pornographic books, tell dirty jokes, go to topless or nude bars, and constantly pander to sensuality are guilty of making themselves impure. Impurity, planted in mind and memory, is notoriously hard to uproot.

The next word is "uncleanness." This word stems from the word *akatharsia.* It means "wantonness," or "licentiousness." It describes the person who is so besotted by lust that he simply does not care what people think or say. He abandons all restraint. He has neither shame nor fear. People who march for so-called "gay rights" fit into this category. On some streets in San Francisco and other major cities, perverts openly flaunt their shame. They are bold and brazen in their wickedness. In the New Testament, this Greek word is used of unclean spirits (Acts 5:16; Rev. 16:13). In the Apocalypse, the coming city of Babylon is described as being "the hold [cage] of every *foul* spirit, and a cage of every *unclean* [same word] and hateful bird" (Rev. 18:2). There can be little doubt that "the works of the flesh" that exhibit such behavior are stimulated by evil spirits.

So, there is a progression. First, there is immorality, then a general state of mental impurity, and finally a scornful disregard of all things decent.

Then there are *spiritual sins,* sins of a more religious nature. The flesh is incurably religious. Paul mentions, "Idolatry, witchcraft" (v. 20a). We do not usually think of idolatry as one of the works of the flesh, but it is. It represents religious flesh at its worst. The unregenerate religious man makes an idol from wood or stone and then falls down and worships it. It satisfies his craving to have a visible, tangible god. No matter that the thing can neither hear, speak, feel, nor talk. It might be a thing of artistic beauty, or it might be as ugly as sin, but it gives visible form to the flesh's idea of God. It might be shaped like a man or a woman, like a wild beast, like a bird, or like a creeping thing. Or it might be a hybrid monster—part man, part fish—a grinning, prancing effigy that is all arms and legs, or a vast, brooding being with cold, callous countenance. Nothing can be more astonishing than man's determination to worship gods that he has fashioned with his own hands. Behind all idolatry are demons. Invisible evil spirits give power to idolatry. This is why graven images hold countless millions of people in thrall. Those who worship idols worship demons that make them slaves to every kind of superstition and suggestion. Idolatry is a work of the flesh and one of which Satan takes full advantage.

Even more subtle is the form of idolatry that substitutes men's own thoughts and philosophies for God. Men become worshipers of themselves. Paul airs this whole subject thoroughly in Romans 1. Humanism, communism, and rationalism are all forms of this kind of idolatry. All of them are works of the flesh. All of them dethrone God and enthrone man.

Then comes *witchcraft.* The empty soul of man, estranged from God, craves some contact with the supernatural. Evil spirits are all too willing to oblige; hence, from time immemorial, witches, mediums, psychics of all sorts, astrologers, necromancers, and soothsayers have offered people contact with the unseen world. The unseen world is very real. Satan, principalities and powers, the rulers of this world's darkness, wicked spirits in high places, fallen angels, and demons haunt it. All of them are willing to oblige men by means of Ouija boards, rappings, séances, trances, incantations, horoscopes, voices, visions, ecstatic utterances, tongues, prophecies, signs, healings, curses, and spells. Witchcraft is very real. It has resurfaced, with all of its age-old fascination and power in our day. The so-called New Age movement is its most popular front. Satan worship, covens, hauntings, and demon possession are all part of the vast deception, launched from the alien, hostile, unseen world. The "works of the flesh" find their religious expression in such things.

The word for "witchcraft" is *pharmakia,* literally "sorcery." Our English word *pharmacy* is derived from this word. The word itself links occultism and the use of drugs. In sorcery, the witch uses drugs, incantations, charms, and amulets to accomplish her aims. One explanation for the hopeless addiction of people who get hooked on drugs is that they fall under the power of demons. The Bible makes clear that occultism will increase in the post-Christian era. In the Apocalypse, we get, indeed, a terrible glimpse of a God-hating, demon-drug culture hardened in its sin (Rev. 9:20–21). The triumph of the works of the flesh is that they finally spawn the Antichrist, that diabolical creature whom the Bible calls the Man of Sin.

Then there are *social sins,* sins that outrage human life and society. Paul speaks of "hatred, variance, emulations, wrath, strife, seditions, heresies, envyings, murders, drunkenness, revellings, and such like . . ." (vv. 20b–21a).

First, we have "hatred." The Greek word is *echthra,* the opposite of love. In view here is the person who entertains and nurtures hostility toward his fellows. The world is full of religious, racial, and political strife fostered by this devilish spirit of hatred and enmity. Why should we hate someone just because of the color of his skin? Why should we cherish enmity of the deadliest sort toward another person because they differ from us in a point of doctrine, over a scientific theory, or over a political issue? We might dislike the other person's position, but why should we also dislike his person? That is the flesh at work. It so cherishes self-love that it can breed promiscuous hate. The Lord Jesus shows us how to react toward those who differ with us, even to the point of hatred and enmity. Jesus loved His enemies enough to die for them. He prayed for them.

D. L. Moody liked, in one of his sermons, to depict the Lord's sending of Simon Peter on a mission of mercy: "Find the man who crowned Me with thorns and tell him I wish to offer him a crown in heaven. Find the man who pierced My side with that spear. Tell him there's a quicker way to My heart." So, we are to love our enemies (Matt. 5:44), we are to feed them when they are hungry (Rom. 12:20), and we are to answer their hatred with love. Impossible? Yes, indeed, if we are relying on the works of the flesh.

Then comes "variance." The word here is *eris,* which means strife, or quarrelsomeness. It is the spirit of rivalry, contention, and wrangling. It originally had to do with rivalry and competitiveness for prizes in athletic events, but, more commonly, it had an evil connotation. The Greeks deified this vice. The goddess Eris exuded a vicious influence on mankind, urging men to war and destruction. The Holy Spirit enthrones this evil spirit, not in some mythical Greek pantheon but in the unregenerate Adamic nature. We see it at work in Cain's animosity toward Abel. It sprang full grown into the world consequent upon the fall of man.

The next work of the flesh is "emultations." The word here is *zēlos,* which gives us our English word *zeal.* It stands for jealousy when it is used in a bad sense. Another man gets the promotion we were anticipating; someone else gets a louder round of applause than we do; another preacher outshines us in the pulpit, draws bigger crowds, pastors a larger church, or drives a better car, and, at once, we face the crossroads where *zelos* stands. *Zelos* can draw us into admiration and a desire and determination to emulate our rival, or it can lure us down the road to bitter animosity and resentment. When it is one of the works of the flesh, it has its source not in love but in enmity. The personal element is always strong in this passion.

Then comes "wrath." The word is *thumos.* In the Apocalypse it is used seven times to describe the wrath of God (Rev. 12:12; 14:8, 10, 19; 15:1, 7; 16:1; 18:13). It speaks of hot anger and passion. God's wrath is always righteous wrath; ours is usually sinful. Here in Galatians, it follows hard on the heels of "jealousies," which, when allowed to ferment in the soul, break out in wrath. The word can be translated as "bad temper," or "outbursts of rage." It describes not so much a smoldering anger as anger that flares up and dies. Even so, it can do a great deal of damage. Bad-tempered people might get over their ill humor, but they leave scars in other people's memories that are not so quickly erased. Moses, in a sudden fit of temper, smote the rock when he had been told to speak to it, and he called God's people "rebels." For this infraction, he was locked out of the Promised Land (Num. 20:10–12). Temper is a serious matter when it blazes out in the lust and energy of the flesh.

The next item in the list is "strife." The word here is *eritheia.* It can be translated "factions," "ambition," or "rivalry." It refers to the party spirit that has so often promoted the splitting of the church into rival denominations. It comes from a word meaning "hireling" and hence came to be associated with the desire to win a following. It is one of the fruits of jealousy. All such things are quite contrary to the spirit of Christ.

The next word is "seditions." It comes from the word *dichostasia.* It means literally "standing apart." It gives us our English word *dichotomy.* In Romans, Paul warns the believers to mark those who cause divisions *(dichoatasia)* and to avoid them (Rom. 16:17). Those who split churches often think themselves spiritual. The Holy Spirit bluntly labels this spirit as one of the works of the flesh. It is often a direct result of the party spirit that is condemned under the previous word in this list. We can see this kind of work in all walks of life. All religious systems split and divide. Scientists split into warring factions over rival theories; politicians differ heatedly, often violently, over political issues; and educators fight over the relative values of opposing programs. Hardly an issue in life exists over which men will not squabble and divide. It is this very divisive factor in the sin equation that ruins every one of Satan's attempts to produce that one-world society toward which he has been working throughout the ages of time. Even when he does manage to force all people into one empire, ruled by his special agent, the Antichrist, it will not last long. The eastern half of the empire will split off and set the stage for Armageddon (Rev. 16:12–15).

Then, we have "heresies." The word used is *hairesis,* and it is used of the Sadducees (Acts 5:17) and the Pharisees (Acts 15:5). This is the word that the orator Tertullus used in his tirade against the apostle Paul and what he called "the sect of the Nazarenes" (Acts 24:5). Originally, the word was not necessarily a bad word. Heresy is a division that is thoroughly established and organized around false teaching. Heresies are a work of the flesh. They abound in religion because of the total spiritual blindness of the unregenerate man (1 Cor. 2:14). Indeed, the more outrageous the error, the more people seem to be disposed to believe it. Mormons believe that a dissolute character named Joseph Smith found some plates written in Egyptian hieroglyphics that he was able to translate—with the aid of some magic glasses—into the *Book of Mormon,* which was composed in imitation King James English style. They believe that God has a body and that Jesus was a polygamist. They believe the lie of the Devil: "Ye shall be as gods."

Christian Scientists pin their faith in the metaphysical meanders of Mary Baker Glover Patterson Eddy, who, despite the fact that she buried three husbands and eventually died herself, proclaimed death to be an error of the mortal mind and pain to be an illusion. Jehovah's Witnesses mock at the Trinity; believe that Jesus was Michael the archangel; deny the biblical doctrine of hell; deny the literal, bodily resurrection of the Lord Jesus; believe that He returned in 1914, claim that only 144,000 people can be born again; and make general mayhem of Bible prophecy.

And so it continues. In the early church, heresies raised their head, Gnosticism being the most dangerous of them, but the brand of teaching that the Judaizers propagated in Galatia was almost as bad. Heresy is the end result of the previous six works of the flesh.

Next, Paul lists "envyings." The word is *phthonos,* which is used invariably in the New Testament in a bad sense (Matt. 27:18; Mark 15:10; Rom. 1:29; Phil. 1:15; 1 Tim. 6:4; Titus 3:3; James 4:5; 1 Peter 2:1). Envy is a malicious spirit of displeasure that results in some people when they see or hear someone else being advantaged or praised. Solomon said that envy is "the rottenness of the bones" (Prov. 14:30). Whereas jealousy desires to have what someone else has, envy simply wishes that he could be deprived of it. Envy motivated the religious leaders of Israel to deliver the Lord Jesus into the hands of the Romans for crucifixion, and Pilate recognized that fact (Matt. 27:18). Envy is malicious and spiteful and has no redeeming features at all.

Next comes "murders." The first sin after the Fall was murder (Gen. 4:8). The voice of the murdered man's blood reached the ears of God. Because of this sin, a further curse was pronounced against the earth. Cain realized that he was now under the divine sentence and had become a vagabond. He feared for his own life and voiced his despair. Rather than make an example of him, God marked him and allowed him to depart protected but henceforth a rebel.

The society that he founded was so filled with violence (Gen. 6:11) that, after the Flood, God instituted capital punishment for the crime of murder (Gen. 9:6). That punishment was formally ratified in the Mosaic Law (Lev. 24:21). God has never revoked this requirement that society execute the murderer. It is ratified in Paul's letter to the church in the legislative capital of the world (Rom. 13:1–4). One reason why murder is so common in our modern society is that modern sociologists think that they know better than God does. They are more concerned with the "rights" of the murderer than with the rights of his victim. Consequently, capital punishment is either outlawed altogether or hedged about with so many delays, appeals, and protests that the murderer usually escapes the due reward of his deed. God places a very high value on human life. When a society condemns a murderer to life imprisonment and then, after a number of years, paroles him or turns him loose, it defies the divine decree. That society reaps what it sows is increasing violence.

Next on the list is "drunkenness." The word is *methē* and stands for overindulgence in strong drink. It is one of the most common of the sins that afflict mankind. Drunkenness weakens a person's control over his words and actions. It leads to all kinds of other sins. Our society is very tolerant of drunkenness. We have whitewashed even the word, preferring to call a person an alcoholic, rather than a drunkard. One prime example of society's indulgence of this vice is seen in its attitude toward drunk driving. People who are under the influence of alcohol are allowed to commit mayhem on our highways, assured that soft laws and indulgent judges will let them off with little more than a rap on the knuckles. Even where sterner laws are enacted, we still allow brewers and distillers to manufacture, advertise, and distribute their poisonous wares. We call alcoholism "a disease," then allow people to do everything in their power to spread it.

The first drunkard in the Bible was Noah. His besotted condition gave occasion to Ham to exhibit his own wicked nature. This brought down God's curse upon Canaan, Ham's son and the progenitor of the vile Canaanite race (Gen. 9:21).

The second drunkard was Lot. Having escaped the overthrow of Sodom by the very skin of his teeth, he sought refuge, with his two surviving daughters, on a nearby hill. His unscrupulous daughters had a conference and then, systematically, made their father drunk on two successive nights and committed incest with him in his stupor. As a result, they gave birth to Moab and Ammon. These children, in turn, became the progenitors of two nations that became Israel's bitterest and most persistent foes.

When David wanted to cover his sin with Bathsheba, he first arranged for Uriah, her husband, to be sent home on leave. To ensure the success of his crafty scheme, he made Uriah drunk. He hoped, of course, that he would go home and have relations with his wife so that David's own sin might be concealed. Bathsheba could then claim that the son, already conceived, was Uriah's. Unfortunately (or fortunately, indeed), David's scheme failed. Uriah was a better man than David, and he had more honor and higher principles, as the story reveals. When Uriah's sense of loyalty was stronger even than his unintentional intoxication, David resorted to murder (2 Sam. 11:1–15).

Zimri, the captain of Asa's guard, murdered him, the unsung and useless king of Israel, while he was "drinking himself drunk" (1 Kings 16:8–10). When Nahum pronounced Nineveh's doom, he foretold that drunkenness would contribute to the great city's downfall (Nah. 1:10). While he was drunk, Belshazzar crossed that hidden boundary line between God's mercy and His wrath (Dan. 5:1–5). Drunkenness is an ill odor throughout the Bible. In the Old Testament, a man who had a drunkard for a son could invoke the death penalty against him (Deut. 21:20). In the church, drunkenness is one of the sins for which a man can be excommunicated (1 Cor. 5:11). One of the classes of people whom Paul says will not inherit the kingdom of God are drunkards (1 Cor. 6:10).

The last sin in the list is "revellings." The word is *kōmos.* It occurs three times in the New Testament, is always in the plural, and is always in close company with drunkenness. The word can be rendered "orgies," or "carousing." The word was used to describe the licentious groups of devotees of Bacchus, the god of wine. It suggests revelry that goes beyond the barriers of restraint, revelry that has degenerated into license. It conjures a picture of all kinds of immorality, a sin that is often a near neighbor of drunkenness.

What a list! It is not exhaustive because Paul adds, "and such like," indicating that it would be possible to expand it. What a terrible portrait the Holy Spirit has drawn of man in sin. He has set before us the picture of an adulterous, foul, and licentious person, one given to idolatry and the dark sins of witchcraft; a hateful, quarrelsome person, jealous and bad tempered; one who causes dissension; and one who is envious, murderous, habitually drunk, and debauched. Truly, God never made man to be like that! Satan caused man to become like that. The flesh is what makes people behave like that.

No wonder Paul adds, "Of the which I tell you before [I solemnly avow], as I have also told you in time past, that they which do such things shall not inherit the kingdom of God" (v. 21b). The word for "do" here is *prassō,* and it means "to practice." It stands in contrast with *poieō,* which is used in verse 17.

According to W. E. Vine, *poieō* signifies an action that is complete in itself; *prassō* signifies, as a rule, the habit that results from continually repeating the action.[2] Both words occur in Paul's concluding indictment of heathen behavior: "Who knowing the judgment of God, that they which *commit* [*prassō,* 'practice,' 'keep on doing'] such things are worthy of death, not only *do* [*poieō*] the same, but have pleasure in them that *do* [*prassō,* 'keep on doing'] them" (Rom. 1:32). The indictment is then carried over to the hypocrite: "Therefore thou art inexcusable, O man, whosoever thou art that judgest: for wherein thou judgest another, thou condemnest thyself; for thou that judgest *doest* [*prassō,* 'keep on doing'] the same things" (Rom. 2:1).

The point is that the people whom Paul here excludes from the kingdom of God make a habitual practice of some or all of these terrible sins. He says the same thing in 1 Corinthians 6:9–11, where he gives a similar list of sins. He differentiates there between the genuine believer and the unregenerate person,

2. C. F. Hogg and W. E. Vine, *The Epistle to the Galatians* (Grand Rapids: Kregel, 1921), 284.

who makes a practice of these sins. "And such were some of you," he says, "but ye are washed, but ye are sanctified, but ye are justified in the name of the Lord Jesus, and by the Spirit of our God" (1 Cor. 6:11). A similar list found in Romans 1:24–32 ends with the blunt statement that "they which commit such things are worthy of death" (v. 32).

We cannot get into the kingdom of God by our own efforts to be good and to keep the Law. But we can certainly be kept out of the kingdom of God by practicing these sins. It is possible to practice these things so long that we actually are identified with them. Thus, we call a person a liar, a thief, or a drunkard, for instance. Such a person has so surrendered himself to the sin in which he is involved that he has become mastered by it.

When we are genuinely saved, the Lord cleanses us from such sins and emancipates us from their hold over our lives (Rom. 6:6–7; Rev. 1:5). As Charles Wesley's hymn "O for a Thousand Tongues to Sing" puts it,

> He breaks the power of cancelled sin
> And sets the prisoner free;
> His blood can make the foulest clean,
> His blood avails for me.

It is possible for a child of God to fall into any of these sins, to his shame, and then to be restored under the chastisement of God, the conviction of the Holy Spirit, or the caring ministry of another faithful believer. The person whose life is controlled by these kinds of sin, however, is in serious peril. Jesus said, "Ye shall know them by their fruits. Do men gather grapes of thorns, or figs of thistles? Even so every good tree bringeth forth good fruit; but a corrupt tree bringeth forth evil fruit. A good tree cannot bring forth evil fruit, neither can a corrupt tree bring forth good fruit. Every tree that bringeth not forth good fruit is hewn down, and cast into the fire. Wherefore by their fruits ye shall know them" (Matt. 7:16–20). The primary application of this lesson is to false prophets, but the passage applies equally to those who have a false profession.

It is true, of course, that every blood-bought believer has two natures, the one incorrigibly bad and the other incorruptibly good. The indwelling Holy Spirit in the believer never ceases to war against both the believer's old Adamic nature and against its works (Gal. 5:17). No genuine believer can reconcile himself to the habitual practice of the works of the flesh. If all evidence of the new birth is absent from the life of the person who professes to be saved, obviously he is not saved. His habitual practice of sin proves it. The New Testament continually warns us not to be deceived along these lines (John 3:20; Rev. 21:8; 22:15).

Paul says of such people that they "shall not inherit" the kingdom of God. The word *inherit* is *klēronomeō,* which is used in a variety of ways in the New Testament. It includes in its embrace all that we have in Christ and that is promised to us as children of God. It takes in the believer's birthright and all that is to be ours in the age to come. The emphasis is on all that is ours as the free gift of God (Matt. 19:29; Mark 10:30; Gal. 4:30; Heb. 1:4; 12:17). If, as the Lord Jesus told Nicodemus, no one can even so much as see the kingdom of God apart from the new birth (John 3:3), still less can one earn its inheritance by the deeds of the Law. It is an inheritance. An inheritance cannot be earned; it is bestowed.

Some people think that the expression "shall not inherit the kingdom of God" refers to loss during the coming millennial age or even, perhaps, exclusion altogether from the kingdom in its millennial phase. Govett argues this view thus:

> There are two things set before the believer; "the *gift* of God," which is eternal life (Rom. 6:21), and "the *prize* of our calling" (Phil. 3). Eternal life is God's assured blessing to all believers. But our obtaining the prize of our calling turns upon our conduct after faith. God will manifest His displeasure with offending sons of His, even though He finally admits them to His bliss. He has appointed a day of a thousand years, in which each shall be dealt with, according to his works.[3]

Other people think that the warning both here in Galatians and in similar Scriptures goes far beyond that. W. E. Vine says, "The practice of the vices is presumptive evidence of the absence of that new birth which is the sole qualification for heirship. This expression cannot be confined to the Millennial period. . . . These things call for 'the wrath of God upon the sons of disobedience' . . . such cannot have an inheritance of even a limited character in the kingdom of God; their end is to endure the wrath of God, their portion is 'the second death.'"[4] To which we might add that the Bible confidently expects that, once a person has been "born . . . of the Spirit" (John 3:5), he will begin to exhibit the evidence of a new life in Christ (2 Cor. 5:17). He will begin to loathe the things that once he loved and will begin to love the things that once he loathed. He will begin to

3. R. Govett, *Govett on Galatians* (London: Thynne and Co., 1930), 198.
4. Hogg and Vine, *Galatians,* 288–89.

show, in some degree at least, the fruit of the Spirit. That is Paul's next theme in this epistle.

b. The spiritual man revealed (5:22–23)

Now comes what Paul calls the fruit of the Spirit. "But!" Oh, that mighty word *But!* Said the prodigal, "I will arise and go to my father, and will say unto him, Father, I have sinned against heaven, and before thee, and am no more worthy to be called thy son: make me as one of thy hired servants. And he arose, and came to his father. *But* . . ." (Luke 15:18–20).

We read of King Uzziah, "And he made in Jerusalem engines, invented by cunning men, to be on the towers and upon the bulwarks, to shoot arrows and great stones withal. And his name spread far abroad; for he was marvellously helped, till he was strong. *But* . . ." (2 Chron. 26:15–16).

We read of David, "And it came to pass, after the year was expired, at the time when kings go forth to battle, that David sent Joab, and his servants with him, and all Israel; and they destroyed the children of Ammon, and besieged Rabbah. *But* . . ." (2 Sam. 11:1–2). David broke his heart in the greatest of all of his messianic psalms: "My God, my God, why hast thou forsaken me? why art thou so far from helping me, and from the words of my roaring? O my God, I cry in the daytime, *but* . . ." (Ps. 22:1–2).

In one of his catalogs of human sin, Paul summarizes, "Among whom also we all had our conversation in times past in the lusts of our flesh, fulfilling the desires of the flesh and of the mind; and were by nature the children of wrath, even as others. *But* . . ." (Eph. 2:3–4).

*But!* That little word is the hinge upon which great events and great truths turn. So it is here: "Now the works of the flesh are manifest, which are these . . . they which do such things shall not inherit the kingdom of God. But . . ." (Gal. 5:19, 21–22).

"But the fruit of the Spirit is . . ." The word for fruit is *karpos,* a word that is often used in the New Testament in its natural sense—that which is produced by the energy of the living organism. It is used here to describe that which is produced in the life of the believer by the energy of the indwelling Holy Spirit. Lust works secretly and displays itself in the works of the flesh. The Holy Spirit works secretly and reveals His presence by the traits of character that Paul now lists.

The first three fruits of the Spirit are *emotional:* "love, joy, peace" (v. 22a). The first fruit of the Spirit is *love, agapē.* The common word for love among the

Greeks was *philanthrōpia,* from which we get our word *philanthropy*. It did not go higher among the Greeks than giving a man his due. The word ranked far lower than the New Testament word *philadelphia,* the love of one believer for another, genuine brotherly love. *Agapē* is spontaneous love, love irrespective of "rights." It is the word commonly used in the New Testament to describe the matchless love of God. Henry Drummond demands,

> What is the *summum bonum,* the supreme good? You have life before you. Once only you can live it. What is the noblest object of desire, the supreme gift to covet? [Love!] The greatest of these is love. . . . A man is apt to recommend to others his own strong point. Love was not Paul's strong point. . . . The hand that wrote, "The greatest of these is love," when we meet it first, is stained with blood. . . . Paul begins by contrasting love with other things that men in those days thought much of. . . . He contrasts it with eloquence. . . . He contrasts it with prophecy. . . . Then Paul contrasts it with sacrifice and martyrdom. . . . You can take nothing greater to the heathen world than the impress and reflection of this Love of God upon your character. That is the universal language. It will take you years to speak in Chinese, or in the dialects of India. From the day you land, that language of Love, understood by all, will be pouring forth its unconscious eloquence. . . . You can take nothing greater. . . . It is not worth going if you take anything less.[5]

Referring to 1 Corinthians 13:4–6, Drummond says,

> Paul in three verses, very short, gives us an amazing analysis of what this supreme thing is. As you have seen a man of science take a beam of light and pass it through a crystal prism, as you have seen it come out on the other side of the prism broken up into its component colours . . . so Paul passes this thing Love through the magnificent prism of his inspired intellect, and it comes out on the other side broken up into elements. And in these few words we have what one might call the spectrum of love. . . . Notice that they have common names; that they are virtues which we hear about every day; that they are things which can be practiced by every man in every place in life. . . . The spectrum of love has nine ingredients: patience ("love suffereth long"), kindness ("and is kind"),

---

5. Henry Drummond, *The Greatest Thing in the World* (London: Collins, 1930), 47–51.

> generosity ("love envieth not"), humility ("love vaunteth not itself, is not puffed up"), courtesy ("love doth not behave itself unseemly"), unselfishness ("seeketh not her own"), good temper ("is not easily provoked"), guilelessness ("thinketh no evil"), sincerity ("rejoiceth not in iniquity, but rejoiceth in truth").[6]

Love! It is the sum and substance of the Christian life. It all began with love. Love flooded this sin-cursed planet even before Adam's fateful fall. The Old Testament prophet first picks up and then puts down that great word from God: "Yea, I have loved thee with an everlasting love: therefore with lovingkindness have I drawn thee" (Jer. 31:3).

When Moses wrote his memoirs, he sought for an explanation of God's extraordinary love for Israel, a love that burst all barriers and triumphed over all provocations, a love that took minimal account of Israel's continual murmurings, complainings, rebellion, and unbelief but that, in spite of all, brought the nation to the Promised Land. God looked at the Hebrews. He knew them only too well. He had "suffered . . . their manners in the wilderness" (Acts 13:18). He could find only one explanation: "The LORD," he said, "loved you, and because he would keep the oath" (Deut. 7:8).

The gospel begins on the same high note. Never have greater words been penned than these: "God so loved the world, that he gave his only begotten Son, that whosoever believeth in him should not perish, but have everlasting life" (John 3:16). Well might we sing Frederick M. Lehman's hymn "The Love of God":

> Could we with ink the ocean fill,
> And were the skies of parchment made,
> Were every stalk of earth a quill,
> And every man a scribe by trade,
> To write the love of God above,
> Would drain the ocean dry.
> Nor could the scroll contain the whole,
> Though stretched from sky to sky.

6. Ibid.

"God is love" (1 John 4:8). Jesus came to demonstrate the truth of that declaration. He exhibited love as a babe, as a boy, as a teenager, and as a man. He manifested love in the home, in the classroom, on the playground, in the synagogue, and at the workbench. He revealed love when tramping the highway, when on the sea, and when in the temple. Ever and always, He displayed this one great truth about God: God is love. He displayed it with every breath He breathed. He demonstrated love in action in a particularly memorable, undiluted, down-to-earth way. There was never a road too rough, never a way too long, never an appeal too faint, never a case too hard, never a sob too late, and never a day too long for His love. Now it was an aristocratic Pharisee coming to Him in the dead of night, then it was a wicked woman at a wayside well at high noon. Now it was a dead little girl, then a demon-possessed little boy. Now it was a loathsome leper, then a woman with an issue of blood. Now it was Nathanael under a fig tree, then it was Zacchaeus up a sycamore tree. Now it was a wedding that had run out of wine, then it was a funeral and a woman who had been robbed of her only son. Now it was a publican, next a peer of the realm. Now it was a hungry multitude, then some frightened disciples in the grip of a howling gate. Always, love found a way to dry the tears and calm the fears.

Love! The word breathed through His teaching. He summarized all 613 commandments of the Mosaic Law in the one word—*love!* He said, "Thou shalt love the Lord thy God with all thy heart, and with all thy soul, and with all thy mind. This is the first and great commandment. And the second is like unto it, Thou shalt love thy neighbour as thyself. On these two commandments hang all the law and the prophets" (Matt. 22:37–40). He said to His disciples, "A new commandment I give unto you, That ye love one another; as I have loved you, that ye also love one another" (John 13:34). But He demanded even more: "I say unto you, Love your enemies, bless them that curse you, do good to them that hate you, and pray for them which despitefully use you, and persecute you" (Matt. 5:44).

Impossible? Not for Him. He loved poor, lost Herod, self-seeking Annas, crafty Caiaphas, and weak and wavering Pilate. He loved them enough to die for them. He loved Peter even as he cursed and swore and denied Him. He loved Judas even as he planted the traitor's kiss on His cheek. He loved the man who punched Him in the face, the man who crowned Him with thorns, the man who smote Him on the head with a reed, and the man who plowed His back with a scourge. He loved the soldier who dropped that heavy cross upon His lacerated back and commanded Him to get going. He loved the men who nailed Him to that tree.

He loved the very men who mocked Him as He died: "Father, forgive them," He said (Luke 23:34). What love:

> Love that no tongue can teach,
> Love that no thought can reach;
> No love like His.
> God is its blessed source,
> Death ne'er can stop its course,
> Nothing can stay its force;
> Matchless it is.[7]

Now then, says Paul, "The fruit of the Spirit is love." It is the love that "many waters cannot quench" (Song 8:7), the love that "suffers long and is kind" (1 Cor. 13:4), the love that "will not let [me] go" (Song 3:4), and the love that is "strong as death" (Song 8:6). Impossible? Of course, it is impossible to us. But it is gloriously possible to the Holy Spirit. Indeed, that is one of His New Testament titles—He is called "the spirit . . . of love" (2 Tim. 1:7).

Let us remind ourselves afresh how the Lord Jesus, as Man, lived His life on earth. He did not live His matchless life in the power of His own deity, although He could have done so because He was never less than God. He allowed the love of God His Father to flow through Him as electrical current flows through a wire, in touch with the power at one end and the need at the other end. As a result, the supernatural, sublime, and superlative love of God flowed through the Lord Jesus at all times, in all places, and under all circumstances.

That same love is to flow through the believer in the same way by means of the Holy Spirit. We cannot manufacture it; neither can the flesh imitate it. The flesh, indeed, can exhibit what it calls love, but it is flawed at best. True love is of God, for God is love. In contrast with the "works of the flesh" is this glorious fruit of the Spirit.

Love took David Livingstone to Africa. "In the heart of Africa," says Drummond, "among the great lakes, I have come across black men and women who remembered the only white man they ever saw before—David Livingstone; and as you cross his footsteps in that dark continent, men's faces light up as they speak of the kind Doctor who passed there years ago. They could not understand him; but they

7. Thomas Kelly, "Glory to God on High!" *Hymns of Worship and Remembrance* (Belle Chasse, LA: Truth and Praise, Inc., 1950), no. 58.

felt the love that beat in his heart."[8] The same was true of Carey in India, Judson in Burma, Hudson Taylor in China, Brainard among the Indians, J. G. Patan among the terrible cannibals of the New Hebrides, George Müller among the orphans of England. Christian love not only has sought to save men's souls but also built hospitals, asylums, leper colonies, orphanages, and homes for the aged. Love sent William Booth to the drunks and derelicts of London's slums. Love led William Wilberforce to strike the blow that freed the slaves in Britain's vast domains. Love sent Lord Shaftesbury to the factories and mines and then to the House of Lords to demand an end to child abuse and harsh labor laws. When all else fails, love never fails. Christianity is Christ, Christ is God, and God is love. Christianity is love in action. The fruit of the Spirit is love.

Then comes *joy*. Joy is not just another word for happiness. Human happiness depends on what happens; joy smiles in the face of even the most adverse of circumstances. Joy takes even Calvary in its stride (Heb. 12:2). Over and over in His last talk with His disciples, with the shadow of the cross black and heavy on His heart, Jesus spoke of joy—His and theirs. "These things have I spoken unto you, that my joy might remain in you, and that your joy might be full" (John 15:11). "Ye shall be sorrowful, but your sorrow shall be turned into joy" (John 16:20). "I will see you again, and your heart shall rejoice, and your joy no man taketh from you" (John 16:22). He said to His Father, "And now come I to thee; and these things I speak in the world, that they might have my joy fulfilled in themselves" (John 17:13). The last thing Jesus did before going out to break His heart in Gethsemane was sing (Matt. 26:30)!

Joy is the stuff of which heaven is made. Joy has its everlasting source in God. The psalmist sang, "Thou wilt show me the path of life; in thy presence is fulness of joy; at thy right hand there are pleasures for evermore" (Ps. 16:11). That statement contradicts the gloomy view that some unsaved people have of heaven as some perpetual prayer meeting that is boring beyond words to describe! Heaven is not like that. In heaven, we shall be in the perpetual presence of God, the One who abounds with exuberant joy. Pleasure was His invention. Heaven rings with song. Heaven is ablaze with light, life, and love. Only once do we read of tears in heaven, and even then one of the high and holy ones vacated his throne to wipe those tears away and point the weeping one to Jesus (Rev. 5:4–6). The only reason John wept at all was because he had not yet caught a glimpse of Jesus in the midst.

8. Drummond, *Greatest Thing in the World*, 50.

Joy is the rainbow, smiling, undaunted, and triumphant in the storm. Joy is the fountain, bursting irrepressibly from the depths of the earth, reaching for the sky. Joy is the sunshine kissing the brow of the mountain far, far above the thunderstorms below. Joy is the happiness of heaven imported by the Spirit of God into a receptive human heart. Joy is the sunbeam lighting the prisoner's cell. Joy is knowing Jesus. Joy is the boundless exuberance of God quickening the pulse of a child of God.

Nobody had more cause to weep and bemoan their circumstances than Paul and Silas in that Philippian jail. They had been seized, stripped, and scourged. Their backs were bleeding; their feet were cramped in the stocks. Their prison was dark and dank, and chains galled their wrists. Their companions were criminals who filled the air with their curses and complaints. They themselves were hungry and thirsty, and they should have been afraid. Outside their enemies would like nothing better than to press even more charges against them. By all human norms, they should have been worried, anxious, and resentful. Instead, they sang! They sang until the prison walls clapped their hands, and the foundation stones beat out the time! Their chains fell off, the doors burst open wide, and the other prisoners were riveted to their beds by awe. That was joy! "Joy unspeakable and full of glory," as Peter would put it (1 Peter 1:8). "Blessed are ye when men shall revile you, and persecute you, and shall say all manner of evil against you falsely, for my sake," Jesus said. "Rejoice, and be exceeding glad: for great is your reward in heaven" (Matt. 5:11–12).

Joy! No wonder the jailor, his wife, and all of his house came to Christ that night! Joy in jail! What that jailor saw in Paul and Silas was more supernatural than the earthquake. What he saw in Paul and Silas was the second fruit of the Spirit—joy. Just that one taste of it, and he wanted more, wanted it for himself and for his family.

Joy! It is what took the martyrs singing to the stake. The proconsul Pliny spoke of it to the emperor Trajan in a now-famous letter. He had found a brand of criminals for whom his most terrible punishments and most dreadful prisons held no terror. The more he persecuted them, the more "the contagion of the superstition spreads!" The imprisoned Christians sang in their cells. The dying martyrs greeted death itself with a cheer. Prisons they transformed into a palace; the meanest food they ate as though it were bread from heaven.

When one of the early Christians, charged with the crime of Christianity, appeared before the Roman emperor, the emperor threatened to banish him. The Christian replied, "You cannot banish me, for all the world is my Father's house."

"But I will kill you," said the emperor.

"No, you cannot kill me, for my life is hid with Christ in God," the Christian said.

"I will beggar you," the emperor said.

"That you cannot do," the Christian replied, "for my treasure is all laid up in heaven."

"I will drive you away from men and see to it that you have no friends left," the emperor responded.

"I have a Friend in heaven who is closer than any brother," replied the Christian. "You cannot separate me from Him. I defy you. There is nothing you can do to hurt me."

Such men do not escape *from* prison; they escape *in* prison. A magic turns prisons into mansions and chains into the glorious bonds of Christ. That magic is the love and joy of the indwelling Christ.

Paul, on the brink of his own martyrdom, wrote, "I am now ready to be offered, and my departure is at hand." He gloried in his approaching martyrdom and faced it with joy. In his martyrdom, he would be as wine (the Bible symbol for joy) poured out. Ignatius, called the Prince of Martyrs, compared the martyr to the meal offering—"God's wheat, ground fine by the teeth of wild beasts, that he may be found as pure bread, a sacrifice to God."

"There is no day in the whole year," wrote Jerome of his own age, "to which the number of five thousand martyrs cannot be ascribed."

"A vast multitude in Rome alone," says Tacitus.

"Inexhaustible wells of martyrs," says another Roman author, "burned, impaled, beheaded."

"Why are you so bent upon death?" an official asked Pionius of Smyrna. "You are so bent upon death that you make nothing of it." The martyr replied, "We are bent, not upon death, but upon life."[9]

The joy of Christ sent the martyrs singing to the most dreadful deaths. It is a fruit of the Spirit. A sour Christian is a contradiction in terms. The only way to keep those joy bells ringing in the soul is to abide in Christ, to walk in the Spirit, and to be filled with all of the fullness of God.

The next fruit of the Spirit is *peace.* There is peace for the Christian in the storm—a calm, untroubled spirit, come what may. Jesus exhibited this peace. He was never in a hurry, never upset, and never disturbed. From the age of twelve,

9. D. M. Panton, *Dawn Magazine,* 15 July 1926, 160–64.

He knew—in terms of His humanity, that is—that He was to die on a cross for the sins of the world. The shadow of the cross crept ever nearer with every day He lived. As the time drew near, He talked about it more and more, but He never showed the slightest fear. It never upset His peace and never disturbed His poise. He lived above the storm.

Simon Peter learned the secret of that peace the day he walked upon the waves. The darkness had come down. The fierce winds whipped the waves into marching mountains, and doom rode the crest of each succeeding billow. Then Jesus had come, walking on those waves as though that was the ordinary way to cross a lake. At the Lord's bidding, Peter himself had dared a step or two. But then a particularly angry wave slapped him in the face. Peter was distracted. He took his eye off Jesus, and, at once, the billows claimed him as their own. He began to sink. He cried out in fear. The Lord reached out and saved him. Back on board, with Jesus by his side, a sense of peace stole into Peter's heart. Peace was having Christ in the vessel and leaving the storm to Him.

"Peace I leave with you," Jesus said, "my peace I give unto you: not as the world giveth, give I unto you" (John 14:27). It is His legacy, bequeathed on the edge of Calvary by the Prince of Peace Himself. His peace was "the peace of God, which passeth all understanding" (Phil. 4:7). He could sleep amid the raging storm. He could await unmoved the approach of a demon-possessed madman, the terror of everyone in that part of the country. He could hold His peace when His enemies baited and badgered, falsely accused, mocked, and railed upon Him. The peace of God garrisoned His heart against all ills and all odds.

It is impossible to think of God being agitated, worried, or upset. He is omniscient, that is, knows all things, including how it's all going to end. He is omnipotent, that is, all-powerful, able to create a hundred billion galaxies with a single word. Nothing can thwart His will or defeat His purpose. He is omnipresent, that is, everywhere; nothing can happen behind His back. The peace of God cannot be disturbed. No man, no combination of men, no demon, and no coalition of demons can break His Olympian calm. It is the unassailable peace of One who is all-wise and all-powerful; who has all things under His control; who overlooks no detail, fears no foe, and makes no mistakes; and One who proceeds majestically onward toward goals and objectives that He Himself has set.

This is the peace that Jesus enjoyed as Man. In every situation, He simply made Himself available to His Father, and the Father, in turn, made His peace available to Him. He had come to do the Father's will and to be "obedient unto death, even the death of the cross" (Phil. 2:8). Quite apart from His own possession, as God, of all the attributes of God, Jesus as Man, drew on the illimitable resources of His Father for all that He needed. As a result, an atmosphere of perfect peace surrounded Him every step of the journey from the cradle to the grave.

After Pentecost, when he had learned how to walk in the Spirit, Simon Peter entered into this peace. Before Pentecost, he bristled at the barest suggestion from a mere serving maid that he was a follower of the Man from Galilee. He could deny his Lord, as much as he loved Him, to save his own skin, even with oaths and curses. After Pentecost, however, we see a different Peter. We see him in person now, arrested by Herod and sentenced to death. His dear friend and colleague, James, had already been beheaded. The date has been set for Peter's execution—tomorrow. Sixteen soldiers took turns ensuring that he wouldn't be rescued. Tomorrow he is going to die.

What is Peter doing? Is he biting his fingernails, breaking out in the cold sweat of fear, and tearing at his fetters? No! Is he pacing up and down his cell, to the end of his tether and back again, plucking up his courage, resolving to die like a man or like a Christian? No! Is he praying that his faith might not fail as it almost had once before? No! He is asleep, sound asleep, rolled up in his cloak and at perfect peace, sleeping like a baby! Peace!

Peace is one of the fruits of the Spirit, ministered to us as we rest in the arms of Jesus as He Himself had rested in the arms of His Father.

World War II broke out in Britain on a Sunday morning. The storm, which had been threatening for years, had come at last. Within the hour, the air-raid warnings were sounding in London. The country was at war, and the world would never be the same again. In one of England's churches, the congregation was just settling down for worship when a member came in and made the announcement: "We are at war." A ripple of consternation swept through the congregation. Soon, loved ones would be torn from their families, herded into the armed forces, and marched off to the front lines. Death and destruction would rain from the skies upon the homes, shops, and schools of everyone, everywhere, without regard for age, sex, or health. A grim silence reigned as people in that church digested the news—war!

Then a man stood up and announced a hymn, Edward Henry Bickersteth's "Peace, Perfect Peace." The song leader must have been inspired.

> Peace, perfect peace, in this dark world of sin?
> The blood of Jesus whispers peace within.

Peace, perfect peace, with sorrows surging 'round?
On Jesus' bosom nought but calm is found.

Peace, perfect peace, with loved ones far away?
In Jesus' keeping we are safe and they.
Peace, perfect peace, our future all unknown?
Jesus we know, and He is on the throne.

Peace, perfect peace, death shad'wing us and ours?
Jesus has vanquished death and all its powers.
It is enough, earth's struggles soon shall cease
And Jesus' call to heaven's perfect peace.

The next three fruits of the Spirit are *evidential.* They provide visible proof of some great work of God that has been wrought in the believer's heart. The first of these fruits of the Spirit is *long-suffering.* The word is *makrothumia,* a compound word derived from *makros* ("long") and *thumos* ("temper"). We know what a short-tempered person is like; he blows up at the slightest provocation. A long-tempered person is the opposite. He has forbearance and plenty of patience. Long-suffering is the capacity of self-restraint in the face of provocation. The person who has developed the fruit of long-suffering does not rush to retaliate or avenge a wrong suffered. Long-suffering, however, is not the same as patience. "Patience is that quality that does not surrender to circumstances or succumb under trial; it is the opposite of despondency and is associated with hope in 1 Thess. 1:3; it is not used of God."[10] Long-suffering is the opposite of anger, and it is used of God (Exod. 34:6; Rom. 2:4; 1 Peter 3:20). It is associated with mercy.

When the children of Israel came to Sinai and Moses disappeared up the mountain to appear before God, the people became impatient. "Up!" they exclaimed to Aaron, "make us gods, which shall go before us; for as for this Moses, the man that brought us up out of the land of Egypt, we wot [know] not what is become of him" (Exod. 32:1). So Aaron made the golden calf and, beneath the very shadow of Sinai, the people sank into shameless idolatry. The sin met with swift punishment, but worse was to follow. God told Moses that He Himself was

10. W. E. Vine, *Expository Dictionary of New Testament Words* (Nashville: Thomas Nelson, 1985), 116–17.

going to abandon the people but that He would send an angel to clear the way for them into the Promised Land. Moses was alarmed. He assumed the role of a mediator and pleaded with God not to abandon His redeemed people: "If thy presence go not with me," he prayed, "carry us not up hence" (Exod. 33:15).

Moses was again summoned to the summit of Sinai. "And the LORD passed by before him, and proclaimed, The LORD, The LORD God, merciful and gracious, long-suffering, and abundant in goodness and truth, keeping mercy for thousands, forgiving iniquity and transgression and sin . . ." (Exod. 34:6–7). Although the people had provoked the living God, the Holy One, beyond anything that we can imagine, He displayed long-suffering. He did not rush to retaliate and avenge. It was necessary, indeed, for God to bring home to the guilty people a sense of His holiness and the outrage of their insolent idolatry; even so, long-suffering was the chief characteristic of His dealing with them.

Paul uses the word *long-suffering* to describe the way God still holds His hand back from visiting His wrath upon the human race for its terrible sins. The long catalog of crimes listed in Romans 1 is capped by the sin of those who, while persuading themselves that they were better than the heathen, nevertheless, did the same things. They were guilty of despising "the riches of his goodness and forbearance and long-suffering" (Rom. 2:4). God's long-suffering, however, is not to be mistaken for weakness, indulgence, or indifference. On the contrary, people who abuse this feature of God's character are really storing up wrath for themselves to be visited surely and certainly at last upon the unrepentant (v. 5).

The great Old Testament example of God's long-suffering is seen in the way He held back the Flood upon the people of Noah's day for 120 years (Gen. 6:3). During that time, Noah preached to the lost world, and God's Spirit continued to strive with men (2 Peter 2:5). It was a time, too, when the ark was being built as a means of salvation for anyone who would heed the message and flee from the wrath to come. But it was all in vain. Peter speaks of those people as being "disobedient, when once the long-suffering of God waited in the days of Noah, while the ark was a preparing" (1 Peter 3:20).

Nobody ever exhibited long-suffering like Jesus. He was long-suffering with His disciples. Even in Gethsemane, when He had especially urged them to watch and pray, they fell asleep. Twice He woke them. The storm was about to break. Judas and the mob were already marching through the night toward them. The disciples needed to pray. At last, He left them to their sleep: "The spirit truly is ready," He said, "but the flesh is weak" (Mark 14:38).

He was long-suffering toward the unbelief of His own generation: "O faithless and perverse generation," He said to the critical crowd at the foot of the Mount of Transfiguration, "how long shall I suffer you?" (Matt. 17:17). That spirit of unbelief would dog His steps all of the long way from the heights of Hermon to the halls of Pilate. Not once did He react.

He was long-suffering with the Samaritans, who, in their religious and racial bigotry and pride, refused Him passage through their village. James and John reacted at once: "Lord, wilt thou that we command fire to come down from heaven, and consume them, even as Elias did?" He replied, "Ye know not what manner of spirit ye are of" (Luke 9:54–55). They had not yet received the Holy Spirit and, consequently, could not exhibit this fruit of the Spirit.

He was long-suffering with Jerusalem (Matt. 23:34–38), staying the well-deserved judgment of God for nearly forty years to give the nation, which had so sinfully rejected Him, a chance to receive His Spirit instead.

He was long-suffering with Judas. Over and over, He let that benighted man know that He knew the full extent of His dishonesty and betrayal and that He was still willing to forgive even at the moment of betrayal itself.

He was long-suffering with Simon Peter and eager to forgive his denial. He was long-suffering with James, His half brother. We shall never know what the Lord Jesus suffered at the hands of this narrow-minded, Pharisaical man during the long years that they lived together in their Nazareth home and while they labored together at the carpenter's bench. But after the Resurrection, when even James's stubborn unbelief could be thawed, He went out of His way to find him and save him (1 Cor. 15:7).

This rare character trait is to be part of our character too. We are to be long-suffering in the face of provocation and insult. How do we react toward that man who is smoking cigarette after cigarette in the nonsmoking section of the restaurant? Or toward that truck driver who bears down upon us from behind on a busy interstate highway, tailgates us, passes us, throws mud from the road all over us, pulls in front of us, blocks our view, and then slows down?

"How often?" Peter demanded. "How oft shall my brother sin against me, and I forgive him?" Then, feeling that he was being magnanimous in the extreme, he added, "till seven times?" (Matt. 18:21). That was the uttermost limit of impetuous Peter's ability to suffer the provocation of a brother. The Lord put it on the plane of the impossible: "I say not unto thee, Until seven times: but, Until seventy times seven" (Matt. 18:22). For that kind of long-suffering, we need a supernatural source of grace, such grace as is to be found only in God. The energy of the flesh might make a fair show of forgiving seven times, but only the Holy

Spirit can enable us to forgive seventy times seven. The Christian life is not just difficult; it is impossible, apart from the Holy Spirit.

The next evidential fruit of the Spirit is *gentleness.* The word used is *chrēstotēs,* the usual word for kindness or goodness of heart. It is goodness in action. It says something for the state of Jonah's spiritual condition that he ran as far away from Nineveh as he could when he learned that he had been commissioned of God to proclaim to the benighted city its impending doom. He was prophet enough to know that the downfall of Nineveh had to be good news for Israel. The words "Yet forty days, and Nineveh shall be overthrown" sounded like sweet music in Jonah's ears. Nineveh was the scourge of the world. Every nation within marching distance of its terrible army lived in fear. Jonah decided that it would take God more than forty days to get him to Nineveh. Indeed, he was willing to die, to be cast overboard and drowned, to ensure that the hourglass of forty days would run its full course.

When, at last, he did go to Nineveh and deliver the ultimatum of heaven, it was to see his worst fears realized. Nineveh repented, and judgment was stayed. The sullen prophet determined to wait it out to the bitter end to see if, perchance, the repentance would prove to be too shallow to change God's mind. Then comes the story of God's goodness and kindness to Jonah. The gourd no less than the gale and the worm no less than the whale were God's instruments to deal with His rebellious prophet. But look at Jonah's bitter complaint against God: "I pray thee, O LORD, was not this my saying, when I was yet in my country? Therefore I fled before unto Tarshish: for I knew that thou art a gracious God, and merciful, slow to anger, and of great kindness, and repentest thee of the evil" (Jonah 4:2).

Jonah knew because Moses knew (Exod. 34:5–7; Num. 14:17–20). He knew because David knew (Ps. 86:5). Jonah knew, Hosea knew (Hos. 11:8–9), and Micah knew (Mic. 7:18–19) that God is good and gentle and kind.

In his memoirs, Moses, reminiscing over God's infinite love and kindness to erring Israel, put it thus: "As an eagle stirreth [the word is *fluttereth*, the same word as in Gen. 1:2] up her nest, fluttereth over her young, spreadeth abroad her wings, taketh them, beareth them on her wings: So the LORD alone did lead him" (Deut. 32:11–12). Many a time, during the days that he had kept Jethro's sheep in the backside of the desert, Moses had observed the ways of the eagle. He had seen those great birds of prey on the wing. He had seen them swoop from the sky, as swift as an arrow, on some unprotected lamb. He had seen those terrible talons sink home and the fierce beak rend and tear. He had seen the massive wings beat as bird and victim soared back skyward before ever he could get there. He had located the eagle's nest, perhaps, maybe had seen the helpless young inside. How different was the eagle now. The fledglings looked up, unafraid, into those piercing eyes and opened their mouths eagerly for what that tearing beak would give. No fear was in that nest, just love, great tenderness, and wondrous gentleness. Even when the time came to break up the nest and to teach the fledglings to fly, it was the same. Kindness broke up the nest. Kindness nudged the young eaglets over the edge and into the yawning abyss below. How else could they learn why they had wings? There was never any fear of a fall. The parent bird itself was there to plunge beneath the falling young ones, to catch them on its outspread wings, and to teach the lesson again. It was all kindness—creature kindness and a faint reflection of the kindness of God.

The kindest man who ever lived was Jesus. And oh, how good and kind He was! Peter summarized his impression of that wonderful three and a half years that he had spent with Jesus in these words: Christ "went about doing good" (Acts 10:38). How kind He was to the mothers of Jerusalem when they sought to bring their little ones to Him, only to be turned away by the officious disciples (Matt. 19:13–15). How kind He was to Jairus and his little girl (Luke 8:50, 55). How kind He was to touch that wretched leper, who came to Him in all of his need (Matt. 8:3). How kind He was to Peter, overwhelmed as he was with guilt and shame (Luke 24:34). How kind He was to the dying thief (Luke 23:42–43). In fact, it is impossible for us to imagine Jesus ever being unkind.

He was the great fulfillment of the Davidic type. Remember how David reached out to poor, lost Mephibosheth! The unhappy man was lame on both of his feet. He had no standing before God or man. Although he was the grandson of a king, Mephibosheth had lost all of his great expectations. He was heir to a lost estate. Worse still, he was the grandson of King Saul, who had tried to murder David on twenty-four different occasions. When David reached out in his grace to Mephibosheth, he said, "Is there not yet any of the house of Saul, that I may show the kindness of God unto him?" (2 Sam. 9:3). That was David! And that, too, was great David's greater Son. He came "out of the ivory palaces, into a world of woe" to show us the kindness of God.

Bernard of Clairvaux caught the truth of it in his great hymn "Jesus, the Very Thought of Thee," which the Christian church has been singing now for some nine hundred years:

Jesus the very thought of Thee
With sweetness fills my breast;
But sweeter far Thy face to see,
And in Thy presence rest.

O Hope of ev'ry contrite heart,
O Joy of all the meek,
*To those who fall how kind Thou art!*
How good to those who seek!

The next fruit of the Spirit is *goodness.* The word used is *agathōsunē.* It refers to that which is characteristically or constitutionally good in itself and beneficial in its effect. The adjective *agathos* is widely used. It is used, for instance, to depict the absolute goodness of God (Matt. 19:17). It is used to describe Barnabas, whom the Holy Spirit says "was a good man, and full of the Holy Ghost" (Acts 11:24). The essential goodness of this man led him to befriend the ostracized Saul of Tarsus after his conversion when everyone else, it seems, doubted the genuineness of it and thought that it was the ploy of a spy (Acts 9:26–27). The same essential goodness of Barnabas motivated him to seek out Saul and bring him to Antioch to spearhead the revival there (Acts 11:21–26). Barnabas, apostolic delegate that he was, must have known that Saul would eclipse him soon. That made no difference to Barnabas. He was interested in only what was good for the church. The same quality of goodness caused him to stand up for John Mark, even to the point of parting company with his beloved friend and colleague Paul (Acts 15:37–39).

The word *agathōsunē* is a synonym to the previous word *chrēstotēs.* In other words, "gentleness" and "goodness" are in the same family of virtues. They are kinfolk, so to speak. The word for goodness, however, is said to be made of sterner stuff. Doing what is *good* might sometimes call for a tougher stand than would be implied simply by the word *gentleness.* The Lord's inherent and essential goodness, for instance, moved Him to use vigorous actions in cleansing the temple (Matt. 21:12). The same essential goodness of the Lord Jesus caused Him to take off the gloves, so to speak, when denouncing the scribes and the Pharisees for their hypocrisy, error, and rejection of Him (Matt. 23). Greek scholars tend to define *chrēstotēs* as the kinder and gentler element in the Lord's perfect character and *agathōsunē* as the sterner element. To be both kind and good is the ideal. This combination causes a loving parent to say a firm "No!" to a child or minor and to back it up with discipline when necessary. Paul commended the Christians of Rome for being "full of goodness" *(agathōsunē).* We know some of them by name, including Jason, Sosipater, Terius, Gaius ("mine host, and of the whole church"), Erastus ("the chamberlain of the city"), and Quartus, whom Paul designates with the delightful description "a brother" (Rom. 15:14; 16:21–23).

Paul says that it would be difficult to find anyone who would die for a righteous man, "yet peradventure [perhaps] for a good man [*agathos*] some would even dare to die" (Rom. 5:7). Men like Barnabas and Gaius are the kind of men for whom other men would die.

Wicked men hate that kind of men too. Something about real goodness is formidable. Real goodness confronts wickedness on a level that strikes to the very conscience of the wicked. In Harold Begbie's case histories of men who, in the early days of the Salvation Army's exploits in the London slums, were converted to Christ from hopeless addiction to drink, Begbie tells the story of "The Plumber." The man was well liked by his workmates. Like the rest of them, he was a foul-mouthed thief and drinking man who was always willing to share a dirty joke. But then he was converted. He no longer drank or swore. He no longer stole. He had suddenly become good, not just a "goody-goody" but a genuinely good man. His goodness first amused, then irked, and eventually infuriated his former companions. They began a program of systematic persecution designed to make his life such a misery that he would be forced to quit his job. His goodness was impenetrable and incorruptible. They came to hate him with a loathing that almost beggars description—just because he was good and they were evil.[11]

Perhaps it is this particular quality of genuine goodness for which we long the most, especially as we get older. We can look back over our lives and see so much that has been spoiled by its lack. We would give anything to be able to go back to this or that particular incident and be able to relive it. To have been good, genuinely good, whereas we gave way to lust, temper, pride, envy, or whatever it was that we did or said. The fact is that we were not good. We had not, as of then, "so learned Christ," despite all of our profession of faith and our reputation as Christians.

The old hymn "There Is a Green Hill Far Away" by Cecil F. Alexander puts it best:

11. Harold Begbie, *Twice Born Men* (New York: Grosset and Dunlap, by arrangement with Revell, 1909), 189–217.

He died that we might be forgiven,
He died to make us good;
That we might go at last to heaven,
Saved by His precious blood.

In one recent edition of a hymnbook, the editor changed that second line to read, "He died to *do* us good." That wording, however, misses the whole point of the verse. Of course, He died to *do* us good, but He died for a far greater reason than that. He died to *make* us good. He died not only to make us good positionally by crediting to our account in glory all of His won impeccable goodness and righteousness (2 Cor. 5:21) but also to make us good practically. Hence, one of the fruits of the Spirit is goodness. It is the work of the Holy Spirit to make us like Jesus. He was good; we are to be good. This goodness is not just a negative quality, a list of the things that we do not do; it is also an active, positive expression of the life of the Lord Jesus in us. It is supernatural goodness. It is the active enemy of all of the works of the flesh. It can be wrought in us only as we, in our humanity, make ourselves available to the Lord Jesus, in all of His deity, so that He, in His incomparable goodness, can be available to us to live His life in us by His Spirit.

The next three fruits of the Spirit are *elemental* (vv. 22c–23), that is, they are the ultimate basics of the Christian life. They are the bare essentials of vital Christianity. They are "the bottom line" of the balance sheet of holy living.

The first such fruit, for instance, is *faith*. The Greek word is *pistis*. This can be either the act or attitude of believing trust or else the quality of faithfulness, dependability, and loyalty. Sometimes "faith" is simply the ordinary, everyday faith that every human being exercises in a thousand ways in the commerce and contacts of normal life. Faith is woven into the very fabric and texture of our lives. Faith has no particular virtue in itself. What is important is the *object* of our faith. Faith can be misplaced and result in disaster. Ordinary, everyday faith becomes saving, securing, and sanctifying faith when it is placed in the Lord Jesus Christ.

Over and beyond this kind of faith is "the gift of faith" (1 Cor. 12:9; Rom. 12:3, 6). Some believers have an extraordinary capacity to trust God and to believe Him for miracles. One such man was George Müller of Bristol, whose whole life and ministry was dedicated to demonstrating to an unbelieving world that God "is, and that he is a rewarder of them that diligently seek him" (Heb. 11:6).

Here in Galatians, the word *pistis* must probably be regarded as the quality of faithfulness and trustworthiness because the other fruits of the Spirit here are all moral qualities. In writing to the church at Rome, Paul said, "What if some did not believe? shall their unbelief make the faith [*pistis,* 'faithfulness'] of God without effect? God forbid," (Rom. 3:3–4). One of God's characteristics is that He is utterly trustworthy, absolutely to be depended upon. He can never break His Word. The dependability of God is manifested in the natural world. The world as we know it was brought into being by ten commandments of God (the words *And God said* occur ten times in Gen. 1, vv. 3, 6, 9, 11, 14, 20, 24, 26, 28, 29). The laws of nature, as we call them, are expressions of this legislative activity of God in creation. We depend on them implicitly. The laws of heat, light, sound, magnetism, gravity, and so on are completely dependable. The laws that govern life, as complex and mysterious as they are, are expressions of the complete faithfulness of God regarding the physical universe. All science is predicated on the assumption that nature's laws are dependable.

God's moral laws are equally fixed. Their outworking in human life and society might be more complex, mysterious, and harder to trace, but they are inviolable. "When lust hath conceived, it bringeth forth sin: and sin, when it is finished, bringeth forth death" (James 1:15). We can be sure that God keeps faith with His own Word as to that. When God makes a promise, He keeps it, whether specifically (to an individual, such as Abraham, or to a nation, such as Israel) or generally. We can bank on the promises of God. God cannot lie (Heb. 6:18). His Word is His bond (Ps. 119:89).

No one was ever more trustworthy than the Lord Jesus. The disciples must have thought that He'd let them down once. After the feeding of the five thousand, "Jesus constrained his disciples to get into a ship, and to go before him unto the other side, while he sent the multitudes away" (Matt. 14:22). Halfway across the lake, they were caught in a violent storm that threatened to sink the ship. "It was now dark," is John's comment as he recalled the incident years later, "and Jesus was not come to them" (John 6:17). He had let them down! Never! We know what happened, and what a thrilling story the disciples had to tell as long as they lived. In retrospect, they would not have missed the experience for worlds!

David Livingstone staked his life on the faithfulness of Jesus. In every great crisis of his life, wandering amid savage tribes, often with death only a hairbreadth away, he would write again in his diary his favorite text: "Lo, I am with you always, even unto the end of the world" (Matt. 28:20). Then he would write down his usual comment: "It is the word of a Gentleman of the strictest and most sacred honor, and that's an end of it!" It never occurred to him to doubt the word of Jesus.

It should never occur to anyone to doubt our word either. The Christian's word should be inviolate. Some years ago, I heard Paul Little, at that time head of InterVarsity Fellowship, tell of a conversation that he once had with a college principal. A young woman had come to an agreement with him to be on the faculty for the coming year. She was a professing Christian, and he had taken her word for it. She was to sign the contract upon her arrival on campus. Shortly before the beginning of the semester, he received a letter from the woman. She had been offered a better-paying position and had decided to take it. She had prayed about it, she said, and had peace about it. Said the college principal bitterly, looking at the gap in his faculty and the problem he would now have in finding a replacement at that late date, "Great! She had the peace; I had the pieces." This young woman knew nothing of even common integrity, much less Christian character. "Who shall dwell in thy holy hill?" David asked the Lord. "He that sweareth to his own hurt, and changeth not" (Ps. 15:1, 4). When a Christian gives his word, he should do what he says for the simple reason that he would not dream of doing anything else. He should be completely dependable. It is a fruit of the Spirit.

The next fruit of the Spirit is *meekness.* The word is *praotēs,* a word not readily translatable into English. The word *gentleness* has been suggested. Aristotle's definition is sometimes cited: "The midpoint between excessive proneness to anger and incapacity for anger." In English, the word *meekness* is often equated with weakness, for which it is not a synonym. The common notion is that meek people are weak people who cannot defend themselves. But meekness in the Bible is the prerogative of strength, not weakness. Meekness is the attitude of heart that accepts the Lord's dealings with us as good, perfect, and acceptable and are not open for dispute or resistance.

The Lord Jesus described Himself as being meek. He said, "Take my yoke upon you, and learn of me; for I am meek and lowly in heart: and ye shall find rest unto your souls" (Matt. 11:29). The Lord Jesus was God manifest in flesh. He possessed in Himself, even when He was living on earth, the inherent power to create a galaxy. As Man, He chose to put Himself at the complete disposal of His Father and the Holy Spirit. He displayed extraordinary power. He had the power to turn water into wine, to multiply loaves and fish, to still the storm, to cleanse the leper, to command the demon hoards, and raise the dead. When Pilate threatened Him, He could look him in the face and say, "Thou couldest have no power at all against me, except it were given thee from above" (John 19:11). When the Sanhedrin sent its minions to arrest Him, all He had to say was, "I AM," and "they went backward, and fell to the ground" (John 18:5–6). He did that to demonstrate the truth of His declaration: "Therefore doth my Father love me, because I lay down my life, that I might take it again. No man taketh it from me, but I lay it down of myself. I have power to lay it down, and I have power to take it again. This commandment have I received of my Father" (John 10:17–18). He further demonstrated His power over His own life when He was on the cross. John tells us that "Jesus knowing that all things were now accomplished, that the scripture might be fulfilled, saith, I thirst" (John 19:28). The word here for "accomplished" is *teleō,* "finished." The Lord Jesus saw them casting lots for His vesture (vv. 23–24) and knew that all that Scripture had foretold of others in connection with His death was finished. Only one more prediction remained for Him to finish (Ps. 69:21). He deliberately fulfilled that prophecy, then "bowed his head, and gave up the ghost" (John 19:30). He had power over every event, even those surrounding His death.

In this context, we must understand His meekness. It was the acquiescence of One who was possessed of unlimited power to all that happened to Him in accordance with "the determinate counsel and foreknowledge of God" (Acts 2:23). Out of great strength He submitted patiently to the terrible indignities and injuries inflicted on Him at His trials and crucifixion.

Archbishop Trench wrote in his sonnet,

> He might have built a palace at a word,
> Who oft-times had not where to lay His head.
> Time was when He, Who nourished crowds with bread,
> Would not one meal unto Himself afford.
> Twelve legions, girded with angelic sword,
> Were at His beck, the scorned and buffeted;
> He healed another's scratch, His own side bled,
> Side, hands, and feet, by cruel piercings gored.
> Oh! Wonderful, the wonders left undone,
> And not less wonderful than those He wrought;
> Oh! Self-restraint passing all human thought,
> To have all power, and be as having none.
> Oh! Self-denying love, cared alone
> For needs of others, never for its own!

The great Old Testament example of meekness is Moses. The Holy Spirit says, "The man Moses was very meek, above all the men which were upon the face of the earth" (Num. 12:3). The Hebrew word for meekness means "to endure with submission what might be evaded," in contrast to another Hebrew word that means, "to bear what cannot be avoided." Moses had not always been meek. There was nothing meek about the Moses who was raised in the courts of Egypt and who was "learned in all the wisdom of the Egyptians." There was nothing meek about that Moses who was "mighty in words and deeds" (Acts 7:22), the man who was the adopted son of Pharaoh's daughter and whom she was grooming for the very throne of Egypt itself. There was nothing meek about the Moses who smote the Egyptian. There was nothing meek about the Moses who stood up to the bullying shepherds at the well in Midian to champion the cause of the daughters of Reuel (Exod. 2:17–18). It took forty years in the wilderness, in the backside of the desert, to distill in Moses' soul the submissive spirit that marked so conspicuously the years of his public ministry. We marvel at how much Moses willingly endured at the malicious tongues and bad temper of Israel for some forty years. Meek indeed! At the burning bush, he had learned that "any old bush will do" to accomplish the purposes of God as long as the fire that burned in that bush is not natural fire but the fire of God.

The incident, which caused the Holy Spirit to draw specific attention to the meekness of Moses, was very personal. Moses' brother, Aaron, Israel's high priest, and his sister, Miriam, Israel's first prophetess, had attacked Moses verbally "because of the Ethiopian woman whom he had married" (Num. 12:1). The typical man will bristle if someone makes a slurring remark about his wife. But Moses displayed such remarkable Christlikeness of character in connection with this insult that God Himself intervened directly, not only to vindicate him and pay tribute to his meekness but also to punish the offenders, Miriam directly (Num. 12:10) and Aaron indirectly (Num. 12:11). Doubtless, the only reason Aaron escaped Miriam's punishment was because he was Israel's high priest, and it was unthinkable that, as such, he should be contaminated with leprosy.

But Moses failed in the area of his greatest strength. In the end, he was kept out of the Promised Land for losing his temper and speaking hastily with his lips (Num. 20:3–12; Ps. 106:33).

Meekness as a fruit of the Spirit is much discounted by most people, but it is a trait eminently to be cultivated. The Lord Jesus promised, "Blessed are the meek: for they shall inherit the earth" (Matt. 5:5). No quality could be regarded as less desirable, according to this world's standards, in those who would conquer the world than meekness. What Alexander, Caesar, Genghis Khan, Napoleon, Hitler, or Stalin ever imagined meekness to be the key to world conquest? But Jesus did. When He finally presented Himself to Israel as the nation's long-awaited Messiah, He rode into Jerusalem in triumph—on a donkey! How the Romans must have laughed. But here is what the Holy Spirit says: "All this was done, that it might be fulfilled which was spoken by the prophet, saying, Tell ye the daughter of Sion, Behold, thy King cometh unto thee, meek, and sitting upon an ass, and a colt the foal of an ass" (Matt. 21:4–5; Zech. 9:9).

Britain's General Lord Allenby finally won the decisive victory that wrested Palestine and Jerusalem from the despoiling hand of the Turks. The day came for his triumphant entry into the city. He rode up to the gate of the city on his horse. There, he dismounted, bared his head, and walked humbly into the city. When asked why he had not ridden his horse into the city, as the Kaiser had on his state visit to Jerusalem years before, Lord Allenby replied, "It was not fitting for me to ride a horse where my Lord was content to ride a donkey."

The final fruit of the Spirit is *temperance.* The word is *enkrateia,* which comes from the word *kratos,* meaning "strength." In modern usage, *temperance* is more or less limited to abstinence from alcohol. However, that use is too restricted for the word as it is used. The word is sometimes rendered "self-control," but one must be careful in using it thus because even unregenerate people can exercise remarkable self-control. As a fruit of the Spirit, it evidently means more than self-control, as that virtue is practiced by the unregenerate and even by carnal and worldly Christians in some areas of their lives. In his letter to the Corinthians, for instance, Paul points out that athletes, preparing for some great event, are "temperate [*enkrateuomai*] in all things," that is, they exercise self-control (1 Cor. 9:25). The reference is to the rigid regime and severe training that athletes impose upon themselves, over many months, to achieve their goals. In the same letter, he advised single people who were unable to restrain their appetites to get married: "I say therefore to the unmarried and widows, It is good for them if they abide even as I. But if they cannot contain [i.e., have not self-control, *engkrateuomai*], let them marry: for it is better to marry than to burn [*puroomai,* literally 'to glow with heat']" (1 Cor. 7:8–9). The word *enkrateia* means self-control in all things, and it was used to describe the person who had powerful passions but kept them under control.

When Paul stood in chains before Felix and Drusilla, making his first great defense before a Roman governor, he not only sought to clear himself of the trumped-up charges brought against him but also characteristically went after the soul of Felix. We read that "as he reasoned of righteousness, temperance [*enkrateia*], and judgment to come, Felix trembled" (Acts 24:25). Well he might. The emperor Claudius had made him procurator of Judea in A.D. 52, but he was noted for his cruelty and treachery. Drusilla was the daughter of Herod Agrippa I, but she had walked out on her husband, Azizus, King of Emesa, in order to marry Felix.

As with all of the other fruits of the Spirit, we turn to the Lord Jesus for a glimpse of this one. Think how perfect was His self-control at the time of His trial. How magnificent was His self-control before Caiaphas, whose mean soul He could read like an open book! How calm He was when confronted by a whole string of false witnesses that the chief priests and elders had hired to testify against Him. He simply "held his peace," Matthew says (26:59–63). How complete was His self-control when, having finally broken His silence to confess His deity when He was put under oath, the members of the Sanhedrin spat in His face and slapped and smote Him, taunting Him, "Prophesy unto us, thou Christ, Who is he that smote thee?" (Matt. 26:67–68).

Think of His self-control before Herod. There sat that godless man surrounded by soldiers. There stood the chief priests and the scribes. Herod would have given anything to see this magician do one of His magic tricks. The Jewish authorities "stood and vehemently accused him." Herod plied Him with questions. But Jesus said nothing. Then "Herod with his men of war set him at nought, and mocked him, and arrayed him in a gorgeous robe, and sent him again to Pilate" (Luke 23:8–11). Nothing disturbed His self-control.

Think of the calm poise with which He confronted Pilate. How seldom He broke His silence and then only to make clear to Pilate exactly with whom he was dealing. The scourging, the ribald mockery of the soldiers, the unjust and cowardly sentence of the governor, the insulting preference of the Jews for Barabbas, and their shrill demand that He be crucified, and that, too, after all of the love and kindness that He had bestowed on them in so many marvelous and wonderful ways. Nothing could break His self-control.

Follow Him to Calvary. See the dignity with which He submitted to the soldiers who were to drive the nails through His hands and feet. Listen to Him pray earnestly for their forgiveness. See Him provide for His mother and hear Him promise the dying thief a home in heaven. Not once did He lose His sublime self-control. His mind, heart, and will were under the control of His spirit, right down to the moment when He sovereignly dismissed that spirit, bowed His head, and died.

Temperance! Self-control! It is listed as a fruit of the Spirit. This is not a result of the mind, the emotions, and the senses being brought under the control of the human will; it is a result of the human will being brought under the control of the Holy Spirit. The Holy Spirit thereby energizes the human will to produce this fruit of the Spirit, self-control.

A delightful person to meet is the person in whom the fruit of the Spirit is well developed and in full display. Such a person is loving, full of joy, calm, and peaceful, come what may. Such a person is patiently submissive to God at all times and under all circumstances. He is gentle, good, completely dependable, strong, and quite above reacting to provocation. We have met such people. We have envied their poise. Paul tells us next how the humblest child of God can cultivate such fruit.

### 3. The practice of Christlikeness (5:24–26)

He underlines two essentials. First, there must be *death to the flesh:* "They that are Christ's have crucified the flesh with the affections and lusts," Paul says (v. 24). He is saying that the fruit of the Spirit cannot be generated by any energy or efforts of the flesh. The Judaizers were offering the Galatians the Law as a means of restraining the evil tendencies of the flesh. Paul knew only too well (Rom. 7) that the Law, far from restraining such tendencies, only stimulated them to greater activity. The fruit of the Spirit cannot be produced by any human efforts to keep the commandments.

The cultivation of the fruit of the Spirit is along different lines altogether: "they that are Christ's have crucified the flesh with the affections and lusts." God's answer to the flesh—all of it and all of its passions and lusts—is the cross. The expression "have crucified" refers to a definite act. We appropriate what was accomplished for us at Calvary. The very figure of crucifixion militates against the idea that we ourselves do anything about it, except accept an accomplished fact by faith. A man can put himself to death in a variety of ways. He can hang himself, drink poison, cut his throat, or drown himself, but he cannot crucify himself. The figure of crucifixion implies that someone else does the putting to death. God crucifies the flesh with its passions and lusts. By identifying us with Christ in His death, burial, and resurrection, God has put us to death, buried us, and raised us again in newness of life. The moment we receive Christ as Savior, we enter positionally into the good of that deed. Paul anticipates here that we now enter experientially into the good of it.

Because the flesh cannot produce the fruit of the Spirit either with or without the stimulus of the Law, and because in God's sight, the flesh is fit only for crucifixion, how can the fruit be developed? The answer that Paul gives is *life in the Spirit:* "If we live in the Spirit, let us also walk in the Spirit. Let us not be desirous of vain glory, provoking one another, envying one another" (vv. 25–26). Evidently the Galatians were quite out of step with the Holy Spirit. They had become boastful and envious. F. F. Bruce thinks that perhaps they were expressing this kind of behavior in challenging one another to theological debate. The peace of the Galatian churches, already upset by the theological nonsense that the Judaizers were propagating, was being further upset by the carnal wrangling of the believers over the issues involved.

The answer was to produce the fruit of the Spirit. But how was this to be done? They already lived in the Spirit (the *if* here is used in the sense of "because"). They needed now to walk in the Spirit, to keep in step with the Holy Spirit. Again we ask, How is this done? The clue is to be found, as we might expect, in Christ Himself.

The Lord Jesus was God manifest in flesh. Because He was God, all of the fruit of the Spirit was inherent in His divine nature. Love, joy, peace, long-suffering, gentleness, goodness, faith, meekness, and temperance were all characteristics of His nature, person, and personality as God, over all, blessed forevermore. It was impossible for Him ever to act in any other way. He could not deny His own inherent, divine nature.

The Lord Jesus came down to earth. He was Man inhabited by God, the kind of Man that God intended man to be. He could say, "I do nothing of myself; but as my Father hath taught me, I speak these things. And he that sent me is with me: the Father hath not left me alone; for I do always those things that please him" (John 8:28–29). And again, "Believest thou not that I am in the Father, and the Father in me? the words that I speak unto you I speak not of myself: but the Father that dwelleth in me, he doeth the works" (John 14:10). Not once did the Lord Jesus act independently of His Father. The Lord Jesus was coequal, coeternal with the Father, self-existent, God over all, blessed forevermore. But in His blessed and glorious humanity, He always submitted Himself to His Father. That was the secret of His life. Therefore, the fruit of the Spirit was produced in the Lord Jesus from the moment of His birth unto the moment of His death because there never was a moment when He, in His sinless humanity, failed to make Himself available to His Father.

A similar principle applies to us in our regenerated humanity. The Lord Jesus makes Himself available to us by the Holy Spirit, in the measure in which we make ourselves available to Him. The Lord's teaching on the vine (John 15:1–11) makes this point clear. We must draw on all of the divine resources of the Lord Jesus. The Holy Spirit will then develop in us the love, joy, peace, long-suffering, gentleness, goodness, faith, meekness, and temperance that so marked the Lord Jesus in His humanity. As we live in the Spirit, so we are to walk in the Spirit.

C. The law of love for Christ (6:1–6)
   1. The love that woos sympathetically (6:1–2)

Love is the law of life. Love is the primary color in the spectrum of human behavior. Paul demonstrates this fact first in relation to *the backslider:* "Brethren, if a man be overtaken in a fault, ye which are spiritual, restore such an one in the spirit of meekness; considering thyself, lest thou also be tempted" (v. 1).

Into all of the squabbles now raging in the Galatian churches, Paul injects this one word: *brethren!* The first mention of this word in Scripture is of interest here. Abraham and Lot had arrived in the Promised Land. Abraham had built his altar and had called upon the name of the Lord. Then had come the unseemly squabble between the herdsmen of Abraham and the herdsmen of Lot, an event that promised to ruin not only the fellowship of Abraham and Lot but also their testimony. Abraham, the spiritual man, took the lead in resolving the problem. He said, "Let there be no strife, I pray thee, between me and thee, and between my herdmen and thy herdmen; for *we be brethren*" (Gen. 13:8). He then made a proposal that proved what a spiritual giant he already had become, a proposal that involved the surrender of his own rights and prerogatives. "You choose and take whatever you want," he said. "I'll take what's left." Lot's prompt and selfish reaction to the proposition revealed how worldly and carnal he was and how backslidden he was in heart.

"Brethren!" In all matters, except the surrender or compromise of some vital doctrine, Paul was the most conciliatory of men. Even then, he was courteous. Interestingly, the first two disciples of the Lord Jesus in the New Testament were brothers (Matt. 4:18). The next two were brothers too (Matt. 4:21). Whatever else we might or might not be in the family of God, one thing is sure and basic: we are brothers and sisters in Christ. "A brother is born for adversity," said Solomon (Prov. 17:17). Mutual love, respect, and assistance are the thought behind the word. We have much in common. We are brothers.

The word here for "fault" is *paraptōma,* which means "a falling aside." It is used of a breach of God's law, of a moral fall, and of a falling away from the truth. The disobedience of Adam is described under this word (Rom. 5:15, 17–18). In the context, it has in view "the works of the flesh" that were just described. It can also embrace the falling aside of those who were heeding the false teaching of the Judaizers. The word is used in the terrible warning of the apostle against apostasy: "For it is impossible for those who were once enlightened, and have tasted of the heavenly gift, and were made partakers of the Holy Ghost, and have tasted the good word of God, and the powers of the world to come, if they shall fall away [*parapiptō,* the corresponding verb, used only here], to renew them again unto repentance; seeing they crucify to themselves the Son of God afresh, and put him to an open shame" (Heb. 6:4–6). Some of the Galatians were in danger of doing this. It was urgent that the spiritual ones "restore" such people before it was forever too late. Whether moral or doctrinal, some kind of fall is envisioned here.

The word for "overtaken" is *prolambanō,* which can mean "to be found out or detected." It might mean that, or it might mean that the person was inadvertently caught by some trespass, being off guard. This is something quite different from the deliberate and premeditated practice of evil.

The word for "restore" is *katartizō,* a word of wide usage. It is used of James and John, whom the Lord found mending *(katartizō)* their nets (Matt. 4:21). It is used of God's creative activity: "Through faith we understand that the worlds were framed [*katartizō,* 'prepared'] by the word of God" (Heb. 11:3). The apostle prayed that the Hebrew believers might be made "perfect [*katartizō*] in every good work" (Heb. 13:21). Peter uses the word similarly (1 Peter 5:10). Paul urged his Corinthian converts to be "perfectly [*katartizō*] joined together in the same mind and in the same judgment" (1 Cor. 1:10). The Greeks used the word to describe the action of a physician setting a broken bone. Such a procedure called for knowledge, skill, and care. It was not a task for just anyone. Mishandling of a fracture could make it worse.

Hence, Paul declares that "ye which are spiritual" must undertake the task of correcting faults and failings among the brethren. The spiritual person, of course, is the person who is exhibiting the fruit of the Spirit in his life. Tenderly, with love and compassion, calmly, with gentleness and because he is good and in a spirit of meekness, the spiritual person addresses himself to the fallen one. He is like the Good Samaritan of the Lord's parable. He pours oil and wine into the open wound, oil to soothe and wine to cleanse. He picks up the fallen, surrounds him with love, is not afraid of the cost, provides for continuing care (Luke 10:30–35).

All of this is done "in the spirit of meekness." This particular fruit of the Spirit is most helpful in dealing with the fallen. It is very disarming and carries with it no atmosphere of blame. It does not lecture or express censorious surprise and disapproval. It is alive to the weakness of the flesh, aware of how easy it is for anyone to fall.

The person who would thus minister to a brother in need will be "considering" himself lest he, too, be tempted. The word for "consider" is *skopeō.* It is translated "take heed" in the Lord's warning that we look out lest our light be turned to darkness (Luke 11:35). The word refers primarily to a watchman. Paul used it in this sense in telling his Roman friends to watch out for cultists: "Now I beseech you, brethren, mark [*skopeō*] them which cause divisions and offences contrary to the doctrine which ye have learned . . ." (Rom. 16:17). Although the spiritual person will be quick to see a brother's peril and need, he will be ever mindful of his own frailty and danger because temptation lurks in the path of all of us. No state of holiness exists in this life that is beyond temptation. More than one would-be counselor has fallen into the very sin from which he has been seeking to rescue someone else.

The second illustration has to do with the *burden bearer:* "Bear ye one another's burdens, and so fulfil the law of Christ" (v. 2). The law of Christ is the all-encompassing law of love. The Judaizers were trying to load the believers with the intolerable burden of the Law and Jewish tradition. The Lord denounced the religious leaders of His day for this very thing. He said to the multitudes and His disciples concerning the scribes and the Pharisees, "They bind heavy burdens and grievous to be borne, and lay them on men's shoulders; but they themselves will not move them with one of their fingers" (Matt. 23:4). At the Jerusalem conference, convened to consider this very issue, Peter said to his fellow Jewish Christians concerning Gentile believers, "Now therefore why tempt ye God, to put a yoke upon the neck of the disciples, which neither our fathers nor we were able to bear?" (Acts 15:10). The Lord Jesus came to fulfill the Law and to deliver us from its burden.

Far from putting additional legalistic burdens on each other, we should look for opportunities to bear the already heavy burdens that some of our brothers and sisters in Christ are bearing. Such struggling believers are all about us. Some are carrying heavy financial burdens, others have physical infirmities, still others are burdened over wayward loved ones, and some carry a heavy load of guilt and shame. Others are burdened because of unsaved relatives and friends. Some are carrying the burden of a broken home. Some are burdened by the deplorable spiritual condition of their local church. There are plenty of burdens to be shared. The law of Christ, far from causing us to add to burdens already borne, will move us to seek ways to alleviate existing burdens.

Think of Simon the Cyrenian. He made a virtue of necessity and carried the cross for Jesus all of the way to Calvary. We can well imagine the shame and resentment that filled his soul when he was rudely arrested by the centurion and pressed into this distasteful service. The stigma attached to a cross in those days was very real. And the cross was heavy, the way long, and the day hot. But we can well believe that, by and by, his resentment was eroded by the dignity and grateful thanks of the Man Jesus, who stumbled along at his side. The sobs of the women, the sad reply of the Savior, the venom of the priests, the howls of the mob, and the callous indifference of the soldiers—the whole terrible scene impressed itself upon him. Likely enough, he lingered at Calvary long enough to hear the Savior say, "Father, forgive them, for they know not what they do." Perhaps he read the title "Jesus of Nazareth, the King of the Jews." In any case, he became a Christian, an elder of the church at Antioch, and the father of two boys whom the apostle Paul much appreciated (Mark 15:21; Acts 13:1; Rom. 16:13). We can well imagine that he would never get tired of telling people how he had borne the cross for Christ and carried that burden for Him all of the way to Calvary.

We can do the same. Jesus said, "Inasmuch as ye have done it unto one of the least of these my brethren, ye have done it unto me" (Matt. 25:40).

### 2. The love that walks softly (6:3–5)

Paul continues with his practical advice for living the Christian life. He has three words of counsel. First, *mark your own boundaries:* "For if a man think himself to be something, when he is nothing, he deceiveth himself" (v. 3). It is just plain common sense to know one's limitations. Secular and sacred history is strewn with the wreckage of people who, for one reason or another, had inflated egos and exaggerated ideas of their own importance. The Jewish judge Gideon, who earned the well-deserved accolades of a grateful people, had a son, Abimelech, who imagined that he ought to be acclaimed king upon his father's death. He died ignominiously when a woman cast part of a millstone at him and hit him on the head (Judg. 9). Great David had a son named Absalom who had an inflated sense of his own importance and led the tribes in rebelling against his father, the king. He, too, came to a bad end (2 Sam. 15:1–18:15). Solomon's son and heir Rehoboam likewise had an exaggerated view of his power and place. He lost ten of the twelve tribes as a result of his folly (1 Kings 12:1–19).

In modern psychology, the phrase "the Peter Principle" has become almost a cliché. It refers to the mistake of promoting a man beyond the level of his competence in some field. A man might be a first-class salesman, but that does not mean he will be a successful sales manager. Many businesses make the mistake of making a man a company director or the chairman of the board just because he is the son of the founder of the firm. A man's son does not necessarily have his father's intuition, vision, and competence.

In Christian circles, many a church has voted a beloved pastor's son to succeed his father in the pulpit and lived to regret it. D. L. Moody founded two schools, the prestigious Moody Bible Institute in Chicago and the Northfield School in Northfield, Massachusetts. The Moody Bible Institute passed into the hands of evangelist and teacher R. A. Torrey and from thence to Dr. James M. Gray and a succession of other able and spiritual men. Northfield, however, fell into the hands of less capable men who had far less conviction than those who ran the Moody Bible Institute. There was no comparison between the two schools. Moody Bible Institute became a citadel of the faith; Northfield lapsed into liberalism.

Paul is quite right, of course. For a man to overestimate himself, or for that matter to let other people overestimate him, amounts, in the end, to self-deception. Even a man of gift and talent must be careful not to get the idea that he is "somebody." Glorying in one's gifts and talents is a mark of carnality, not spirituality. "No flesh should glory in [God's] presence" (1 Cor. 1:29). Paul says that even if a man speaks with the tongues of men and angels, has the gift of prophecy, understands all mysteries, has all knowledge, beggars himself to minister to the poor, even prepares for martyrdom, and does it all without love, the first fruit of the Spirit, it is all worthless. It is all counterfeit coin, not the true currency of the kingdom (1 Cor. 13:1–3). When the activities of his enemies drove Paul to defend his apostleship, he was careful to conclude his comments by adding, "I be nothing" (2 Cor. 12:11).

So, then, we should mark our boundaries. Love walks softly. Those who are determined to live the Christian life should also *mind their own business.* "But let every man prove his own work, and then shall he have rejoicing in himself alone, and not in another" (v. 4). This is simply a caution to everyone who is engaged in some form of Christian ministry. We should not be addicted to the approval of others. On the contrary, we should continually assess for ourselves the value of our own work. It is not the province of one believer to assess the ministry of another. Each of us is answerable to the Lord Himself. Because our service is to be assessed, and either rewarded or rejected at the judgment seat of Christ, the imperative need for Spirit-directed self-examination is evident (1 Cor. 3:12–15; Rom. 14:10–12).

There are two extremes. One is to have an exaggerated idea of one's own importance; the other is to have such an inferiority complex as to be constantly depreciating one's gifts and ministry. The classic example is Moses. At the end of the first forty years of his life, he was a Hebrew at heart. He had already made the great decision that cost him the throne of Egypt and earned him the high praise of God (Heb. 11:24–26). As a result of his social position, educational background, personal ability, and good looks, he had an extremely good opinion of himself, his importance, his influence, and his ability to do the Lord's work. He thought that he could take on the whole of Egypt single-handedly. He imagined, too, that his brethren had as good an opinion of him as he had of himself. So, he struck a blow for God—with disastrous results. Instead of being Moses the missionary, he became Moses the murderer and woke up belatedly to the fact that he had acted in the flesh, had earned the active hostility of the world, and was liable to criminal prosecution. All of his talents and good intentions were tainted by worldliness. Moreover, the people of God disliked him (Exod. 2:5–14). It must have been a rude awakening for him.

For the next forty years, he was in God's school, unlearning much that he had learned as a young prince in Pharaoh's court. He wandered as a shepherd on the backside of the wilderness. But then he went too far in the opposite direction. When the call of God came, he at once began to make all kinds of excuses. "Who am I?" he protested. "I don't even know your name. The people will not believe me or listen to me. I am a poor speaker. Send somebody else" (Exod. 3:10–4:13).

By the end of his life, however, he had come to a realistic assessment of his life and ministry. His last words, before his great song and final blessing of the tribes, reveal this fact. He handed his lifework over to others. He handed over the Law, especially the book of Deuteronomy, to the Levites with the conscious knowledge that what he had written was divinely inspired: "Take this book of the law, and put it in the side of the ark of the covenant of the LORD your God," he said, "that it may be there for a witness against thee" (Deut. 31:26). However, he knew only too well how little long-lasting effect he had made on the people whom he had served so loyally and for so long. "I know," he said, "thy rebellion, and thy stiff neck: behold, while I am yet alive with you this day, ye have been rebellious against the LORD; and how much more after my death? . . . For I know that after my death ye will utterly corrupt yourselves, and turn aside from the way which I have commanded you . . ." (Deut. 31:27, 29).

Or we could think of Peter's boasting of his love for the Lord one day (Matt. 26:33–35) and of his deprecating himself almost to the point of rendering himself useless in the Lord's work another day (John 21:15–19). Think of King Uzziah's inflated ideas of his own importance, for instance, and the pride of self that made him think that he could take over the priestly ministry in Israel (2 Chron. 26:16–21). Or think of Barzillai's many excuses for not going to Jerusalem to be one of David's counselors (2 Sam. 19:31–37).

Perhaps nobody needs to learn balance more than an author. The comments he receives along the way run all of the way from extravagant praise and eulogies from people who have been helped and blessed by his books on the one hand to sarcastic, biting, unfair, and sometimes malicious comments by critics and reviewers on the other hand.

We must walk above the praise of men on the one hand and the abuse of men on the other hand. Our sole aim should be to please the Lord.

Paul has another word of advice—*move your own burden:* "For every man shall bear his own burden" (v. 5). Some burdens cannot be shared. In verse 2, Paul said, "Bear ye one another's burdens." The word there is *baros,* which denotes a weight, something that presses on one physically (Matt. 20:12). It speaks of that which makes an exhausting demand upon one's resources. But here in verse 5 the word is *phortion,* which is simply something that we have to bear regardless of its weight. The Lord tells us that His burden *(phortion)* is light because no matter how heavy the load He puts upon us, He will take the heavy end (Matt. 11:30). By sympathy and help we can assist someone who is carrying a *baros* kind of burden, but everyone must carry his own *phortion* kind of burden. A person carrying a *baros* kind of burden affords us an opportunity for sharing in the burdens of the Lord's people.

But here Paul reminds us that, at the judgment seat of Christ, we will be on our own. Each will be responsible before the Lord for his own life. Each of us will have to account to the Lord for what we have done, for better or for worse, for richer or for poorer, with the burdens that the Lord has given us to bear. The Lord will not compare Paul's efforts with Peter's and ours with someone else's. In a sense, our *phortion* burdens are a great opportunity to lay up treasure in heaven personally and individually. Indeed, the word actually is used to describe a ship's cargo (Acts 27:10). No captain would want to share that! It is his job to carry that load. He is responsible to carry it as long and as far as the bill of lading declares. His hope of reward and remuneration depends to a large extent on the way he handles that weight. It is his responsibility; he is personally accountable for it.

3. The love that works sincerely (6:6)

Still along the same line, Paul adds, "Let him that is taught in the word communicate unto him that teacheth in all good things" (v. 6). Those who receive instruction in the Word should be willing to help support their teachers financially. The word for "communicate" is *kōinoneō,* which means "to share." Paul uses the word to urge the Roman believers to give to the Lord's work: "Distributing *(kōinoneō)* to the necessity of saints; given to hospitality" (Rom. 12:13). He thanked his friends at Philippi for their generosity to him: "Now ye Philippians know also, that . . . when I departed from Macedonia, no church communicated [*kōinoneō*] with me as concerning giving and receiving, but ye only. For even in Thessalonica ye sent once and again unto my necessity" (Phil. 4:15–16). "The labourer is worthy of his hire," Jesus said (Luke 10:7). Those who teach the gospel are entitled to get their living from the gospel (1 Cor. 9:14).

Paul himself much preferred, personally, to be independent of financial support and often took a job to pay his expenses rather than be a financial burden on an infant church. He never wanted people to say that he was in the ministry for the money. At the same time, he recognized that the Lord's people have a moral and spiritual responsibility to support financially those who minister the Word to them. The full-time worker in the ministry must be sincere in his motives. He does not work for money, and his calling is not just another job. At the same time, those who are blessed by his ministry must be sincere in expressing their appreciation for his labors in the Word. One way to express that appreciation is by giving appropriately toward his financial support.

D. The law of life in Christ (6:7–10)

1. The law logically explained (6:7–8)

The Mosaic Law is no longer binding on the believer. Paul wants his Galatian friends to know that. Love has replaced law as the driving force behind the behavior of a believer. But laws and principles do operate in the life of a believer, and we need to know them. Paul has been spelling them out along the way—the law of liberty in Christ, the law of likeness to Christ, the law of love for Christ, and now, finally, the law of life in Christ.

First, he explains this law. He draws attention to it as, for example, a well-known *law of the soil:* "Be not deceived; God is not mocked: for whatsoever a man soweth, that shall he also reap" (v. 7). The principle is so evident in farming and gardening as to be obvious. The word for "deceived" is *planaō,* meaning "to cause to wander or go astray." The English word *planet* is derived from this word. The ancient astronomers thought that the planets wandered through space in contrast with the fixed stars. Although that word is often used of deceivers, doctrinal error, and religious deceit, it is also used of self-deception.

The word for "mocked" is *muktērizomai.* It occurs only here. It means literally to turn up one's nose at someone. An intensified form of the word *(ekmukterizō)* is used to depict the scorn with which the Pharisees rejected the Lord's teaching regarding the love of money. Luke says, "they derided him" (16:14). The same word is used to describe the mockery of the rulers of Israel at Calvary: "The rulers also with them derided [*ekmuktērizō*] him" (Luke 23:35). Paul warns, "You cannot fool God."

Our hearts are deceitful above all things and desperately wicked (Jer. 17:9). We can flaunt God's laws in His face and think that we can get away with it, but we reap what we sow.

The classic example is David. His high-handed sin with Bathsheba and his subsequent murder of her husband, Uriah, was to bring down upon his head the severe retribution of God. When Nathan the prophet denounced David, he told David that he would pay fourfold. And so he did. Four of his sons died in fulfillment of this terrible prophecy. He sowed adultery and murder, and he reaped adultery and murder in his family. There was the terrible, immoral, and unprincipled behavior of Amnon with his unfortunate half sister, Tamar, the sister of Absalom. But how could David invoke the death penalty on Amnon, as the Law of Moses demanded, when he himself had committed adultery with Bathsheba? When it became evident that David was not going to uphold the Law and punish the unprincipled Amnon, Absalom took the law into his own hands and murdered Amnon. Again, how could David invoke the death penalty for murder, as the Law required, against Absalom when he himself had on his conscience the murder of Uriah? What he sowed, he reaped. It is most instructive to trace the law of sowing and reaping in David's life and to see David laying down with his own hands the paving stones along which the judgment of God traveled. God is not to be mocked, even by the choicest of His saints.

Then, too, there is the parallel *law of the soul:* "For he that soweth to his flesh shall of the flesh reap corruption; but he that soweth to the Spirit shall of the Spirit reap life everlasting" (v. 8). The law of sowing and reaping is just as much a law of the soul as it is a law of the soil. We cannot escape the moral and spiritual consequences of our behavior any more than we can escape the physical consequences of our behavior whether it be for good or for bad. The law of sowing and reaping is sure.

Abraham sowed to the flesh and reaped Ishmael. Isaac sowed to the flesh and reaped Esau. Jacob sowed to the flesh and reaped Simeon and Reuben. Lot sowed to the flesh and reaped Moab and Ammon. Samson sowed to the flesh and reaped blindness and bondage. Eli sowed to the flesh and reaped Hophni and Phinehas. David sowed to the flesh and reaped Ahithophel (the grandfather of Bathsheba and thereafter Absalom's chief adviser in wickedness). Solomon sowed to the flesh and reaped Rehoboam.

On the other hand, Enoch sowed to the Spirit and reaped rapture. Noah sowed to the Spirit and reaped salvation. Abraham sowed to the Spirit and reaped "a city which hath foundations whose builder and maker is God." Joseph sowed to the Spirit and reaped the most Christlike character and disposition in the Bible. Moses sowed to the Spirit and reaped a place on the Mount of Transfiguration. Joshua sowed to the Spirit and reaped the conquest of Canaan. Hannah sowed to the Spirit and reaped Samuel. David sowed to the Spirit and reaped a royal covenant. Hezekiah sowed to the Spirit and reaped the deliverance of Jerusalem. David sowed to the Spirit and reaped the high praise of heaven. Mary sowed to the Spirit and reaped Christ. Jesus sowed to the Spirit and reaped a multitude that no man can number whose names are written forever in the Lamb's book of life. Peter sowed to the Spirit and reaped Pentecost. Paul sowed to the Spirit and reaped a crown. Stephen sowed to the Spirit and reaped an open heaven. John sowed to the Spirit and reaped the visions of Patmos.

And so it has gone from the beginning. We reap what we sow. When I first joined the staff of the Moody Bible Institute, the radio pastor of the Moody network was a godly man named Robert J. Little. The more one came to know this beloved brother, the more one appreciated him. He was a giant in the Scriptures, a humble and able man with a big heart and a catholicity of interests. A vast and varied radio audience loved him, and the church respected and revered him. His knowledge of the Scriptures was encyclopedic. We often put him to the test during our coffee breaks; like the queen of Sheba with Solomon, we plied him with hard questions. We never knew him to fail.

One day, in his later years, an elderly brother came up to him after a service and said, "Brother Little, I wish I had your knowledge of the Bible." R.J. looked at him for a moment. Then he said, "My dear brother, you are too late. In fact, I would judge that you are about fifty years too late. If you wanted my knowledge of the Bible, you should have started fifty years ago. I did. I have been studying my Bible diligently and intensively for fifty years. That's how I gained my knowledge of the Bible. I'm sorry to tell you, my brother, that you can never have my knowledge of the Bible. You have left it for too late." It was a case of sowing and reaping. It always is.

2. The law logically exploited (6:9–10)

The apostle almost takes for granted that those who have been baptized and indwelt by the Holy Spirit will cultivate the things of the Spirit. For this, *patience is required:* "And let us not be weary in well doing: for in due season we shall reap, if we faint not" (v. 9). Nobody who plants something in the garden expects to reap a harvest a week later. One of the fundamental laws of sowing and reaping is patience. It takes time for the seed to germinate, to put out its first little roots and its first green shoot. Then it takes more time for the plant to develop and grow. Then it has to flower, and the fruit has to form. It takes a whole growing season for annuals; it takes years for trees. The one requirement imposed impartially on everyone is patience.

We are in such a hurry. Our fast-paced age encourages impatience. Whereas our grandparents traveled by horse and buggy—or, at the fastest, by train—we board a jet and travel thousands of miles in a few hours. We cross time zones as casually as our fathers crossed the street. This is the age of fast foods, instant communication, high-pressure business, and forced produce that is urged to swift maturity, picked today in California, and sold tomorrow in Japan. We have learned how to rush even Mother Nature herself.

But God refuses to be hurried. He always takes His time. We cannot speed up the rotation of the earth upon its axis or hurry the planet on its journey around the sun. We cannot shorten a day or alter the mathematical alternation of day and night. We can shorten our workweek, but we cannot shorten a real week nor abbreviate a year. God has His own pace for accomplishing His purposes. Although He Himself transcends all time, He knows the value of time—for us. He has made us creatures of time. It takes time to mature Christian character just as it takes time to grow a rose.

The problem that Paul confronts here is the problem that we all face at times—

we get weary in well doing. So many factors are involved in this particular equation. Our motives and efforts are often misunderstood and unappreciated. People are so slow to respond, or they react to our efforts with anger or indifference. The flesh gets in the way. Our own physical resources can become depleted. Satan puts discouraging thoughts into our minds. Our own spiritual life has its own highs and lows. Other people can get in the way.

The word for weary here is *ekkakeō*. It can be translated "to lack courage," "to lose heart," or "to be fainthearted." "Well doing" is *kalopoieō,* "to do well," or "to act honorably." Paul was a great encourager. He is constantly urging us not to slack off in our efforts to cultivate the life of Christ.

"In due season we shall reap, if we faint not," Paul assures us. "To every thing there is a season, and a time," Solomon observed (Eccl. 3:1–8). God's purposes take time to ripen. Jonathan requested that David, come what may, would show kindness to his family (1 Sam. 20:15–17). The years came and went, but when he at last was securely established on the throne and Jonathan was long since dead, David reached out in love to Mephibosheth and treated him as a member of the royal family (2 Sam. 9). But there was a time—when Mephibosheth was in distant Lo-debar, hiding for fear of his life—when it must have seemed that Jonathan's request would never be granted. How often it is so with our prayers for our children at the throne of "great David's greater Son."

Think of how many times David himself narrowly escaped death at the hands of King Saul. On some twenty-four different occasions, in one way or another, directly or indirectly, King Saul tried to murder David, whom Samuel had anointed to be Israel's next king. But David was unwearying in his patient refusal to take the law into his own hands. On two distinct occasions, he had Saul in his power but resolutely refused to smite his enemy although some of his men urged him to do so. Even when David had his own private army of guerillas, he would never fight the king. He chose rather to flee.

The years came and went. The throne had been promised to David by divine decree; yet Saul—his mad rages, jealousy, and senseless hatred notwithstanding—continued to reign. David had to stand by and watch the kingdom degenerate. He had to watch while evil men whispered their slanders into Saul's ears. He had to watch helplessly as hereditary enemies laid God's people low. He waited. During this period, he wrote some of his greatest psalms. He grew in grace and increased in the knowledge of God. He formulated his convictions and trained a cadre of able men to help him run the kingdom when the time came. And, in due time, he reaped. His patience was rewarded.

Then, too, *persistence is required:* "As we have therefore opportunity, let us do good unto all men, especially unto them who are of the household of faith" (v. 10). That was Paul's settled policy. How brightly he shines on board that ship that was being driven by the gale down the Mediterranean. He was a tower of strength when all hope was gone and shipwreck was looming. It made no difference to Paul that some of the men were his jailors or that some of the sailors were treacherous cowards. He spoke words of cheer to everyone. He gave bold testimony to God. He urged people to eat something to keep up their strength. Then, when all 276 people were safe ashore, he took the lead in gathering wood for a fire, went out of his way to heal the father of the pagan chief of the island, and did much to earn the goodwill of the whole island—so much, indeed, that when the time came for the castaways to leave the island, the people heaped provisions upon them.

Evangelicals should be in the forefront of efforts to do good things. And so they have been. Before Christianity burst upon the world, there were no hospitals, no orphanages, no asylums, and no schools for the children of commoners. Christian missionaries have taken both the gospel and good works to many lands. The Salvation Army's early successes were due as much to their social activities as to their gospel preaching. D. L. Moody was as interested in the development of the Young Men's Christian Association as he was in citywide evangelistic crusades. So many of the thrilling *Unshackled* stories, which come out of Chicago's Pacific Garden Mission, begin with some deed of kindness done to a drunkard, a drug addict, or a derelict.

Law? You cannot legislate kindness. Nowadays, the government has become the arbiter of social activity. People look to the government to take care of the sick, the homeless, the unemployed, and children from broken homes. Social workers, psychologists, and institutional and government programs have usurped the church's historic role of caring for the needs of men. And, all too frequently, the average Christian is content to leave these things to the State.

Well, plenty of homeless people, sick people, old people, young people, and poor people still long for someone to love them, help them, and minister to them. Paul sees all such people as so many opportunities for doing good—especially when the needy are members of the body of Christ.

PART 5

# Conclusion

## Galatians 6:11–18

A. Paul emphasizes the truth of Galatians positively (6:11)

Paul has just about finished his letter. Now he summarizes in five steps. First, Paul emphasizes the truth of Galatians *positively:* "Ye see how large a letter I have written unto you with mine own hand," he said (v. 11). The apostle now takes the pen into his own hand. To this point, he seems to have followed his customary practice of using the services of a secretary to write down what he dictated. But for the closing verses, he wants to give positive, personal emphasis to his closing remarks. He draws particular attention to the large letters with which he writes. Possibly an eye ailment made such writing necessary. "Look at these large letters I am writing," he says. This could mean: "Note how heavily I have pressed upon the pen in writing this." Or the words may point to Paul's heavy underlining of his words.

The truth of Galatians is of supreme importance to the church. This epistle is our *Magna Charta,* our *Declaration of Independence* from the shackles of the Law. Paul had thought through the great truth of the Christian believer's total emancipation from the Law. He had championed the truth in every forum available to him. On this very issue, he had withstood to the face the greatly loved, highly honored, and widely respected Peter. He had fought for the truth in Jerusalem. He had suffered unremitting persecution at the hands of the Jews for his stand. Now he seizes the pen to add, in his own handwriting, his final endorsement.

B. Paul emphasizes the truth of Galatians persuasively (6:12–15)
 1. The treacherous motives of the adversaries (6:12–13)

Paul knew his enemies only too well. He knew *their insincerity:* "As many as desire to make a fair show in the flesh, they constrain you to be circumcised . . ." (v. 12a). The word for "constrain" is *anakazō.* It conveys the idea of putting pressure on someone by means of threats, entreaty, force, or persuasion. Paul knew all about that kind of thing. In his unconverted days, he had used similar high-handed, high-pressure tactics against the infant church. In giving his testimony to King Agrippa, he said, "And many of the saints did I shut up in prison, having received authority from the chief priests; and when they were put to death, I gave my voice against them. And I punished them oft in every synagogue, and compelled [*anakazō*] them to blaspheme . . ." (Acts 26:10–11). There, as here, the verb is in the present continuous tense. He kept on doing it, just as the Judaizers kept on trying to get the Galatians to submit to circumcision.

Paul sees through their motives. They wanted to "make a fair show in the flesh." They wanted to put up a pleasing front. It was a means of currying favor with people whom they wanted to impress for some reason or another.

This kind of coercion is common in religious circles. Every group has its particular set of shibboleths, things that simply aren't done, or things that must be done if one is to remain in good standing with the powers that be. With some groups, it is a legalistic insistence that women wear a head covering when attending church services. With others it is the requirement that a person be baptized before being allowed into the fellowship. With some the passport for acceptance is speaking in tongues. With others it is a vow to use no edition of the Bible but the King James Version. With some it is a prohibition against women wearing certain kinds of clothes. With others it is an objection to men wearing beards. The list goes on and on.

Some of the criteria for acceptance would be ludicrous if they weren't so tragic. Some amount to "much ado about nothing." Some are a distortion or exaggeration of a legitimate biblical position. Some are completely heretical. Always, those who want to be "in" try to impress those whom they consider important with their zeal in trying to coerce others to conform to the particular oddities of the group. At Galatia, this kind of silly, religious nonsense was dangerous because what the "in" group advocated was heresy, namely, circumcision as a means of salvation and the badge of acceptance into the club. Paul saw through the insincerity of its propagators. They were trying to put up a pleasing front to those whom they considered worth conciliating. Insincerity was at the heart of it.

He knew also *their insecurity:* they "desire to make a fair show in the flesh, they constrain you . . . only lest they should suffer persecution for the cross of Christ" (v. 12b). A great deal of unpleasantness was being shown to those who refused to conform. Such usually is the case. In Jerusalem itself, the zealots were quite willing to manhandle people whom they considered off-color for having fellowship with Gentiles. If the Judaizers could persuade Gentile converts to Christianity to submit to circumcision, it would not only be a feather in their cap but also would take the heat off. The zealots would be satisfied—or so they hoped.

Paul knew that the antagonism went deeper. The real issue was the cross of Christ. There would always be an offense to the preaching of the cross. It had taken Paul himself a long time to come to the place where he could say, "I am not ashamed of the gospel of Christ: for it is the power of God unto salvation to every one that believeth; to the Jew first, and also to the Greek" (Rom. 1:16). And there could be no gospel apart from the cross. The preaching of the cross was foolishness to the world (1 Cor. 1:17), although it was the very essence of the wisdom and power of God. "Christ crucified" was "a stumblingblock [*skandalon,* "a scandal"] to the Jews (1 Cor. 1:23).

What the Judaizers wanted was to get away from the offense of the cross. It was the preaching of the cross that so outraged the religious Jews of Paul's day. It was the cross that raised the Jewish enemies of Christianity to such a passion of ill will against the Christian community that the outright persecution of those who held to it was considered an appropriate response. Paul had once thought so himself (Acts 26:9).

Every group, with its own particular ax to grind, has ways and means of displaying its disapproval of those who refuse to conform. If they are allowed to remain within the group, they are given the cold shoulder. Usually, they are ostracized or excommunicated. Sometimes they have to face even harsher persecution. No wonder there is a strong urge to take the easy path and conform. Paul takes advantage of the opportunity, wielding his pen himself in bold capitals, to expose the treacherous motives of the adversaries.

He exposes *their inconsistency:* "For neither they themselves who are circumcised keep the law" (v. 13a). It was bad enough that they should be trying to clamp the chains of the Law on the Gentile converts, who were born free. It was worse yet that such capitulation to the Law was the mark of an apostate and proved the proselyte never to have been genuinely saved and now to be beyond the pale of salvation. But, worst of all, the very Judaizers who were painting law-keeping in such rosy colors were canting hypocrites. They themselves were not keeping the Law; they never had and never could. The vast machinery of Judaism was not only bulky and unwieldy but also didn't work—and it never had worked. Nobody could make it work. Nobody had tried harder than Paul, in his unconverted days, to make it work (Phil. 3:2–7). But, in reality, the Judaizers not only did not keep the Law but also made no attempt to keep it. They were nothing but a group of hypocrites.

Then, too, he exposes *their inferiority:* "They . . . desire to have you circumcised, that they may glory in your flesh" (v. 13b). The full force of this indictment will be seen when the contrast of the next verse is studied. All that the Judaizers wanted to do was boast about the submission of the Galatians to their rules. They would be able to write glowing letters back home: "Today several hundred Galatians walked the aisle to express their willingness to be circumcised." Apart from all other considerations, what an inferior sort of thing it was about which they wanted to boast. Paul says to his Galatian friends, "Do you want to be a mere statistic in someone's head count of proselytes?" He is using every argument of which he can think that might make his beloved Galatians awake to the way they were being exploited.

2. The transparent motives of the apostle (6:14–15)

In contrast to the utter phoniness of the Judaizers was the unchallengeable honesty of Paul. The Galatian churches could readily recall Paul's unimpeachable behavior when he evangelized their towns and cities.

He reminds the Galatians that *he lived with his eye on Calvary:* "But God forbid that I should glory, save in the cross of our Lord Jesus Christ, by whom the world is crucified unto me, and I unto the world" (v. 14). If we are going to boast in anything, Paul says, let us glory in the cross. Odd words from a man who did not hesitate to remind a corrupt magistrate that he was a Roman (Acts 25:9–12). No Roman would glory in a *cross,* which was an instrument of shame. It would be like boasting in a gallows or an electric chair.

No one can glory in the cross who has not seen the cross from the standpoint of eternity. The cross is God's answer to sin. The cross has a significance in the plans and purposes of God that transcends time. The Lord Jesus is described as "the Lamb slain from the foundation of the world" (Rev. 13:8). The great theme of the anthems of the blessed in glory is the cross. They sing, "Thou art worthy . . . for thou wast slain, and hast redeemed us to God by thy blood" (Rev. 5:9). Paul says that all of the wisdom of God and all of the power of God are centered in the cross (1 Cor. 1:23–24). Paul had seen the preaching of the cross reach all kinds of men and women and boys and girls and save them from their sins and transform them into saints of God, exemplary citizens, and trueborn members of the very aristocracy of heaven.

But the cross has a very practical application. It is the watershed, the Great Divide, that separates the carnal believer from the spiritual believer. A proper vision of the cross will put an end to compromise with this wicked world in which we live because the cross was this world's answer to Christ. He "went about doing good." He healed the sick, cleansed the lepers, cast out demons, raised the dead, and fed the hungry multitudes. He loved people, all kinds of people—good people and bad people, religious people and ungodly people, people who loved Him and people who hated Him. He rejoiced with those who rejoiced, wept with those who wept, and prayed for those who despitefully used Him. The world had never known a man like Jesus—absolutely good, unfailingly gracious, the visible expression of the invisible God. And what was the world's answer? A cross.

As the cross was the world's answer to Christ, so the cross is the believer's answer to the world. The world will sometimes mask its face and pretend friendship for the Christian. It will offer us its pleasures, money, methods, and applause—but always at the price of compromise. The Christian's answer is the cross. As Margaret Mauro put it in her poem "The Young Christian,"

> Nay, world! I turn away,
> Though thou seem fair and good;
> That friendly outstretched hand of thine
> Is stained with Jesus' blood.

Paul lived with an eye on Calvary. He never lost sight of the cross. The world held no glamour for him. To him, the cross was the symbol of what the world had done to Jesus. It was a constant reminder of the world's undying underlying hatred for all who name the name of Christ. A proper view of the cross puts an end to all compromise with the world.

Then, too, *he lived with his eye on Christ:* "For in Christ Jesus neither circumcision availeth any thing, nor uncircumcision, but a new creature" (v. 15). Again Paul comes back to the central issue in Galatia—circumcision. Circumcision was what put a Jew into the Abrahamic covenant (Gen. 17:9–14). The Abrahamic covenant was for the Jew, not the Christian. When a righteous Jew died, he was envisioned as being "in Abraham's bosom" (Luke 16:22–23). The Christian believer is party to a different covenant, the new covenant (Matt. 26:27–28; Heb. 12:24). God does not see us as being in Abraham but in Christ. The Abrahamic covenant was concerned with the Promised Land (Gen. 15:18). In the Old Testament, the believer had to be in Canaan; in the New Testament, the believer has to be in Christ. In the Old Testament, the believer has to be in a place; in the New Testament, the believer has to be in a Person. In the Old Testament, the believer had to be in the land; in the New Testament, the believer has to be in the Lord.

"In Christ," circumcision is wholly irrelevant. This rite was wholly Jewish in significance and has nothing whatever to do with Christianity. Paul has already fully argued the point in his epistle. Now he underlines it in his own handwriting.

What matters now is that the believer in Christ is "a new creature," literally "a new creation." The word for "new" is *kainos.* It does not mean new in terms of time but new in terms of character. Judaism was wrapped up in a system of rules, rituals, and regulations. Christianity is something entirely new. It is a wholly new departure from "religion." It is new life in Christ. It is supernatural from start to finish. It begins with a supernatural experience called the new birth, and it is developed in a supernatural community called "the body of Christ," into which the believer is introduced by a supernatural "baptism of the Spirit." It is matured by the supernatural ministry of the Holy Spirit by means of His filling and anointing. All of this is radically new and different from Judaism. Circumcision has nothing to do with it.

C. Paul emphasizes the truth of Galatians practically (6:16)

Here is *the rule:* "And as many as walk according to this rule . . ." (v. 16a). Here is *the result:* "peace be on them, and mercy . . ." (v. 16b). Here is *the realm:* "and upon the Israel of God" (v. 16c). This is Paul's summary statement, written with large letters in his own handwriting. He has just stated that the principle by which to live in Christ is that there is neither circumcision nor uncircumcision. The whole question of rules, rites, religion, and regulation is irrelevant. In Christ, we are a new creation, new creatures, ruled by higher laws and loftier principles. For everyone who has entered into this new life in Christ and is seeking to cultivate in this new sphere a daily walk with God, this is a benediction of mercy and peace! Paul can see only trouble and heartache for those who are deluded into accepting the religious nonsense of the Judaizers. For those who take a firm stand in Christ, he can see God's mercy and God's peace wrapped all about them. Continued persecution might occur. Indeed, the hostility and hatred of the enemies of Christ might well intensify and increase. But that will only mean a greater supply of God's grace. Paul knew what he was talking about. He had been battered and bruised in the cause of Christ. Some of the believers in Galatia would remember the stoning that he had received at Lystra in their own country. They would remember, too, the fearless way in which he had continued with his mission, rejoicing in the peace and mercy of God.

The "Israel of God" is the antithesis of "Israel after the flesh" (1 Cor. 10:18). God gave Jacob the name "Israel" at the Jabbok when he wrestled with the Jehovah angel when God broke him to bless him (Gen. 32:24–30). During that contest, God touched the hollow of Jacob's thigh so that all of the fight left him. In the morning watch, he could only cling. Thereafter, he walked with a limp. The change in his outward walk indicated a change in his spiritual walk. Thereafter, although he had an occasional fall and abundant troubles and trials, he walked with God. The name "Jacob" is linked to the patriarch as a natural and carnal man; the name "Israel" is linked to him as a spiritual man.

Similarly, his descendants are variously called Hebrews, Jews, and Israelites. Generally speaking, the name "Hebrew" points to *their character.* Abraham was the first one to be called a Hebrew (Gen. 14:13). The name means "migrant." It describes Abraham as a believing man, a "pilgrim and a stranger" on the earth, one who was just passing through, one whose hopes and affections were fixed on things above. The language spoken by God's Old Testament people was Hebrew. Jonah described himself to the frightened mariners as "a Hebrew," one who feared God (Jonah 1:9). The confession only added to the fear of the pagan sailors. Paul described himself as being, in his unconverted days, "an Hebrew of the Hebrews" (Phil. 3:5). At least he was sincere in pursuing his religious beliefs, mistaken though he was.

The name "Jew" points to *their carnality.* Until the Babylonian captivity, the word was not often used. We find it in 1 Kings 16:6, but by then, the handwriting was already on the wall for the northern ten tribes, unworthy claimants to the name "Israel." After the captivity, the name came into common use and actually embraced remnants of all of the tribes, not just the tribe of Judah (from whence, of course, the name was derived). The word *Jew* is common in the New Testament. It designated both the country in which they lived and their nationality (John 4:9). The expression "the Jews' religion" was used in a derogatory sense of their degenerated faith (Gal. 1:13). Pilate held the Jews up to derision by putting the title "King of the Jews" over the head of Christ on the cross (Matt. 27:37). Paul indicted the Jews for their hypocrisy in the practice of their religion (Rom. 2:17) and stated that really to be a Jew required an inward spiritual experience (Rom. 2:28–29).

The name "Israel" points to *their calling.* When Jesus met Nathanael, He said, "Behold an Israelite indeed, in whom is no guile" (John 1:47). God referred to Himself as "the Holy One of Israel" (Ps. 78:41). Paul said, "They are not all Israel, which are of Israel" (Rom. 9:6). Just because a person was a natural-born descendant of Abraham did not make one an Israelite indeed. A personal experience with God is what made one a true Israelite, just as it took an encounter with God to change Jacob into Israel. The name "Israel" had spiritual connotations that were not always recognized because of the sin, rebellion, and apostasy of so many people who bore the name in Old Testament times. The apostle, in his great doctrinal discussion of the problem of the Jewish people (Rom. 9–11), looks forward to the millennial age, when "all Israel shall be saved" (Rom. 11:26). He anticipates the day when the redeemed remnant of the nation, in love with Jesus at last, will fulfill among the nations the high destiny and holy calling that God always had in mind for His people.[1] But this passage refers to "Israel" after the flesh, to native-born Israelis of the future.

Paul's introduction here, in his own handwriting, of the title *"the Israel of God,"* is highly significant. Paul intends what he says as a slap in the face of the Judaizers, who were trying, by means of circumcision, to make Jews out of Gentiles. Paul says to his Gentile converts, "*You* are the Israel of God." Why try to become Jews when you are already Israelites? By accepting Christ, you have entered into the ideal. In Christ, there is, of course, neither Jew nor Gentile (3:28). In Christ, both Jews and Gentiles become the spiritual seed of Abraham and fulfill the ideal of Israel. Believers in Christ, regardless of their nationality, are "the Israel of God."[2] The expression is Paul's final, clinching argument with his old Judaizing foes.

D. Paul emphasizes the truth of Galatians personally (6:17)

Paul's last argument was himself. He writes, "From henceforth let no man trouble me: for I bear in my body the marks of the Lord Jesus" (v. 17). The word for "marks" is *stigma,* the usual word for a tattoo or a slave brand, something that was burned into the flesh. It was customary to brand slaves. Paul was the bond slave of the Lord Jesus. On many occasions, his body had been branded by beatings in the cause of Christ. The Galatians who had known him personally had probably seen some of the honorable scars that he wore as testimony to his fearless devotion to the cause of Christ. The enemies of the cross wanted to plant

1. See John Phillips, *Exploring Romans* (Grand Rapids: Kregel, 2002).
2. This is a far cry from the amillennialist view that the church is "spiritual Israel," that God has finished with the Jewish people, that all of the great and glowing Old Testament prophecies regarding the world's golden age and Israel's national future in the Millennium are canceled, that they are now being fulfilled spiritually in the church. To maintain this position, the amillennialists have to abandon the literal interpretation of prophecies concerning the coming kingdom of Christ. They have to allegorize them, spiritualize them, explain them away, and ignore the rebirth of the state of Israel. This kind of "exegesis" wreaks havoc with the Scriptures. It is certainly not what Paul has in mind here.

their particular slave brand in the flesh of Paul's Gentile converts by means of circumcision. Did the Galatians want to be branded? Let them seek the honorable brands that he wore, not the dishonorable brand of the Judaizers, which would mark them as apostates from the faith and not true Christians at all.

"Let no man trouble me" he said. There was really no more to be said. He was tired of the constant nagging of the Judaizers. They criticized Paul's personal appearance, his style of speech, and the content of his message. They questioned his integrity and slandered his good name. His final answer? The battle scars he bore in his body! If they were not eloquent enough, genuine enough, or convincing enough that he was prepared to die for his convictions and for the Lord, then there was no more to be said. Let people leave him alone; stop interfering with him.

E. Paul emphasizes the truth of Galatians pastorally (6:18)

Only his pastoral benediction remains: "Brethren, the grace of our Lord Jesus Christ be with your spirit. Amen" (v. 18). So the first word is the last word too—*grace!* Not law, grace. The great message that Paul preached was the grace of our Lord Jesus Christ. There is no other message. The gospel is concerned from beginning to end with that marvelous grace of the Lord Jesus, which brought Him down from the pinnacle of glory to die in agony, tears, and blood upon the cruel cross of Calvary. That grace is greater than all our sin. That grace picks up poor, lost, hell-bound sinners of Adam's ruined race and puts them into the body of Christ. It makes them children of God and joint heirs with Jesus Christ. Grace guarantees them a home in heaven and seats them above all principalities and powers and every name that is named, not only in this life but also in the life to come. Grace is amply sufficient for every circumstance of life. It is as inexhaustible as the love of God.

"The grace of our Lord Jesus Christ be with your spirit." All that the Judaizers had to offer was some kind of "ministry" to the *flesh.* The grace of the Lord Jesus, however, quickened the *spirit* and made it once more the throne room of the Holy Spirit.

"Amen!" says Paul as he flings down his pen. That is also how he had begun (1:5), and thus he ends. Amen! There was no more to be said. Now it was up to them. We can well believe that he longed, with all of his heart, to hear a resounding "Amen!" echoing from his beloved and beleaguered brethren who were far away.